SHADES OF WELCOME

Kenneth Payne

UPFRONT PUBLISHING
LEICESTERSHIRE

SHADES OF WELCOME
Copyright © Kenneth Payne 2002

All Rights Reserved

ISBN 1 84426 007 0

First Published 2002 by
MINERVA PRESS

Second Edition 2002 by
UPFRONT PUBLISHING
Leicestershire

SHADES OF WELCOME

I dedicate this book to all those mentioned within its pages and to countless others, not specifically mentioned, who have helped and inspired me over the years. In particular, I would especially like to mention Judith Bentley for her advice and comments, Jose Murdoch for the proofreading and Nani van Kroonenburg who spent many hours sorting everything out, together with Mary Lowe, Katherine Chappell and Sandy Sidney, who so willingly took on the task of deciphering my scrawl and setting it out on the computer, and finally, to the editor at Minerva Press for the careful and useful editing.

Proceeds from this book will go to the Missionaries of the Poor, who serve the poorest of the poor in Jamaica, India, Uganda, Haiti and the Philippines (see Chapters V and VI).
Thank you.

Foreword

This is a book based on my own experiences as a priest, both since my ordination as well as going back to years prior to that and even before becoming a Catholic. It is an attempt to show the importance of hospitality in our lives and how both the giving and receiving of hospitality is an enriching experience and is essential to the life of a Christian.

I have tried to show through various travel experiences and having an 'open door' wherever I have been, that my own life has become fuller, barriers have been broken down, and great friendships have been formed. At a time when we hear so much about the negative side of the lives of some clergy, I hope that it shows that the life of a celibate priest can be full, exciting, inspiring and at times hilarious.

It begins with some details of my family background and the seeds sown in the bloodstream many years ago. This is followed by some early experiences, with which some readers will no doubt empathise. I have then inserted a chapter on how I was welcomed in the Catholic Church and the tradition of hospitality to be found in the Scriptures and amongst the inhabitants of the Holy Land today. One of the highlights of the book is, I feel, the account of my visits and work amongst the poorest of the poor in downtown Kingston, Jamaica. This I have recounted in some detail, as the experiences were vivid and moving.

There then follows a selection of presbytery experiences which, I hope, reveal another side to the life of a busy priest. Through the 'open door', many contacts were made, some of which resulted in interesting happenings when I was welcomed in other countries. Finally, there is a chapter on the final welcome that we all hope for at the moment of our death.

It is thus a very personal book which, without going into a lot of theology, hopefully reveals something of a deeply happy life spent in the service of God, and in which seeds sown in the past have been allowed to germinate and continue to bear fruit to this very day.

About the Author

The author, a Catholic priest with a love of travel, has worked mainly in the Northampton diocese, in Bedford, Aylesbury and Northampton, with a spell as chaplain to the RAF in both England and Cyprus. He was then administrator and parish priest at Northampton RC Cathedral and, in addition to running a busy town parish, was involved in local ecumenical activities, family groups and the support of the destitute in Jamaica and elsewhere.

Much of this work continues to occupy him in his present parish of St Aidan's, Little Chalfont, Buckinghamshire.

Contents

Introduction		11
I	A Family Tradition: Return to Waterloo	15
II	First Experiences: Real Life Appetisers	20
III	A Welcoming Church: A Journey in Faith	37
IV	Middle-Eastern Hospitality: The Scriptures and Today	53
V	The Poorest of the Poor: Jamaica	87
VI	Jamaica Again: Five Years Later	112
VII	Attempts at Home Hospitality: 56 High Street, Aylesbury	127
VIII	Further Attempts: Cathedral House	146
IX	A Hundredfold Return: Five Continents – Africa	168
X	Five Continents Continued: South America, Australia, Europe and Asia	189
XI	The Welcome of Death: The Climax of Our Lives	218
Conclusion		230
Bibliography		233

Introduction

Many books find their roots and origins in the early thoughts, feelings and events in the author's life, and we are told that the first five years of our lives are of paramount importance.

One of my own early childhood memories is that of gazing, not without some puzzlement, at a black and white rather dark print of Holman Hunt's *Christ the Light of the World* which hung in my grandmother's room. I have often, over the years, thought of this picture and the words written beneath it: 'Behold, I stand at the door and knock.' For me it seemed to spell out mystery and gloom – not what the artist intended. Perhaps this was partly because it was a black and white print; its colour and brightness were absent, as also was the handle on the outside of the closed door.

I only realised the full meaning of the picture much later on, but it somehow became linked in my child's mind with the ever open door of my grandparents' home – but more of this later. What follows is an attempt to show how the closed door can be opened; how mistakes have been made, but how encounters and opportunities have enriched both my own life as well as the lives of many others. My hope is that it may inspire others to break through the barriers of reserve and explore the rich depths to be found through the open door and the practice of welcome and hospitality.

I found on reading Henri Nouwen's excellent little book *Reaching Out* that many events in my own life seemed to form a refrain many times repeated. Nouwen writes about three movements in the spiritual life: the movement from loneliness to solitude, from hostility to hospitality, and from illusion to prayer. They reflect the threefold love embodied in Jesus's command to love God and to love one's neighbour as oneself. It is the second of these movements that I hope to explore in drawing, somewhat pragmatically, from my own experiences. These have entailed, as we shall see, many journeys, both in body and spirit.

This, therefore, could be described as a travel book – but with a difference; it is also a book about faith and trust – but with a difference; it is autobiographical – but with a difference; but perhaps even more, it is a book about love – but, again, with a difference. It may be summed up in the small picture on my desk of three rucksacked young people striding along a road beneath a gloriously blue sky. Beneath is a quotation from Brother Roger of Taizé: 'If at the dawn, we were able to welcome the new day like the beginning of a new life, whoever advances towards God goes from one beginning to another.' Our life is a journey of trust and of love in which we stretch out our hands to one another and, at the same time, hopefully, to God.

Philoxenia is the Greek word for hospitality. It means love of the stranger. The opposite, xenophobia, is fear of the stranger. Most of us oscillate between the two, depending to some extent on whether we are classed as extrovert or introvert; whether perhaps we come from a warm Mediterranean country or the cooler north; or, strangely inverted, the north of England or the south; or whether we are Irish, who are renowned for their hospitality, or English who are more reserved.

The word hospitality (linked with similar words: host, hospital, hospice, etc.), although usually suggesting the idea of welcoming someone into the home, goes deeper than that. It is expressive of a basic attitude to others. Nouwen says, 'Hospitality means primarily the creation of a free space where the stranger can enter and become a friend instead of an enemy. Hospitality is not to change people, but to offer them space where change can take place.' This means then that we do not necessarily have to talk to or continually entertain our guests, nor take them on innumerable outings! 'Let there be spaces in your togetherness,' says Kahil Gibran, and that means highlighting the value of stillness and silence.

The similar word, welcome, which comes from the old English *wel*, meaning will, desire, pleasure, and *coin*, meaning comer, or guest, gives further depths of understanding to this theme. This is again illustrated from a childhood memory. One of my favourite books as a child – and, indeed, still one of my favourite books which I often reread – is *The Wind in the Willows* by Kenneth Graham.

It begins with Mole finding his way down to the riverbank, being captivated by the river, and then meeting with the Water Rat, who was on the opposite bank.

> The two animals stood and regarded each other cautiously.
> 'Hullo, Mole!' said the Water Rat.
> 'Hullo, Rat!' said the Mole.
> 'Would you like to come over?' inquired the Rat presently.
> 'Oh, it's all very well to talk,' said the Mole, rather pettishly, he being new to a river and riverside life and its ways.
> The Rat said nothing, but stooped and unfastened a rope and hauled on it, then lightly stepped into a little boat which the Mole had not observed. It was painted blue outside and white within, and was just the size for two animals; and the Mole's whole heart went out to it at once, even though he did not yet fully understand its uses.
> The Rat sculled smartly across and made fast. Then he held up his forepaw as the Mole stepped gingerly down. 'Lean on that!' he said. 'Now then, step lively!' and the Mole to his surprise and rapture found himself actually seated in the stern of a real boat.
> 'This has been a wonderful day!' said he, as the Rat shoved off and took to the sculls again.

Here we have a superb example of hospitality. There is the encounter of strangers – two very different beings; an immediate response on the part of Rat to the enquiring gaze of Mole; the help and understanding shown by Rat to the uninitiated Mole; and the appreciation and gratitude of Mole for the warmth and attention of the Rat's generous welcome.

In a recent sequel to this, William Horwood captures the character of Mole and delves into the inner thoughts of man and the strange dichotomy of wanting to be both open to others and yet needing solitude and control over one's surroundings. I quote at length:

> The Mole sat toasting his toes in front of the fire. The winter wind howled safely outside sending occasional flurries of soot

down his chimney. He was thinking that things were nearly perfect, but not quite.

'I must not be uncharitable,' he said to himself though a slight and uncharacteristic frown showed he was finding it difficult not to be. 'I have my health, I have my home and I – I must not be unfriendly.'

He darted a glance across the hearth towards the smaller and less comfortable chair that was ranged there, looked briefly at the cause of his ill-temper, and looked away again.

'No, I must be patient. My heart must be compassionate. I must put up with it. I must – O bother!'

The wind blew suddenly more violently all round the outside of his house, which was snug among the roots of a fallen old oak tree, and doors rattled, and an ember of the beech log that was burning brightly on his fire cracked and shot onto his rug and smouldered there.

'Don't worry!' said the unwelcome guest who sat in the chair opposite. 'I'll move it!'

The purpose, then, of this little book is to explore through many personal experiences some of these ideas. Hospitality, after all, is really about our relationships with one another and the love of our neighbour – never an easy commandment to put into practice. It is also about seizing, without hesitation, opportunities as they present themselves, and this too can be difficult, depending, as it often does, on our temperament and circumstances.

Finally, I should add that some names, to save embarrassment, have been changed, but I would like to thank every single person mentioned for their inspiration and example. I have learned so much from the loving concern of others who have aided me in my own journey through life, and have shown me the importance of the 'open door'.

Chapter I

A FAMILY TRADITION: RETURN TO WATERLOO

Look for opportunities to be hospitable.

Romans 12:13

Handed down to me by my father are two medals: one is a Waterloo medal which tells me that my great-great-grandfather, James Payne, was a soldier in the 7th Hussars and fought in one of the bloodiest battles of all time. He was fortunate to have survived, although today anyone visiting the peaceful green undulating countryside south of Brussels would find it difficult to picture the scene in mid-June 1815 when Napoleon was finally defeated. Over forty thousand lost their lives and the Duke of Wellington is quoted as saying that few things could be worse than winning a battle and losing so many friends. The inn where Wellington stayed over the three nights prior to the battle is now a museum and on visiting it with my father, the latter had the thought-provoking experience of sitting on the bed used by Wellington while he was anxiously pondering his immediate strategy for overcoming the French army.

Shortly after this incident, whilst accompanying some close friends from France around Woburn Abbey in Bedfordshire, I found myself looking at a scarlet sash worn by Lord George Russell when he was wounded during the Peninsular campaign in 1809, a few years before Waterloo. My friend, Monique, commented that her great-great-grandfather was killed there. James Payne's other medal was awarded for his part in the Peninsular War. They could so easily have been fighting against each other on the same battlefield. Such is the utter foolishness of warfare, of not only closing the doors to others, but of pointing a gun at them.

After James Payne had recovered from the horrors of Waterloo, he was billeted, with those of his regiment who had survived, as part of the army of occupation in north-eastern France. The men were lodged in the village homes of many of the French inhabitants. This was a delightfully pleasant contrast to the rigours of the previous years. It is recounted in one place that the men received a pound of meat a day, a pound of bread, both of good quality, plus a pint of gin to six soldiers, and in general they gave their rations for cooking to the person on whom they were billeted.

James spent most of these two and a half years in Wormhout. He had a room in the house of a widow, Jeanne Thérèse Bouve, who lived in the main street of this little country town in French Flanders. She was a maker of wigs, a popular and essential skill at that time. Her husband had died at home seven years earlier. He, too, had been a wig maker, and his widow had continued the trade, and was helped by her son, Philippe, and her daughter, Marie Jeanne Thérèse. After the defeat of Napoleon and peace being assured by the army of occupation, she undoubtedly found it financially helpful to offer accommodation to the British soldiers stationed in the area. My father writes in his autobiography:

> The headquarters of the 7th Hussars was for part of the time at Cassel, a town set on a high hill just ten kilometres south of Wormhout. James Payne would have many times traversed this distance, probably on horseback and returning to the welcoming homestead of the Bouve family in the evening. It was during this time that he fell in love with Marie Jeanne Thérèse, who was nearly two years his senior, but James was by this time twenty-four years old, and a difference of less than two years was of little account. Gradually, through living with the family, he mastered a little of the spoken French language.
>
> Then the news came in November 1818 that the British army of occupation was to withdraw from France. The 7th Hussars were to leave. James had been with the regiment just ten years. What was he to do? After much discussion with Marie and consultation with her mother, he decided on returning to Ipswich to consult his own parents, or, rather to tell them that he wanted to

return to Wormhout to marry Marie, whom he dearly loved.

He was discharged from the army at Shepperton on 14 December 1818, and spent Christmas with his parents and family. No doubt there was much discussion and no little disagreement around the table that Christmas as to the wisdom of James returning to France to marry someone who had been until not long previously the enemy. Finally, however, his parents, William and Susan, agreed, and James went to London, collected the official act of consent from the French Consul General, and journeyed on, by stagecoach to Dover, across the channel by boat and thence to Wormhout.

There, Marie and James presented themselves with all the necessary papers, at the Mayor's office and the marriage was arranged for nine o'clock in the morning of 3 March 1819. Marie and her family were all good practising Catholics, whereas James was baptised in the Church of England. It would seem that in France at this time, marriages in the Catholic Church could only take place between two Catholics. Thus it was that an otherwise happy and joyful event was nevertheless marred, not only by the absence of James's parents and family, as the journey would have been too costly, but also by the fact that it could not take place in the church.

James, on his wedding certificate, is described as a former soldier and by profession, a candle maker. No doubt he took up this occupation on his return to Wormhout, but how long he was able to pursue it is not known; nor how long it was before he persuaded his wife, Marie, to return to England with him. What is certain is that by 1824 they were both living in Middlesex, north of the Thames, and it was there that their first child was born: James Joseph. By the time the second child, William, came into this world, the family had moved south of the river to Brixton, then to Dulwich where their third son, John, was born and later to Walworth, all addresses being within easy reach of the Dover Road! This made the not infrequent journeys back to Wormhout easier.

From both Brixton and Dulwich, Mary, as she was known on this side of the Channel, trudged up to the nearest Catholic Church in St George's Road, Southwark, to have her babies baptised. It is interesting that at James and Mary's wedding in Wormhout and at the baptism of William, friends from Ireland were in prominence. There was a Patrick Kelly – a resident at Wormhout of independent means who witnessed their marriage –

and a Mary Murphy who was godmother to William.

It was now Mary Payne's turn to have the problem of learning the language, of making new friends, and of becoming integrated into the life of a busy and somewhat overcrowded South London suburb. She had insisted on having her three sons baptised in the Catholic faith, but beyond that it was undoubtedly not easy to bring them up in that faith. Nevertheless, she managed to pass on to them much of her own deep convictions, and even some of her French ways! William, for example, remembers returning to France to visit his relatives and, also throughout his life, insisted that he preferred the green beans at lunch cut up in the French way, and not sliced as is done in England.

In Protestant England, there was not very much demand in the churches for candles, so James made use of his skills learned with the cavalry and became a 'carman'. This probably involved driving a carriage, a stagecoach, or horse omnibus. Horses, at that time, were a common sight everywhere, often standing tethered in front of houses, and James would certainly have felt at home with them.

Their second son, William, married a Henrietta Wortley, and probably due to the fact that they lived almost within earshot of the great Baptist preacher Spurgeon, whose tabernacle was nearby, the whole family came under his influence. William became, for a time, a Baptist deacon.

When Mary from Wormhout died, her husband James moved in to join William's family, which eventually numbered thirteen. Their tenth child was named Henrietta after her mother, and she, like some of her sisters, inherited the somewhat round, high-cheek-boned features and motherly build of their French grandmother. It was due to the close family links that even when William and Henrietta and their children moved north of the Thames to Islington, they kept in constant touch with other members of the family south of the river. These included James-Joseph and his son, John Thomas Smith Payne, with whom Henrietta fell in love. Thus it was that two first cousins, my grandparents, married and were destined, through force of circumstances, to have an open door and a welcome to other family members and to all in need.

Soon after their marriage they cared for the baby of Henrietta's younger sister who had died in childbirth. Later, the widowed William moved in and lived to the considerable age of ninety-seven years. He was succeeded by Henrietta's older sister Emily, who was disabled and very deaf and also lived to a good old age; and when my own mother was ill with tuberculosis for nearly three years they also gave me a loving home. I recall my grandfather near to complaining one day when he commented that he and my grandmother had hardly ever had any time in their married life when they had been alone together. Hospitality, even and perhaps more particularly, within the family can have, as we all must know, many drawbacks. Acceptance of the foibles of close members of the family can be difficult, as also the creation of the necessary space, both material and psychological, in a small household. Notwithstanding all this, my own parents continued the tradition and gave me many tastes of the fundamental importance of being open and welcoming.

Chapter II

FIRST EXPERIENCES: REAL LIFE APPETISERS

'...Come and stay with us.' And she would take no refusal.

Acts 16:15

Most people can recall, usually vividly, the first occasion something happened in their lives, a first experience, which is frequently accompanied by fear – fear of the unknown that lies ahead.

Gwen Ffrangcon-Davies, a well-known actress in the early part of the twentieth century, was interviewed on television at the age of ninety-seven. She was partially sighted, and the interviewer had visited her in her cottage in the country. She was seen on screen walking barefoot across the lawn, guided by the interviewer. 'I love the feel of the grass beneath my feet,' remarked Gwen.

The interviewer then, with slight hesitation, asked, 'Well, Miss Davies, you must at your age have thought of dying. Are you afraid of death?'

Gwen Ffrangcon-Davies paused for a second and then, with a thoughtful smile, replied, 'Well, I suppose you're always a little nervous of doing something for the first time.'

I will return to this later. Meanwhile, my first experience of leaving home and being welcomed into another family, whom I had never before met, was when a school friend, Richard Parsons, invited me to spend a few days after Christmas at his family's home at Wadhurst, near Tunbridge Wells. I was just thirteen years old and it necessitated a journey by train on my own. Richard was one of the small number of pupils who were boarders at Farnham Grammar School where I attended and one of his forebears was the inventor of the steam turbine. Richard's mother was from Belgium. For me, at the time, this all constituted a strange upper-middle-class environment, especially when I was introduced to unfamiliar continental Epiphany customs.

There were nine or ten of us around the dining table: many more than I, an only child, had been used to. Towards the end of the meal the twelfth-night Epiphany cake was placed on the table. A sixpenny piece had been hidden somewhere within it and the cake was duly divided up amongst all present. It was explained to me that the one finding the coin would be the king or queen for the rest of the day. Furthermore, they would have to choose their opposite number, queen or king. Fear engulfed me. Being shy and out of my depth in this highly educated and intelligent family, I dreaded the idea of finding the sixpence in my portion of cake.

The worst happened. I bit on something hard, and immediately wondered if I could remove it from my mouth without being noticed. Then I saw Richard's mother watching me closely. I suspect that she had intentionally planted it in the piece she'd placed on my plate. There was no means of escape. I was the king, and I had to choose my queen! Beyond an overwhelming feeling of embarrassment and shyness, I no longer recall how the evening progressed. However, when I finally returned home I remember feeling a sense of relief combined with the beginnings of a growth of independence and self-assurance.

Soon after this, at the height of the bombing in London in World War Two, Elsa, a first cousin of my father's, together with her husband, Cyril, and their three teenage sons, came to live with us as their house in Beckenham had been destroyed. 'My' bedroom became a dormitory for all four of us boys. This was a further step in my formation in the importance of hospitality, which was to continue with other relatives and friends who were in trouble during those war years.

Teenage years, nevertheless, were marked by a certain sense of loneliness, compensated for by avid reading. Part of the menu seemed to be serious literature, religion and the classics, but also some lighter fare, in particular novels by a prolific lady who wrote under two pseudonyms: Oliver Sandys and Countess Barcynska. She was described in the 1940s as 'England's best-loved woman novelist'. I enjoyed her novels and was especially interested in her autobiography, *Full and Frank*, in which she describes her second husband, throughout, as 'the man'. I was intrigued by this mysterious unnamed person and decided to write to her to enquire who he was. To my amazement and delight – I was only fourteen at the time – she replied in her own handwriting:

> Your charming letter has given me the same kind of pleasure as a handful of freshly picked wild flowers. Thank you for writing to me.
>
> Go on with your studies, for the way to literature is hardy and stony, but do not abandon the idea of writing. Study the short story. Study the great short story writers – Guy de Maupassant particularly.
>
> I am quite sure, after reading your letter, that you will do something in the world of books, so keep sight of your star.
>
> You ask for the name of 'the man'. He was the greatest modern exponent of the short story – Caradoc Evans.
>
> He died a year ago – and that is the end of my story. I have written a biography concerning him – *Caradoc Evans* by Oliver Sandys – and when it is out you will be able to find out all about the life of a genius.

And a year later she wrote:

> I am so glad you liked the biography and the last book. If my writing helps you in any way in the future to become a writer with a view or a message then it will be alone worthwhile that I ever took up a pen.
>
> What are you destined for as regards a career?
>
> You have, I think, an extraordinary maturity of thought and expression. How few people of your age think at all?

And in 1948:

> You know, Kenneth, I am quite certain you are going to do something really worthwhile and, if you keep this letter from fifteen to twenty years, it might prove interesting reading.

And the same year:

> And now about religion – you say you feel you will have to make a choice.
>
> I myself should not be surprised if you become an RC. It is a religion which still produces saints and has much mercy for sinners. I have met two saints in my own time. I feel that in countless ways it sustains where other religions fail. Chesterton's acceptance of it proves that. His great mind could not have followed anything claptrap or trivial.

This was the beginning of an exchange of letters, which continued until shortly before her death in 1964. During that time, whilst on one of many cycling holidays, I visited Caradoc Evans's grave at New Cross in South Wales. The inscription on the tombstone read: 'Bury me lightly so that the soft rain may reach my face and the fluttering of the butterfly may not escape my ear.' The following year I cycled again to Wales and decided to visit my novelist penfriend who lived near Aberystwyth.

On finally finding the address I was looking for, a bungalow, which went by the name of Heddle meaning Peaceful Place, I propped my bicycle by the hedge, but was then dismayed to find no one at home. As it was already evening, I asked a lady living opposite whether Mrs Caradoc Evans was away on holiday. To my relief, 'No,' she had only a few moments ago walked up to the post office, which, even in the smallest of villages, used to keep open until 7 p.m. I was also told that Nickie, her son, was there in the adjacent field. Filled anew with a flood of shyness, I crossed over to the field indicated and saw a man with a gun approaching. As we came within speaking distance I was just about to introduce myself when he said, heartily shaking hands, 'Kenneth, Kenneth, er Payne!' For the moment I was taken aback that he should seem to know me. I discovered later that it was from my photograph, which some time previously I had sent to his mother.

We walked up to the post office where I met his mother, an attractive and colourful lady in her fifties. They both wanted to know more about this strange young man who read the novels, had made a 'pilgrimage' to see them, was interested in religion, and who had begun finding out about the Catholic faith. They invited me to supper the following evening when we talked a lot about the Catholic Church – Nick had recently become a Catholic. By contrast, towards the end of the evening, all three of us visited a certain well-known astrologer who contributed a weekly column to one of the popular newspapers. He lived in a caravan on the lower slopes of Cader Idris and not far from Penrhyncoch. Inevitably, in the course of conversation, his work in astrology was mentioned. He then showed us a large chart that he had devised. It was divided into squares and in each square was written a prophecy. For any given day he would merely stick a pin into a square at random, and whatever was written there would become the prophecy for that day for the astrological sign indicated! He explained that it earned him his bread and butter!

The friendship with Mrs Caradoc Evans, sustained by occasional letters and visits – she moved later to Church Stretton in Shropshire – had a lasting effect upon me, and taught me the importance and influence that an older person outside the family can have on a younger person, through their welcome, their interest and their encouragement.

Severing more conclusively the ties with home occurred when I began studying at university. Hull, which was then a university college, offering an external London degree, accepted my application, and I embarked on a course in pure and applied mathematics, logic and scientific methodology – a combination of subjects for which I was not particularly able. What was then a considerable train journey to a hitherto unknown destination was a very definite severing of the umbilical cord, and I felt very alone on arrival at Cottingham on the edge of Hull where the men's hall of residence was situated. This was a former army camp. Laden with two large suitcases, I reported my arrival at the entrance lodge. The warden looked down a long list of student names, found mine, and with a pronounced Yorkshire accent, said curtly, 'Hut sixty-six.' I glanced through the window only to see a vista of black semi-circular Nissen huts looking like black-cassocked clergy lying flat on their faces to avoid a bomb blast. 'Where's that?' I nervously asked. 'Opposite Hut thirty-three,' was the reply, as if that solved the whole problem.

Each hut was divided up inside by cream-painted breezeblock walls into four or five rooms, with a washplace at the end. I soon discovered that the slightest wheeze or whisper could be heard in the adjacent rooms. I was fortunate to have an end room and my only neighbour was an Indian from Kenya, Aziz Khasim-Laka, who was studying economics. He was a devout Muslim and, most of the time, observed the traditional Muslim times of prayer, beginning at 5 a.m., when I would often not only hear his voice in prayer, but also detect the smell of incense. This was not unpleasant, and he was quite apologetic about the early hour! Aziz's family lived in Mombasa, owning what was then the big Oceanic Hotel on the sea front. They belonged to the Shia group of Muslims, and he explained to me that they believed the Aga Khan to be the manifestation of God here on earth now.

I recalled this when many years later I was hearing confessions in a Catholic school and a little Indian girl from Mombasa came in, sat down, and told me she wanted to confess and say that she was sorry for being naughty, 'But,' she added, 'I'm not a Christian!' She then proceeded to tell me about her naughtiness. I explained to her that I would pray for her and ask God to bless her very specially. I chatted with her a little longer, and then prayed over her. In the course of the conversation she said that a few of the children called her nasty names because she was coloured, and she didn't like it but she felt she had to accept it.

So I said to her, 'Well, you know what to say next time: that Jesus – you've heard of Jesus haven't you?'

And she said, 'Oh yes, I've heard a lot about Jesus in this school.'

'Well, next time you tell them that Jesus was exactly the same colour as you; indeed he may have been just a bit darker than you.'

I think she liked that, and I fell to wondering if maybe her parents had known Aziz's family.

A few days later in Hull a typical north country welcome awaited me when I called on a lady whom I had met through the Dickens Fellowship. I had for the previous year been secretary of the local branch of this organisation in Guildford. This had evolved from my interest in the writings of Charles Dickens and, through my mother, a friendship with a lady who was the national secretary at the Dickens's house in Doughty Street, London. I looked in at a meeting of the Fellowship in Hull and a certain Mrs Broadbent spoke to me. On hearing that I had recently arrived in Hull, she immediately invited me to her home. A week later I decided to take up her invitation, found her house which was near the college, knocked at the front door once, and then again and waited. There was no answer. A third time I knocked, but still no reply. I went to the side of the house, found another door, and then heard a voice call, 'Come in, come in.' Somewhat nervously I entered. 'Oh,' exclaimed Mrs Broadbent, 'I wondered if you'd come. Sit down. I'll get some cake and tea. Don't knock in future,' she added, 'the door's always unlocked: just come in,' and as she said this, someone else, without warning, entered. Such was my initiation into real Yorkshire hospitality. It is sad that the dishonesty and violence of our present-day society has replaced the open door with bolts, spyholes and alarms.

Many stories could be told of such hospitality, characteristic of Yorkshire, which I, as a student from the south, learned to appreciate and revel in. However, happily I was to find that it was not limited to Yorkshire, for two years later Karl Ruffman, a mature German student, arranged for the English Department of four West German universities to invite our Dramatic Society to perform Sheridan's Renaissance classic *The Rivals* in Munster, Gottingen, Kiel and Bonn. Antony Brown, who later took to the stage as his profession, was in charge of the Dramatic Society and it was he who produced the play, also taking the part of Sir Anthony Absolute. I, in addition to playing Captain Jack Absolute, looked after the administration and arrangements, linking up with the preparatory work done by Karl, who was unable to accompany us.

Our first stop was at Munster in Westphalia where we were accommodated in student digs, the bedsitters being expanded to house a further mattress, lilo, settee, or, if lucky, another bed. The journey from England on hard wooden-slatted third-class railway seats together with the excitement of our first night performance made the welcoming celebration drinks at Pinkus in Munster unforgettable. I vaguely recall chopping away at the long heavy oak table in the pub to record our passing – the inscription 'University College Hull Dram. Soc. 1951'. Many years later I revisited Pinkus and tasted once again the potent Muller, a brew of beer with, I think, strawberries, and inspected the carved table still bearing witness to our evening of celebration. The publican, I hasten to add, had encouraged us in our woodcarving efforts.

During one of our performances on a somewhat improvised stage, I was distracted from my part by the sound of something metallic, at short irregular intervals, hitting the floor near the side of the stage, and simultaneously, to my horror the curtain was slowly descending into a crumpled heap near the wings! We concluded the act by hastening as quickly as possible out of sight backstage whilst the curtain-puller struggled with a rope attached to a non-existent curtain.

The welcome we received at Gottingen was memorable and resulted in a long-lasting friendship with Hans Stoffregen with whom I lodged. He gave me his bed whilst he slept on the sitting-room floor of his small student lodging. Gottingen, in the south of Germany looked towards the Hertz mountains, and one evening the English-speaking students took us to a meal and a dance at what was, for impecunious university students, a fairly lavish do. There was plenty to drink and, emboldened by this, I took the girl who played opposite me in *The Rivals* – Lydia Languish – out on to the balcony and, quite seriously, as I had fallen for her in a big way, proposed marriage. She said, later, that she was so surprised that she nearly fell off the balcony! Such was the effect of German hospitality added to their potent beer. Some time later we did become unofficially engaged until the idea of priesthood began to loom large on the horizon, and our relationship broke up. She found another partner and was happily married, and I went off to do two years' military service, followed by five years at the seminary.

However, prior to that, I took over the Dramatic Society and not only acted in, but also produced several plays. One was an ambitious production of Shaw's *Pygmalion*. It was too ambitious a choice for an immature and inexperienced young producer, so I consulted Ida Teather, an elderly lady who was the college tutor in drama. Ida came to a rehearsal. It was only two weeks before the first night. We were rehearsing the scene in which Freddy Eynsford-Hill meets Eliza Doolittle who, for the first time, is displaying her cultivated English accent. Bernard Shaw was very verbal and Ida pointed out that there had to be accompanying visual effects. We had to make much more of the sophisticated afternoon tea party. This would bring out the drama and humour of Freddy's invitation to Eliza to walk with him across the park. 'Walk! Not bloody likely, I'm going in a taxi!' replies Eliza Doolittle. Ida rehearsed with us the movements and intonation of Eliza's exit and her sensational reply to Freddy. We rehearsed it again and again. Ida was not satisfied, and finally, to my alarm, the whole afternoon's rehearsal time was devoted to just that small part of the tea-party scene. We certainly benefited from her expertise, but the rest of the play suffered somewhat through being generally unrehearsed and lacking the spark that she had given to those few minutes of acting time. Fortunately Carmela Dawidowicz, who took the part of Eliza, just survived without walking out on us after having repeated her line some sixty times!

Associated with the world of drama, hospitality was not only seen on the stage, but also experienced in real life. Sir Lewis Casson and Dame Sybil Thorndike had agreed, amongst others, to be vice-presidents of our drama group. On one occasion when they were on tour playing in the local theatre in Hull, we decided to invite them to tea to meet other members of the Dramatic Society. We sat with them in a corner of the students' common room and found them interested in all that we were doing. They, in their turn, regaled us with some of their experiences. At one point I asked if they ever became bored by acting out the same part night after night. 'Oh no,' replied Dame Sybil. 'You see, every audience is different. You can smell an audience!' And she placed a particular emphasis on the word 'smell'. 'Have you noticed that?' she added. We knew what she meant.

As we bade them farewell, expressing our enthusiasm at the prospect of seeing them in the play that evening, Dame Sybil sank back on the seat of the taxi we had ordered for them (students didn't have cars in those days!), laughed and, thanking us, said, 'Well, I hope we can smell you tonight!'

An entirely different expression of welcome occurred

countless times in visiting religious communities. One of the first was that of a few days spent on retreat in a convent near Worcester. I recall nothing of the retreat, who was leading it, nor why I was there. It was before the days of our present 'throw away society' when socks were darned several times over before being discarded. One morning I must have left a dirty and holey pair of socks on the chair in my bedroom. That evening I found them on the chair neatly folded, washed and mended. One of the nuns had noticed my need – actions speak louder than words.

Religious communities are noted for their hospitality and Benedictines in particular. St Benedict wrote in Chapter 53 of his Rule: 'Let all guests that come be received like Christ, for he will say, "I was a stranger and you took me in, etc."' Church members and pilgrims were to be especially welcomed, and were to be worshipped as Christ himself.

The priest who helped me most towards the priesthood whilst I was doing my national service at Halton, near Aylesbury, was a Benedictine from Downside. After gaining a commission I reported to the senior education officer at RAF Halton, who looked at me and then at the file on the desk in front of him. 'I see your subject is mathematics.'

'Yes, sir,' I replied.

'Well,' he continued, 'we've enough officers already teaching mathematics, but we need more to take engineering drawing.' He paused.

'What's that, sir?' I countered quite seriously.

'Oh, it's an easy and interesting subject to teach. Flight Lieutenant Durrant is an expert. Go and talk to him, and then there are books in the library.' Then, to my further alarm he added, 'Today's Tuesday. You could start next Monday! By the way,' he continued, 'I see you're an RC. There's a very fine RC chaplain here, a Father Brookes. See me in the bar before lunch and I'll introduce you to him.'

This he duly did, and I found immediately that Father Brookes was someone who was open and approachable. We became good friends and through him I was able to experience something of the Benedictine spirituality at Downside, meet Abbot Christopher Butler, who later became a bishop and, what was most important, clarify my thoughts about the priesthood.

One Sunday evening Father Brookes suggested that we go over to St Joseph's in Aylesbury for the evening service. We arrived a few minutes late, crept in and knelt in the back row. The parish priest, a Canon McHugh, whom I was later to learn was a good and holy man, was in the pulpit, leading the rosary. However, it would only have been the initiated who would have identified it as such. Almost unintelligible sounds issued from his mouth. 'Aiel Mre ool oface the aawd iswi hee: blerssed art how amongst wimn and blerssed frooooot woomb, Jsus.' On nearly every alternate syllable there was an unusually emphatic emphasis, with occasional unexpected pauses. I have never heard anything like it before or since. A rush of mirth welled up within me. I had to bite my lips to stop laughing aloud, but this became more difficult when I noticed Father Brookes take out his handkerchief and stuff a quarter of it between his teeth. Everyone else seemed to be devoutly praying without the problem we were experiencing. The regular parishioners were clearly quite used to the Canon's speech impediment. The rosary ended and the sermon was about to begin. We felt we could cope with no more. We guiltily crept out and let the laughter explode. As we came down the steps Father Brookes remarked, in the event prophetically, 'There, Ken, one day you may be parish priest in that church!' Twenty-one years later this prophecy was to come true!

A common failing today is to forget a person's name. This may be partly due to the lack of early memory training skills, or it may be because we are bombarded with so many facts and images through the various media that the human mind becomes waterlogged. It has also been said that most people are unable to say they know more than about eight hundred people. It remains, however, that the use of a person's name can be a powerful tool and makes a person feel welcome and accepted.

This was brought home to me in my first few days of the five year's preparation for the priesthood at Séminaire St Sulpice in Paris. Over seventy new students arrived on the same day. We represented nine different countries, although the majority were from Paris itself. Two days after my arrival, whilst speaking with another student, our superior, Père Dornier, came up and greeted us with, 'Bonjour André, Bonjour Kenneth.' I was astounded that he knew our names, and I soon discovered that he had memorised the names of all of us, although not until later did I find that he had spent several days before our arrival studying the passport photos we had sent in advance. 'Sometimes,' he subsequently told me, 'I make a mistake as the photo is not very good!' His greeting, I recall, immediately made me feel at home and gave me a sense of belonging.

After five very happy, although in some ways difficult, years in Paris, I began to think about my ordination. Forty-three of us were to be ordained in Notre-Dame Cathedral. Others were ordained in their own dioceses in France and elsewhere. My parents were interested in coming over for it, as also were several other friends. The ordination was scheduled to begin at 8.30 a.m.

The Parisians all had family luncheon celebrations organised in their homes. What was I to do? I began to make enquiries for a modest restaurant with a private room available where I could gather with some fourteen or so people.

Then, one Thursday whilst I was tidying up after the weekly catechism class in the local parish, Madame Jeanne Lochet, an energetic and skilled catechist in her mid-forties and whom I was understudying, came up to me and asked, 'What are you going to do after your ordination – with your parents and friends?' I explained my predicament, and then, without a moment's hesitation she said, 'Venez chez moi! (Come to my home) – and I will prepare the lunch for you all.' In the event we all went to her cousin's flat nearby as her own in the Rue du Bac would have been too small. Jeanne had six offspring and was widowed soon after the birth of her sixth. Her eldest son had begun training for the priesthood, another was in law and a third was destined to be a veterinary surgeon. The three daughters followed various professions, and in later years I came to know the whole family as a sort of French extension to my own. The English Channel saw many crossings to and fro, by air, by boat, and more recently by train; and all that was a result of that spontaneous and understanding phrase, Venez chez moi!

The lunch itself on that day of ordination was a happy event for all, especially appreciated by my parents as they had had to survive a four-hour ceremony in the cathedral. The laying-on of hands by not only Cardinal Feltin, the officiating bishop, but also some two hundred priests attending, alone lasted over half an hour. It was for my two non-Catholic parents a somewhat mystifying experience, especially as it was entirely in Latin. The one thing they could perhaps really appreciate was the organ playing and some of the singing.

Following a short holiday, I spent six weeks 'on supply' at Northampton Cathedral. As I had only once before been to Northampton, and had no idea where the cathedral was in relation to the railway station, it was with a certain nervousness and apprehension that I arrived with my two suitcases, wondering if I would have to take a taxi. As the train steamed gently into the station I saw a tall black-suited, Roman-collared gentleman, with rolled umbrella and an Anthony Eden hat looking expectantly up and down the coaches. He could be none other than a Catholic priest, I thought. I descended and, espying me, for I too wore a Roman collar, he approached and introduced himself, 'I'm Father David Woodard. The Canon said you'd be arriving this afternoon, but didn't say what time, so I thought, on the off-chance I might meet this train.' He bundled me into his somewhat dilapidated old car and, apologetically said that he had to call on the way at the house of Tom Peck, the headmaster of the Catholic school. I had hardly stepped inside Tom's house before his Irish wife, Kaye, had placed tea and cake and sandwiches in front of me.

The welcome at Cathedral House was more formal. In those days the parish priest was always addressed as Father or Canon, even by his colleagues. Some five years later, leaving Northampton, Father Eric Phillips, my parish priest, made a special point of saying to me, 'Ken, you can now call me Eric.' There were, happily, exceptions to this when, on my second morning in Cathedral House, I was sitting in my room on the second floor, a depressing room painted dark blue, which competed badly to form some sort of contrast with the many shades of brown woodwork. No one had told me what I should be doing as a newly ordained priest at 10 a.m. on a Monday. The Canon had counted the collection, the schools had broken up, there were no sick calls at the hospital, and it was too early to visit families. Then, as a happy exception to the dismal formality of the cathedral, there was a knock at my door. An ascetic-looking clerical figure entered. 'I'm Val Elwes,' he introduced himself. 'I heard you'd arrived. I'm in a great hurry just know, but I just wanted to say that I'm only a few miles away at Great Billing, so do come over anytime. It's quite easy to cycle there. Just give me a ring before you set out. Here's my card!' Val, who was one of the notable Elwes family, became a good friend and confidant for many years.

In spite of the copious ordination lunch arranged by Jeanne, a further reception at St Edward's, Sutton Park, Guildford, after my first Mass, and various other celebrations, followed by the few weeks at the cathedral, when I arrived at my first parish, St Gregory's, Northampton, as curate, I still weighed only eight and three-quarter stones (55 kilos), not overmuch for a six footer! The resident housekeeper (in those days most parishes had one) was a lady of copious proportions, which she clearly thought those around her should emulate. She came from a village on the west coast of Ireland and gave me my first real taste of Irish generosity, humour and goodness. She took one look at me and decided that her immediate vocation in life was to fatten up the curate. I was plied with a glass of milk every time I set foot in the house after a spell of home visiting – which priests used to do by contrast to the plethora of meetings that demand their presence today. In three months my weight had increased by three stones.

Change and new experiences in unfamiliar situations loom large in our memory bank and often influence our later behaviour. One such event was when I arrived in Cyprus just four days before Christmas. After five years in Northampton, I had spent several happy months helping at the shrine in Walsingham, welcoming pilgrims from all over the country, and even abroad. Then, at the request of the bishop, I renewed my link with the Royal Air Force by becoming a chaplain, and was posted to the idyllic island of Cyprus where I was told that you could swim in the sea and ski on the mountain in the same day. I did not attempt the latter, but did, one year, manage to swim in the sea every month.

The Britannia aircraft on which I travelled, landed at Akrotiri one mild, sunny morning. One of the chaplains met me and drove me up to Nicosia where I was to be stationed. On the journey we skirted the Troodos mountains and were assailed with the mild, sweet smells of the local vegetation. We passed through several villages, but most of the way there was nothing but barren infertile rocky country and a few crazy local drivers who drove down the centre of the road.

It was 1965 and at that time there were two Sovereign Base areas in the Republic of Cyprus: Akrotiri and Dhekelia. At Nicosia the RAF rented the airfield from the republic, an arrangement arrived at when independence was granted in 1960. The RAF base was grouped together with the civil airport and the United Nations Headquarters on a plateau to the west of the town, and it was here that I finally arrived just before Christmas.

My predecessor, Father Leander Duffy, had been posted three months earlier and the authorities were looking to the closure of Nicosia as an RAF base. The chaplain's work had been ably done by several lay personnel in conjunction with a local Italian Franciscan priest – the nearest British priest was some sixty miles away. I soon discovered that some were asking why a replacement had been appointed. Furthermore, I certainly was not the person to fill the shoes of Father Leander who had been immensely popular. He had been considerable in girth, a great rugby player and the proud owner of a powerful motorbike, which gave him the name of the 'ton up priest'. When he drove through one of the sleepy Cypriot villages on his way to Pergamos, another station for which we were responsible, sheep and goats, to say nothing of humans, fled for their lives. On one occasion, I learned soon after my arrival, he had brought his bike into the officers' mess on a dining-in night, and ridden it around the tables. I soon tired of hearing how fantastically popular Father Leander had been. However, settling in had to be rapid with the Christmas festivities about to begin. Then, only hours after my arrival, the phone rang and a voice on the other end said, 'This is your commanding officer. Just to say welcome. I don't expect you know anyone yet, and I'll meet you officially quite soon, but as it's nearly Christmas perhaps you'd like to join my wife and a few others for lunch on

Christmas Day.'

This was a warm and thoughtful gesture which I was pleased to accept, although in the event, my innate shyness surfaced amidst the totally new faces, the 'in' talk which I was unable to share in, and hearing, of course, more stories about Father Leander. I discovered that the CO's nickname was Humpty Dumpty, in part due to his rotund proportions. He was a non-practising Catholic, but could not do enough to help and support the Church.

Some years later I returned to civilian life and worked in the Northampton diocese, partly because I felt a growing conflict between my views on war and peace and the compromise evident in wearing a military uniform. There was plenty of work on a new housing estate and nine villages on the edge of Bedford. In order to build up the sense of community, house groups were set up and people got to know one another and realised the importance of welcoming one another into their homes. Then, on the larger arena of the whole parish a vibrant folk group animated the parish under the guidance of Gordon Rock. Hymns were projected up on to a screen with an overhead projector. This not only resulted in an improvement in the congregational singing, but also enabled newly composed songs to be rapidly learned. Some of the latter were written by Father Richard Ho Lung, a Jesuit who taught and lectured in Jamaica and came over several times to spend a holiday with his sister and brother-in-law, who lived in the parish. The welcome we were able to give him sowed seeds that had far-reaching consequences for the future, as we shall see later.

After six years I was on the move again. This time it was to Aylesbury. I was greeted by being told that my predecessor on his last Sunday had preached against the use of guitars or any such instrument in church. A few hours later I sat at the desk and discovered a quantity of unpaid bills, the current account heavily in the red and in general a closed and sombre feel about everything. There was just one shaft of light in the form of a sealed envelope, and inside a card with the words, 'Welcome, Father Ken, to Aylesbury!' It was from John and Joy Parr whom I had met a year or so previously at a folk music day. I felt lost and very lonely and not a little depressed until I read that card. A small gesture such as that can be quite powerful.

From then on I was gradually able, for my part, to follow in action the many inspiring examples of hospitality that had been shown to me. The priest has been rightly described as the servant-leader – although for some he is still the pre-Vatican model of the cultic cleric. By attempting, though time and time again failing, to practise the servant-leader model through openness and a 'welcome to all', I have found great fulfilment and hopefully have been of help to others. It has led me to have close friendships with both sexes. For a celibate priest there have been times when this has not been easy, but few things worth attempting are without difficulties and dangers. As you will see from the ensuing chapters, it should be apparent that the journey was well worthwhile.

However, before embarking on this it will be as well to recount how I was first welcomed into the Catholic Church. This is a question often asked, Why did I become a Catholic? and it is not easy to answer as there is invariably in a conversion story an intangible, mysterious and indefinable way in which God just pulls us along – and in.

Chapter III

A WELCOMING CHURCH: A JOURNEY IN FAITH

You did not choose me, no, I chose you…

John 15:16

I have sometimes asked myself the question, Why did the Church welcome me? Why did Christ welcome me? The simple answer is, I don't know.

There is a deep mystery in divine choice. In reality, I suppose, I read myself into the Church. However, I will enlarge on this and try to describe the various states of mind experienced before I finally started reading Catholic books and, as a consequence, went to Mass. In some ways this chapter is in parentheses and may be omitted if the reader wishes.

Conversion is 'the turning of sinners to God' or 'the bringing over to a faith'. It is a complete switch over to something different. Even in the case of Anglo-Catholics who come over to Rome there is still this change in their whole outlook and way of looking at the world. For most converts, unlike St Paul, the period of conversion is long and painful and it is hard to find when and how it all began.

Perhaps one fundamental belief that has only for a short time ever left me has been a trust in the power of prayer, inculcated in me largely by my grandmother on my father's side. She was a woman of tremendous faith who, together with a certain Miss Coles, my first class teacher at an elementary school at Burnham-on-Crouch, helped to sow the seeds of a deep faith, though perhaps not always through quite the best means! While I was living for nearly three years with my grandparents, every Sunday we'd go for a walk, and I'd listen to the humming sound in the telegraph poles down the road. Grandma would interpret these and explain what messages my mother – who was away ill in a sanatorium – was sending me through Jesus. We'd then go home, and each night pray to Jesus for Mother to get well again. I sometimes asked how Grandma could understand what Mother said through the humming, but she always evaded the question!

I had always been interested in anything to do with the supernatural which explains, I suppose, why one November day in 1944 (I was then thirteen) I became enthralled in a weird and wonderful book of fiction by Colin Brooks, with the disturbing title of *Mad-doctor Merciful*. It told the story of a man who had found a way of casting out evil spirits possessing mad people by an operation on the pineal gland. In a diary of about that time I find the following summary of my beliefs:

> The pineal gland is the receiving and transmitting set of telepathic waves. An elemental is a living entity, which has never had a body. It is evil and with no intelligence other than the intelligence of evil. At the first opportunity these beings spring into the habitation – which is the mind – of the first human shell they can find which is sufficiently vacant or vain to accommodate them. If vacant the victim will become a lunatic subject to violent paroxysms, when he may commit crimes of unparalleled horror. The medical term for this is a split mind. If the victim is vain, he may turn into such a monster in the form of man, such as Hitler. A person may become possessed by one of these evil spirits while he is under anaesthetic. Christ 'willed' these elementals from people, as is read of in the New Testament. A person with a strong enough will can 'project' an image to a fixed person anywhere, so that that person can swear he has actually seen the thing. There is no barrier between the present and the future. Noting one's dreams on awakening can prove this. The world is gradually becoming more like 'heaven'.

Most of these ideas had of course been gleaned from Colin Brooks's book, and also from another book read at about the same time, *An Experiment with Time* by J W Dunne. I remember that I only partly understood this last one. These views appealed to me, and without any questioning I lapped them up. It may be that the idea of being surrounded by a whole host of spirits, be they good or evil, in some way developed from a firm faith in fairies, which I had had as a child. It is certain, however, that the book convinced me of the reality of the powers of good and evil and of a very real world of spirits, which often acted on our own world. I also became interested in telepathy and carried out simple experiments on my mother and a cousin who was then living with us. Most of them consisted of 'willing' a particular shape or design into the mind of the recipient who would then draw whatever came into her head. In most instances this seemed to work moderately well.

At this time my parents, who were at heart Non-Conformists, dragged me along every Sunday to a nearby broad Anglican church. It was during the war and it was impossible to go far by car owing to petrol rationing, and the nearest Non-Conformist church was two miles distant. The Anglican church was much nearer, although I do recall walking occasionally to a Congregational church and seeing Lloyd George, who attended there, sleeping throughout the long sermon. I disliked going to the Anglican church, especially as the sermons were uninteresting and mostly consisted of a tirade against all those who did not come to church. They came nowhere near the highly emotional and stirring preaching I had heard at Baptist and Methodist churches. The latter were absorbingly interesting. It was amazing the way in which a good preacher would animate a seemingly dry text of Scripture and make it so real and alive. To this day I can remember quite clearly the details of many of the sermons I heard from Non-Conformist pulpits when I was about ten or eleven. One particular one thrilled me more than the others. The text was 'I am the Bread of Life, etc.' from St John's Gospel. A Welshman in a small Baptist chapel at Criccieth where we were spending a holiday preached it.

But to return to the Anglican days, several times my parents had tried to get me to go to various youth organisations connected with the Church, but I would invent many excuses in order not to go, just as I did on Sunday mornings. However, eventually parental authority won, and I started going to a youth fellowship on Sunday afternoons. I found that it was little more than a trysting place for early teenage boys and girls. There was a continual sniggering and fidgeting and nudging through the prayers and Bible readings and hymns.

At church very little penetrated my young cranium. God Himself was far away. In fact I was scarcely conscious of His existence. Throughout Matins I would listen, engrossed by the vicar's or lay reader's way of speaking, their intonation and pronunciation. Even now I sometimes find myself oblivious of the meaning behind the words of a speaker, but intent merely on the music of the words and their voice.

However, in spite of all this, a vague belief in the efficacy of prayer still possessed me. Doubtless the bombing and its consequent fears and worries helped to keep alive this spark of faith, just as it caused millions of others to pray, often for the first time in many years. Another book, which I was soon to read, rekindled the spark of faith and set me along the way to Christianity.

This was Lloyd C Douglas's book *Dr Hudson's Secret Journal* which is the story of a man who lives his life according to a literal interpretation of Our Lord's Sermon on the Mount. He thereby enjoys to the full both peace and prosperity, as well as spiritual and worldly advancement. The chief character in the novel is a doctor who, through looking for a suitable epitaph for his wife's gravestone, meets Randolph, a sculptor. They get talking and Randolph suggests an epitaph, 'Thanks be to God Who Giveth Us the Victory'. Dr Hudson remarks that it means nothing to him and that God, if He exists, is probably no more interested in any man's so-called victory than in the victory of a cabbage that does well in a favourable soil. Randolph takes up the challenge and says that he used to think like that once, but he made a little experiment and changed his mind about it. Victory? Oh yes, for he now had everything he wanted and could do anything he wished. All one had to do was to follow the rules! There was a formula: he had only come upon it by accident. He then asks Hudson if he wants to become the best doctor in the town. Hudson thinks he is mad but Randolph tells him to call at his house that night and he will tell him what he has to do. Well, after much hesitation, and mostly out of curiosity, Hudson keeps the appointment and is let into the secret. He carries out the instructions and becomes the happiest of men and the most successful brain specialist in the country. These 'rules' are actually in the New Testament, but throughout the whole book the actual passage in the New Testament is not mentioned.

Thus I was led for the first time to the Bible itself in my search for this formula for success. At last I found it – St Matthew's Gospel, Chapters 5, 6 and 7 – The Sermon on the Mount. Yes, it was most convincing and all very wonderful. I was thus led to an acceptance of the truth of certain of Our Lord's teachings.

It is the one and only really satisfactory way of life. I recognised it as such and tried to adopt it myself. I carried the three chapters of St Matthew's Gospel about with me wherever I went. Of course, for this way of life to work out satisfactorily one had to shut oneself away 'in a closet' and pray quite a lot. This was difficult – so I found. It was difficult, too, to do a good turn and not tell anyone about it. Thus it was not, I suppose, surprising to find that very soon the influence of the book waned, until more than a year later when I became engrossed in spiritualism. I almost forgot Dr Hudson. However, I must have gleaned quite a lot from it as, to this day, I have the details of the Sermon on the Mount well fixed in my mind, standing out boldly as the right way of living.

Shortly after I began corresponding with the previously mentioned novelist, Oliver Sandys (Mrs Caradoc Evans), I was in the library and opened a book on spiritualism by Dennis Bradley. There on the page in front of me was the name Caradoc Evans. I was immediately interested and discovered that it was the account of various séances at several of which Caradoc Evans had been present. I began to find a lot of what was written convincing, and I soon went on to read books by well-known spiritualists: Sir Oliver Lodge, Shaw Desmond, Hannen Swaffer, to name but a few. I argued with nearly everyone I met and tried to show that spiritualism was in perfect harmony with the teachings of Christ. Of course in spiritualism there is a certain amount of truth, but it is exaggerated and distorted and dabbled in so that it ends up as a very dangerous commodity. However, at my very impressionable age, I accepted most of what I read without questioning the authority of the author.

In spite of this great interest in the occult I never once went to a séance to see and hear for myself, though on several occasions I got as far as the very doorway of a spiritualist 'church' and then experienced an inexplicable desire to run away. Spiritualists hold a semi-materialist conception of what happens to the soul after death. Christianity offers a more spiritual future than that proposed by Red Eagle, or Lone Star and the rest.

It was about this time that I met Dudley Dulwich who lived on his own in a large house in Woking. I forget who introduced me to him. I visited his home a number of times and suspected from certain newspaper cuttings in the toilet that he was not only homosexual, but also behaved in an unorthodox way with some animals. He always hugged me when I went there, was great at discussing religion, tended to mock the Catholic Church, and I suspect he was once an Anglo-Catholic. I recall with distaste that one day we were eating ice cream with a wafer biscuit, and as he broke the wafer he asked me what it reminded me of. I hadn't at that time been to many Catholic Masses and was bewildered at what he was referring to, so he explained it was the priest at Mass breaking the wafer, and then he proceeded to mock the whole affair. I think my mother was a little concerned about my seeing him, although nothing untoward happened. The last time I saw him was in January 1950 when I promised him not to become a Catholic. He died shortly after.

Another book which I read about eighteen months after the Bradley book, and which had a great influence on me, was R W Trine's classic, *In Tune with the Infinite*. This described the way to inward peace of mind and it also stressed the importance of prayer. Its great danger lay, however, in treating all religions as of equal value – and this was the next pit into which I stumbled.

Christianity, Buddhism, Islam, the philosophy of the Vedanta and the numerous Eastern religions were all different paths to the Truth. They all led us to the Ultimate Cause of the universe. I do not think it would be remiss of me to quote here a story from a book of Sufi wisdom. *The Mathnawi* of Jalalu'ddin Rumi, called 'The Disagreement as to the Description and Shape of the Elephant'. Kenneth Walker, the Harley Street kidney specialist, commences his book *Diagnosis of Man* by quoting it. It runs as follows:

> The elephant was in a dark house: some Hindus had brought it for exhibition. In order to see it, many people were going, every one, into that darkness. As seeing it with the eye was impossible, each one was feeling it in the dark with the palm of his hand. The hand of one fell on its trunk. He said, 'This creature is like a water-pipe.' The hand of another touched its ear. To him it appeared to be like a fan. Since another handled its leg, he said, 'I found the elephant shape to be like a pillar.' Another laid his hand on the back. He said, 'Truly this elephant was like a throne.' Similarly, when anyone heard a description of the elephant, he understood it only in respect of the part that he had touched. On account of the diverse place of view their statements differed, one man entitled it 'dal', another 'alif'. If there had been a candle in each one's hand, the difference would have gone out of their words. The eye of sense perception is only like the palm of the hand; the palm hath not power to reach the whole of the elephant. The eye of the Sea is one thing, and the foam another: leave the foam and look with the eye of the Sea. Day and night there is the movement of foam-flecks from the Sea: thou beholdest the foam, but not the Sea. Marvellous!

This, according to Kenneth Walker, goes to the centre of the problem of knowledge – not only knowledge of the world but also knowledge of God. Our hands fumble over the surface of the elephant, each of us proclaiming what we have found, and none of us being able to relate the part to the whole. If a light had been in each one's hand, then 'the difference would have gone out of their words'. Many years later, on reflecting on the Easter Vigil held in the Catholic Church, it was so apparent, as all stood there with lighted candles, that we have that light through Christ, and we can see the fullness of God's revelation – see it though not, of course, understand it. I have since used that same story many times in a Christian context.

I gradually came to see that believers in the equality of religions must neglect, in consequence, the value of the Gospels as true historical records, and the only logical conclusion that can be derived from their study is that Jesus Christ was not only man, was not only a prophet, but was God Himself: and Christianity is the logical result of belief in the Incarnation.

I spoke to pagans, atheists and agnostics, and with one accord they agree that if one accepts Christ as God, then Catholic Christianity is the obvious result of this belief.

At this point in my wanderings a great Christian prophet, G K Chesterton, stepped in through his books and helped me out of the confusion which classed Christ, Buddha, Krishna and the rest in one lump labelled 'prophets', or 'revealers of God'. First of all, I read his *Everlasting Man*, but for many months of further reading I was not convinced that there was any distinction between Christ and Buddha, until after reading Chesterton's *Orthodoxy*. This, together with a paragraph in one of C S Lewis's books, caused me to be intellectually convinced of the Incarnation. This was a momentous step forward.

Meanwhile, until I went to university, I attended fairly regularly the local Anglican church with my parents. The rector there was a liberal-evangelical and was a close friend of my parents, often coming to the house for supper. Although he put to me many of the points supposedly against the Roman Church, he failed to justify his own beliefs, but in all fairness, never once tried to persuade me to become an Anglican. His faith seemed to consist, paradoxically, of doubts regarding the main points of the Christian religion. He seemed certain of practically nothing!

At my mother's suggestion I also attended some of the Christian Union meetings at school, and through this went once to an evangelical tea squash; at least I think it was a tea squash for I recall munching a bun, and then before I had time to collect myself from the joys of bun eating, we were all standing up singing a hymn. After this one of the visiting evangelisers arose and told the story of his conversion to the Lord Jesus. Then a prayer and a hymn, and yet another conversion story – and so it went on. With the final hymn we were asked after each verse to sing the following one even louder as a sign of our joyfulness in the Lord.

I had attended this with a friend who was – and I think remained – agnostic. He had accompanied me out of curiosity and I went because I was still seeking God and groping towards some sort of Christianity. At the end of the meeting, when we were both about to escape, we were waylaid at the door and asked if we were interested in buying a pamphlet. My companion very wisely, but rather abruptly, replied, 'No, thank you,' and walked out. Not wishing to hurt the poor fellow's feelings, I stopped and looked at several of them. Immediately one of those who had told us about his conversion strode over and got into conversation. I told him I was in some doubt about many things, and that I couldn't see how spiritualism could be reconciled with Christianity. This was my main worry at that particular time. I was convinced that people could contact spirits on another plane – and that conviction remained with me, and later reached its fulfilment, in a sense, in the Catholic doctrine of the Communion of Saints. The evangelist, however, told me that there was no proof of such contact, and that it was all faked and fraudulent, and, anyway, it had nothing to do with Our Lord's teaching. This did not satisfy me. I was seeking a more comprehensive belief, which neglected nothing.

After an initial disagreement on these and other matters, I was quite anxious to get away, and so (as I thought) to enable this to happen, I nodded yes to everything he said. Unfortunately he took this as a sign of agreement and immediate conversion, and before I knew what was happening, he had me sitting on a bench in a quiet corner of the hall, and, leaning forward, without realising what I was about, repeating after him words of surrender to the Lord Jesus, dedicating myself to Him, and saying that I believed in Him.

As I cycled home afterwards in the clear country air, I came to my senses, and felt thoroughly alarmed and ashamed at what I had done. I had led this intensely sincere man, who was probably a far better Christian than I would ever be, to believe that he had been the means of another conversion. I myself had been dishonest and had not only deceived the man but also, in a sense, God. I worried for several days about it, but kept the whole incident to myself. The courageous thing to do would have been to have got in touch with him and confess that I had been insincere, and that I no more accepted the Lord Jesus than the devil himself. However, this would undoubtedly have meant that he would have come to see me to have another attempt at conversion. This I could not stomach. I had seen all he had to offer, and was not convinced. It was all so vague. What really was meant by saying that Christ was Lord, or the Son of God? I didn't know, but deep down I wanted to know.

I am reminded here of what Arnold Lunn once wrote on the subject, but which I wasn't to read until some years later: 'An evangelical friend said: "Do you know the Lord Jesus Christ?" "I do not, but I am quite sure that He knows me, and this assurance is not without its influence in my life."' And that was as far as I could then honestly go to meet his fervent demands for complete surrender. It is, I am convinced, a great mistake to sweep aside as irrelevant and unimportant the reasoned arguments for Christianity, and to concentrate on urging people to find Christ with all possible speed. It is no use imploring people to try the Christian way of life until you have convinced them that Christianity is true. The attractions of this way of life are not self-evident. The Christian way of life is a way of self-denial and self-discipline, which are worthwhile if, and only if Christianity is true. The first duty of the evangelist, therefore, is to show that Christianity is true.

It was soon after this that I attended a Catholic Mass for the first time. I was having extra French lessons after school with Suzanne Ackermann, the French wife of a former colleague of my father's who had since retired. She was a very devout Catholic, second wife to her husband who was nominally Anglican, but who had once been a Theosophist and who still followed many of their precepts, much to his wife's displeasure. This was particularly so when the French lessons terminated with lengthy talk and discussion about religion with her husband. However, Suzanne must have been praying for me even then, and certainly used to insert the odd word of orthodoxy into our conversation. Thus it was that I asked her one day if I might accompany her to Mass the following Sunday. She was, of course, delighted, and hoped that I would hear a good sermon. It was 20 June 1948 at the Catholic church in Woking. I found the service very difficult to follow, and people seemed to be continually genuflecting, trying to make the sign of the cross and listening to little bells tinkling. It was all most confusing and I had no idea at all what was going on. The sermon was on the subject of divorce, and when we came out afterwards, Suzanne expressed her disappointment in it. I, on the other hand, was very impressed. It was so different from the sermons I had heard in Protestant churches. The priest spoke with authority. He appealed to reason and the Scriptures to support what he was saying, and he showed, not only why the Catholic Church was right in this matter, but also where all the other Churches must be wrong if they allowed divorce. It was all quite definite and conclusive.

During the next year I went several times to Mass, which was then in Latin, and slowly became familiar with its meaning and ceremonies. I also popped into Catholic churches to pray alone, for I seemed to be able to pray much more easily that way. I would often just sit for some minutes, without thinking about anything in particular, and find an indescribable sense of peace and happiness. I was drawn to the Blessed Sacrament reserved in those churches. I continued reading about Catholicism, especially G K Chesterton's books. *Manalive* left a deep impression on me, and the philosophy weaved into the Father Brown stories also helped a lot. This was about the beginning of 1949. The character Father Brown, himself, showed me something of the significance of sin and of evil. I was rapidly coming to the conclusion that the answer was in Catholicism – or nothing at all. There could be no halfway stopping place.

Subsequent to attending Mass for the first time I devoured many books about Catholicism, several of which were somewhat critical regarding other forms of Christianity. It was the age of apologetics, of defence as a form of attack, and especially levelled at the Anglican Church. It occurred to me then that it might be a good idea to see what the Anglicans had to say about it all. So I began to read some decidedly anti-Catholic books, starting with Gore's *Roman Catholic Claims*. This had in fact the effect of turning me even more towards the Catholic Church as the one founded by Jesus Christ, and expressing his teaching. Thus it was that by October 1949 when I went off to study at Hull, I felt quite sure that there was only one course of action to take, namely to become a Catholic. There were a number of reasons, however, why I did not take the final step for another year.

Certain dogmas of the Church I found difficult to stomach. One of these was devotion to Our Lady. However, talking with the novelist Mrs Caradoc Evans and her son Nick, also a convert, helped me to pray to Our Lady and to appreciate her place in the Church and in my own life. Some years later at the Vatican Council, the Church clarified the place of Our Lady, and cut through the aberrations and exaggerations common amongst many Catholics, albeit understandable. Later, Nick sent me a small missal and a rosary, and with the latter wrote a long letter of advice telling me how to use it and meditate on the mysteries.

Papal infallibility had never troubled me, but a certain obstacle which caused me to delay taking the final step was an inbred Protestant prejudice against Catholics. Vernon Johnson in his *One Lord, One Faith* which I was soon to read, expresses it accurately when he writes:

> I am just a very ordinary Englishman, and, as such, I had within me, bred in my very bones, all the dread and fear and suspicion of Rome, and the distrust of what I considered ecclesiastical intrigue and Italian government – the latent hostility which I had inherited as part of the usual English education and tradition – and all this I had to a quite extraordinary degree.

From college I once wrote of this to Suzanne Ackermann, and asked for her prayers. I realised later that she had never once ceased to pray for my conversion, and I am sure that it is largely due to her prayers that I at last took the step. Mother did not approve of what I was intending to do. At home we had many arguments on the subject, some, I regret to say, not without heat on both sides. This, I suppose, was inevitable. Mother thought she would lose my confidence and that it would cause an estrangement within the family, with its strong Non-Conformist links – her father was a Baptist deacon and her brother a Methodist lay preacher. As far as I could see, neither of these things needed to happen. My father kept a low profile through-out, and I was never very clear on what he himself believed at the time. I suspect there was a faint streak of agnosticism in his attitude, as there had been in his father. This was to change in his later years when, without becoming a Catholic, mainly because he found it impossible to accept the doctrine of the Real Presence, he nevertheless never missed Sunday Mass in the Catholic Church. Neither my mother nor he knew at that time that his not so distant forebears had been Catholics!

On returning home to Jacobswell, near Guildford, for my first long vacation in 1950, I went, with my parents' reluctant consent, to Mass and afterwards went to the sacristy to ask Father Gordon Albion, the parish priest, if I could become a Catholic. Up to that point I had kept away from priests, and although I had been many times to the college Catholic Society meetings, I had never once had a talk with the chaplain. John Thornton, a friend at college, had helped me, and particularly his family whose way of life had impressed me deeply. They lived just outside Stone in Staffordshire and were so clearly detached from material things; their lives being centred around their daily Mass at Oulton Abbey. Suzanne Ackermann was, of course, a constant support, as also was Maddie Hammond, the Belgian Catholic wife of Aubrey Hammond, journalist and political correspondent on the *Morning Post* and the *Observer*, who lived two doors from us at Jacobswell. It was 25 June 1950, after the 8.30 a.m. Mass that I knocked at the sacristy door and very nervously blurted out, 'I want to become a Catholic.' I didn't even prefix my statement with 'Father'. This, with my Non-Conformist background, stuck in my throat!

Father Gordon Albion was a gifted Church historian who was often away lecturing, as well as being a frequent and popular broadcaster with *Thought for the Day* and various Sunday broadcasts. He showed no particular surprise at my request, but invited me to come for a chat a few days later. Because of his commitments and my own holidaying I had three further sessions with Father Albion, read several books he recommended, began, but began only, to work through the Penny Catechism – I think we looked at just three or four of the 'questions' – when the end of September approached and the beginning of the new term at Hull. I wanted to be received into the Church before returning to college.

Father Albion's church and presbytery were situated on a part of Sutton Place just outside Guildford. All that time, it was the home of the Duke of Sutherland. St Edward the Confessor had a hunting lodge there, and the ancient well attached to this is still to be seen. It was here in the little church dedicated to St Edward that after minimal preparation I became a Catholic on

27 September 1950. Having been only dedicated in the Baptist Church as a baby, I was fully baptised as a Catholic, and then received my first Communion. At my reception at St Edward's my mother attended with Dora Eates, a close friend of hers, an Anglican, who said to me afterwards, 'One day you'll be up there on the altar!' To which I replied with full conviction, 'Oh, no, never!' However, God thought otherwise.

Soon after being received into the Church, with some audacity, but also with a conviction that has never left me, I wrote a letter to the *Catholic Herald*. It expressed my strong feelings against the custom I had observed of taking a second collection immediately after receiving Holy Communion. The letter was printed. In subsequent weeks several other letters appeared supporting my plea, including a letter from a Mlle Ginette Gillman who also wrote to me personally. I found that she lived in Paris with her father who was English and her mother who was French. An intermittent correspondence ensued until, five years later, I arrived in Paris to prepare for the priesthood, and found a most wonderful welcome at their flat where, on my afternoons off, her mother plied me with soft juicy tomato sandwiches and cake.

In those days confirmation for an adult being baptised usually took place later. In my case it was two years later at Southwark Cathedral, which one hundred and thirty years earlier had been a parish church and where, I later discovered, my paternal forebears had been baptised! I put off going to confession for as long as I dared. This is often a difficulty for converts. My talks with Father Albion had hardly touched on it, and so it was with considerable nervousness that I went into the confessional box in the Catholic church in Cottingham and confessed to a little Irish priest. I began, as I had read in the book, 'Bless me Father, for I have sinned. This is my first confession.'

'What's that, what's that?' came the response from the other side of the grille.

I realised later that he had never before encountered a deep male voice saying that it was his first confession. He had probably only heard first confessions of children. At the time, of course, I became almost speechless, but managed to explain that I had only been baptised some few months previously. He then proceeded to go through the Ten Commandments. Had I uttered the name of God in vain? Had I honoured my parents? Had I killed anyone? Had I committed adultery? And so on.

I became even more nervous and confused, but as far as I remember it all ended with the sought after absolution, the sign of God's forgiveness.

Welcome by the priest in the confessional is a highly sensitive situation, and not always easy to show when it is through the grille. This is one reason why, today, the alternative face-to-face method is to be recommended. Later, as a priest, I recall two less usual situations. One was during the vigil before the midnight Mass at Northampton Cathedral. After each part of the commentary I was giving I stepped down and the subsequent carol was then sung. As I did so at one point the father of one of our parishioners stepped up to me clearly in some distress and asked if he could go to confession! 'I've done a dreadful thing, a dreadful thing,' he said. I decided that while I could not in any way go into the confessional, partly because I was doing the commentary and partly because I would probably become trapped in it, I whispered to him, 'Tell me what it is,' and there standing close together just below the lectern, and only inches from the front row of people, I briefly heard his confession and gave him absolution – just before the last verse of the carol, when I was to go back to the lectern again!

Another occasion was more unusual. I had just had one of my regular swims and had decided to follow it with a sauna, when I met Sam who had come in from a nearby town also to have a sauna. He was married and struggling to bring up his family as Catholics. I had met him previously on a number of other occasions. This time it was shortly before Christmas and he explained to me that he was soon to go into hospital to have a back problem sorted out. Then he added, 'I must come and see you for confession some time. When do you hear confessions?'

'There are certain times on Saturdays,' I replied, 'but any time really.' And then, as there was no one else in the sauna at the time, I added on the spur of the moment, 'I could even hear your confession now if you wished.'

'Could you really?' he replied.

I doubt whether it had been administered in such a situation before, but I proceeded in a somewhat unorthodox manner to give him the sacrament of God's love and mercy.

As a Catholic and, later, as a priest, I have found myself frequently caught up, as it were, in many expressions of God's love shown in and through the Church. This surely is the sign par excellence that the Church, in spite of its many unfortunate blemishes, is nevertheless the true presence and voice of Christ in the world today. Since those days in 1950 and later, subsequent to the Catholic Church's second Vatican Council in the 1960s, many things have changed, but the essential remains unchanged and unchangeable; and I thank the Lord that He called me and welcomed me into His Body, the Church, the People of God.

Chapter IV

MIDDLE-EASTERN HOSPITALITY: THE SCRIPTURES AND TODAY

> Anyone who welcomes you welcomes me; and anyone who welcomes me welcomes the one who sent me.
>
> Matthew 10:40

The history of every group of people, every family, and indeed, every individual, exhibits examples in varying degrees of that opening out to others in love and in friendship, in welcome and in hospitality. This is particularly true of the Middle East. It is a characteristic of the Hebrew/Israelite/Jewish peoples as we see them depicted in the Scriptures. This makes it all the more paradoxical and tragic that probably nowhere in the world has there been a people more prone to tension and conflict around them.

Some would claim that religion is the cause of violence and war. It is true that there have been crimes and conflict linked with religion, and some of the most appalling instances of this are directly connected with distorted and fanatical religious attitudes. However, to claim that religion is the cause of war is like saying that football is the cause of hooliganism. There would be hooliganism if there were no football. There would still be warfare and conflict if there were no religion. The underlying attitude that usually causes war is greed and injustice. It is illustrated in the story of Abraham Lincoln who was seen walking along the road holding the hands of two small boys. Someone passing stopped and asked, 'What's the matter, Mr Lincoln, with the boys?'

'Just what's the matter with the whole world,' replied Lincoln. 'I've got three walnuts and each wants two.'

However, on a more positive note, in the Holy Land the age-old tradition of 'water for the feet, oil for the head, and wine that makes glad the heart of man' continues to be the ingredient of hospitality and feasting. In the Hebrew story of the origins of the universe, in common with many other similarly ancient accounts, we read how God through his astounding love which, as it were, saturated the whole of creation, welcomed the development of *Homo sapiens* into our world. And as Eamon Duffy described it: 'We are guests of the world and we share with the sea-birds a precarious moment's rest on the cliff-face.'

Further on in the book of Genesis, in one of the earliest sections set down in writing, we read of Abraham, with promptitude and simplicity offering two complete strangers food and hospitality. As a result his and Sarah's prayer for a child was unexpectedly and belatedly answered. It is a typical account of the welcome given by people of that culture and time, but it has become well known in no small measure due to the famous icon by Andrej Rublev. At Taizé, the ecumenical community in France where thousands of people, mostly young, come together to search, to commune and to pray, it is known as the icon of hospitality. Other examples in the Old Testament abound and even extend to the account of a prostitute, Rahab, who sheltered two spies and whom Clement of Rome described as the story of one who was saved 'by faith and hospitality'.

We also find that hospitality has at times to be combined with prudence and self-defence, as in the case of King Hezekiah and his defence of Jerusalem, which in the eighth century BC was threatened with an Assyrian invasion. The city of Jerusalem had originally been constructed in relation to the water supply. The main source was a fountain, now called, somewhat mysteriously, the Virgin's Fountain. This, in former times, was outside the city wall, and it would have been disastrous if an enemy had laid siege to the city and cut off the water supply. The Assyrians were advancing and the enterprising Hezekiah, in great haste, got his men to hew an underground tunnel from the spring outside the wall to a pool, now called the Pool of Siloam, inside the wall. Today both the spring and the pool are outside the old city as the wall was resited after the destruction of Jerusalem in AD 70.

Hezekiah covered over the fountain and thus safely secured the supply of water.

The tunnel still exists and its history intrigued me. One afternoon whilst in Jerusalem I decided to explore it. Two young members of our group, Brendan and Linda, agreed to accompany me. The three of us set off via St Stephen's Gate, turning immediately right through the Muslim cemetery. The path led just below the city wall and past the Golden Gate, which formerly led straight into the temple area. Jesus would have entered the city by this route on Palm Sunday, and many other occasions. Further on we passed above Absalom's tomb and then dropped down into the valley of Josaphat where we eventually came to a flight of stone steps with the inevitable souvenir shop at the top and the Pool of Siloam at the bottom.

We avoided the souvenir shop and descended immediately to the pool. A woman was there doing her washing, and judging by the state of the water it might well have been her annual wash. There, just by her, was the entrance to the tunnel. We paused to read again the brief account of its construction in the pages of the Old Testament as well as the Gospel account of how Jesus had healed the man born blind by telling him, after having had his eyes anointed with clay and spittle, to go and wash in the Pool of Siloam. We had no sooner finished reading this when an old man and a boy appeared at the scene.

'You want to go through the tunnel?' asked the boy. He must have been about thirteen years of age and spoke English quite well.

'Oh no,' I quickly replied, looking at the murky pool, which appeared quite deep, and recalling that one of the Franciscans at lunch had warned us that there was probably too much water after the recent rainfalls.

'It's okay,' countered the boy, 'up to your knees.'

I looked at Brendan and could see that he was as interested as I in exploring the tunnel, which, after all, was about the oldest remaining part of Jerusalem. So, we rolled up our trousers and took off our shoes.

'You're quite sure it's no deeper than up to our knees?' I asked the boy again, as I saw him come out of the souvenir shop wearing swimming shorts.

'Well,' he replied, 'it might come up to there in parts,' and he indicated the upper part of his thighs.

The one and only pair of trousers I had with me in Jerusalem were to be totally ruined. I hesitated, weighing up the pros and cons. Meanwhile, Brendan had disappeared into the souvenir shop. I entered to see what was going on. He had managed to borrow a pair of somewhat dilapidated shorts. This clearly seemed a good idea if we were to continue with the adventure. I asked if yet another pair of trunks could be had. At first the proprietor of the little shop said no, and then he rummaged in a corner and finally extracted a small faded pink pair of damp shorts. I made a good act of contrition and struggled into them. Brendan and I then, feeling not a little awkward and embarrassed descended again to the Pool of Siloam. We stuffed our trousers, shoes and socks into the briefcase I was carrying, and, each being given a lighted candle by the boy, we were ready to set off.

The boy led the way, then Linda, who decided she would risk getting wet, Brendan and I brought up the rear. The beginning was difficult and the water by the Pool of Siloam came nearly to our waists. Carrying a briefcase under one arm and a lighted candle in the other hand was not easy, and the boy, seeing my difficulty, suggested that his grandfather, who until that moment had been standing at the side watching us, should carry the case to the other end of the tunnel. He would walk round by the road and meet us there. This was clearly a good idea, so, with some hesitation, I gave the old man the case. My hesitation was due to the fact that we were entrusting our identity cards, money and camera to a complete stranger. However, this risk was soon forgotten as we splashed our way through the dark, damp ancient tunnel that twisted and bent its way in an extraordinary fashion through the solid rock. It was no more than two feet wide, and the height varied from eight or nine feet to as little as four and half feet. After walking what seemed an interminable distance, and having problems with the candles going out, the boy stopped and explained that we were just halfway. One could see how the workmen had started to cut the tunnel from both ends and had met in the middle, finding the meeting point by listening for the sounds of the others' axes. The join in the middle, as can well be imagined, was not quite true; but it was quite amazing how it had been done, especially considering the haste with which it was constructed for fear of the invading Assyrians.

We proceeded on, and finally arrived at the other end, at the Virgin's Fountain. There the water was crystal clear, in considerable contrast to the dirt at the Pool of Siloam. And there also was the old Arab waiting with my case, which he insisted that I should check to ensure that nothing was missing. I thanked him and the young lad who had been our guide, and he seemed quite pleased with what I gave him. It was, he told us, the first time he'd shown anyone through the tunnel for the past six weeks. This I could well understand. Brendan and I changed into dry clothes, and Linda, who was short, was also dry by the time we had walked a little way in the hot afternoon sun up the path back to the Mount of Olives.

There, I reread H V Morton's comments on this famous tunnel which saved the lives of the inhabitants of Jerusalem. He points out how astonishing it is that, while so much of old Jerusalem has perished, this tunnel of Hezekiah, one of its earliest relics, should exist today almost as it was seven hundred years before Christ. It is mentioned three times in the Bible, but a mystery about it has remained unsolved. Why, 'at a time when every moment was precious did the workmen cut a winding tunnel 1,749 feet in length, when the direct measurement from the two points is only 1,098 feet? Why should they cut through an unnecessary 651 feet of rock? A once popular explanation was that they bent the tunnel to avoid the rock tombs of David and Solomon. This theory has fired the imagination of archaeologists and treasure hunters and has led several men to dig for these tombs; but nothing has ever been discovered.'

This account of Hezekiah's protection of Jerusalem cannot be concluded without underlining my vivid recollection of the old man and the boy – their helpfulness and honesty towards a group of strangers. It was typical of so many I met on different occasions in the Holy Land. Arabs are for the most part Christian or Muslim, and for both, hospitality spells out the attitude of God towards us humans. Hospitality is a sacred duty and involves compassion, which extends to the depths of 'the other'. However, for those of another culture, and especially we more reserved English, it may involve crashing through the barriers erected by shyness and reserve. It can be difficult. How many look 'eye to eye' at their neighbour or friend when clinking glasses over a convivial drink or as a Christian in church exchanging the sign of peace? Even more, would we ever suggest, spontaneously, that someone, especially if living alone, might like to join us for Sunday lunch? We hold back and are more concerned as to whether there will still be sufficient meat or potatoes! Does this really matter? The innkeeper at Bethlehem found something in the way of food and shelter, and so will we.

I reflected on this after celebrating Mass on the first of many visits to the Holy Land, and to Bethlehem in particular. Paradoxically, the first impression of Bethlehem and Jerusalem consists of a blend of smells, the noise of human bargaining in the souk, the Arab market, and the insistent calls of shopkeepers telling you what your needs really are. To find the traces of Our Lord, you have to penetrate beyond this camouflage, although remembering that much of the atmosphere has remained unchanged over the centuries. Penetrating beyond this façade is the inspiring encounter with the remaining traces and reminders of Christ's life and the origins of Christianity.

And so one can recollect the hospitality of the innkeeper and visit the cave where Jesus was born, which was, as it were, the backyard typical of many dwellings around Bethlehem at the time. On a steep hillside a dwelling would be built covering the outside of a natural cave of which many still exist. There was no room in the main living area and so Mary and Joseph were relegated to the back where often the animals were kept and the food was stored. The cave in question is undoubtedly that preserved beneath the Basilica of the Nativity of Bethlehem. This, too, is camouflaged with its Orthodox and Catholic appendages, but nevertheless provides a moving setting for the celebration of the Mass of the Nativity.

The Eucharist in this setting brings to mind its celebration in many other places at Christmas time – by candlelight in some smaller churches; or with a certain degree of ceremony and dignity with the bishop in the cathedral; or when we all prayed for my mother who seemed to be dying but by New Year's Day had revived and walked out of the nursing home; or the occasion when as a young priest, exhausted after the confessions and midnight Mass, I overslept on Christmas morning until a violent ringing of the telephone and a voice from the hospital chapel enquired where the priest was!

I thought also of another occasion when one Christmas morning the telephone woke me up at 2.25 a.m.: a sick call from a Special Care Unit of a local maternity hospital. A baby of twenty-five weeks had just been born and the mother wanted it baptised. The Sister got the water and the cotton wool ready for me, and just as I was about to do the baptism two doctors zoomed in and completely took over with their tubes and blowers and special apparatus. One, I think, was Indian and the other possibly Chinese or Japanese, and they, in spite of my greeting, completely ignored me as if the Church was an utterly irrelevant element in life. I was amazed at the way that they pulled and tugged at the baby in their efforts to test and to see how life could be sustained. Science is really quite wonderful but there are occasions when it is given a false priority. I whispered to the Sister that I'd perhaps do better to spend a few minutes with the mother in another ward and pray with her, which I then did and she was grateful. When I returned the doctors had just finished and I was able to baptise the baby. I then prayed over him – Christopher John – and as I did so his tiny hand was touching the palm of my hand and trying to grasp me. I wondered, if he survived, what effect all this traumatic disturbance in his life would have on him. Traumatic enough to be born, but then, within an hour or so, to be caught up in the latest techniques of modern science. Christopher was a Christmas gift from God.

Not far from the basilica in Bethlehem there used to be a Cheshire Home, and on pilgrimage we would take parcels of toys for the handicapped children who always gave us a warm and emotional welcome. This was the celebration of the Mass in the flesh: the sufferings and the joys of Christ in these children today.

The celebrations at Christmas have in many parts of the world smothered the real meaning of the feast. Man, as Harvey Cox has remarked, is a celebrating animal. Celebration distinguishes him from lower forms of life. However, his animal instincts surface when he no longer knows why he is celebrating. This was not the case one memorable Christmas when nearly a dozen friends crowded into a tiny bungalow my parents were renting on the island of Cyprus. The bungalow was owned by two elderly sisters, Maria and Galadia, who lived just to the rear. My parents were living there for about ten months whilst I was stationed in the RAF nearby.

Some two weeks before Christmas I had gone to see my parents and taken with me Thelma, my secretary, and her brother, Mervyn. They both originated in India but had lived in Cyprus for twelve years. It was Thelma who had found the bungalow for my parents. We were all discussing our various plans for the Christmas celebrations and the inevitable question arose of what sort of bird to have for the lunch. Mervyn suggested that Maria and Galadia might be able to help, so they were invited in to discuss the matter. The result was that we agreed to Maria's suggestion that a turkey should be purchased locally and that she would cook it and bring it to us on Christmas day. This suited my mother as her oven was quite small. It was then thought best to buy the turkey without delay, as prices would rise rapidly as Christmas approached. At this Maria suddenly got up and disappeared down the road. Within ten minutes she had returned bearing a turkey hanging with its head down and its legs tied.

'Feel, feel,' she cried, thrusting it forward for me to take.

I held it, told her that it seemed to be a very good one – it weighed about 17 lbs – and then, to my surprise, I saw that its head had moved round and it was looking up at me in a dazed fashion. It was still alive. Mervyn, who acted as interpreter, explained that Maria would let it run around the yard and fatten it up even more until a couple of days before Christmas. It would then be killed and prepared for the oven. My father promised to keep an eye on it in the yard, although I think he only caught a glimpse of it once during the whole week. Christmas day arrived and we all wondered if the lunch would be marred by teeth cracking and jaws aching over a tough old bird badly cooked. However, it was a case of G K Chesterton's ninth beatitude,

'Blessed is he who expects nothing, for he shall be gloriously surprised.' It was the best, the tastiest and the tenderest turkey any one of the twelve of us had ever enjoyed, cooked in olive oil in an outdoor clay oven. Maria and Galadia had indeed opened up to us the potentialities of good simple living. The atmosphere and climate at that Christmas celebration was simple and homely, without unnecessary extravagance, and fairly typical of many a festive occasion in that part of the world.

We know little of Jesus's childhood, but his first miracle was at a wedding feast to which he and his family and his disciples had been invited. In Cyprus, near to the Holy Land, I found that weddings, whether Greek or Turkish, were similarly simple, joyful events with everyone being welcomed, whether especially invited or not. There always seemed to be ample food to share.

Such was the case at Cana – although in this case they did run out of wine, doubtless due to the influx of unexpected guests. However, trust in God's power, through the presence of Jesus, resolved the difficulty, and this continues to be true today, although so often we want to plan and be in control. 'Do whatever he tells you,' were Mary's words to the servants and to us.

Today, unfortunately, many weddings are far from happy and relaxed celebrations. There are tensions caused by the problem of divorced parents and where to place them, and irritation generated by sergeant-major-type photographers attempting to control the whole timetable of events. However, in spite of this, humour can often raise its head. This was the case on one occasion when a bridegroom, standing at the altar in front of me, instead of saying, 'I promise to take thee, Anita Rose Nolan, to be my lawful wedded wife, etc.' said, 'Anita Nose Rolan.' His wife to be was immediately convulsed with giggles, as were most of the guests, to say nothing of myself. Then there was my own embarrassment when, at my third wedding on one afternoon, I absent-mindedly turned to the bridegroom and said, 'William Jones, will you take Mary Smith to be your lawful wedded husband?' And a later occasion when the best man dropped the wedding ring and it rolled down a nearby hot-air heating grid!

Marriage is the welcoming of someone else into our life in a permanent and totally loving way, but, as with other less intimate relationships, always a certain distance must be preserved. Kahil Gibran expresses it well when he writes that there be spaces in your togetherness. Our welcome of another into our lives must always include the love and respect we give to Christ. Repeatedly in the Gospels we are reminded of this.

When a stranger entered a village, it was the villagers' duty to offer hospitality as soon as they saw the visitor. It was not the traveller's task to ask for it. Jesus instructed the twelve 'to take nothing for the journey except a staff – no bread, no haversack, no coppers for their purses…' and he said to them, 'If you enter a house anywhere, stay there until you leave the district. And if any place does not welcome you and people refuse to listen to you, as you walk away shake off the dust under your feet as evidence to them.' (Mark 6:8–11)

In the first of my pilgrimages to the Holy Land shortly before the six-day war in 1966 our group comprised a multiple of seven people, as we travelled from place to place in seven-seater diesel-driven taxis. On one occasion we were ahead of schedule and the driver of the taxi we were in returning to Jerusalem from Jericho invited us to stop down at his house just outside Jerusalem. There we met his wife and three children as well as several other relatives whom he introduced as his brothers and sisters. However, in the course of conversation, I realised that they were in fact first or even second cousins; and I was reminded of the reference in the Gospels to Jesus's 'brothers and sisters' – a generic term in many parts of the world for near relatives.

Jesus himself was 'the host' on a number of occasions when he multiplied the loaves and fish. This was a miracle, which probably occurred several times when he was talking to his followers out in the country 'in a lonely place' (Mark 8:14–21). He also makes a point of emphasising the importance of not wasting food. So often in our own attempts at hospitality we over-cater. After baptismal, wedding and funeral celebrations the dustbins the following morning reveal our extravagance and waste.

Then frequently Jesus received hospitality from his followers, the most notable being when he stayed at Simon Peter's house (Mark 1:29–34). This was situated between the lake of Galilee and the synagogue at Capernaum. It was in the latter that he expounded on some of his most significant teachings. We read of him seated in the synagogue where he taught the Jews. To be seated when teaching was a sign of authority. Sometimes he sat in the boat offshore so that the crowds could hear. This is the origin of our current expression, the professor's seat at the university – the seat of learning.

There were other instances when he was in a house surrounded by tax collectors and other outcasts (Mark 2:15–17) and in a leper's house (Mark 14:3–9). Then, due to the prejudice of some of the Samaritans, he was not always shown the traditional form of hospitality (Luke 9:51–55).

There were also occasions when Jesus invited himself. 'Hurry,' he said to Zaccheus, the wealthy tax collector, 'I am going to stay at your house today' (Luke 19:1–10). How would some of our middle-class comfortable and sophisticated fold today react to that? Instances abound of where he was a guest in the houses of all sorts and conditions of people: Luke 7:36–50; Luke 14:1–14. Frequently he would relax with friends, as when he called in at the home of Martha, Mary and Lazarus at Bethany. This is just a short distance out of Jerusalem. Martha was the organising, practical type, and it was she who initially welcomed Jesus, and later it was she who rushed out of the village to meet him when he had heard of the death of Lazarus (John 1:11–14). To mark these happenings, and in particular the bringing of Lazarus back to life again, Christians have built both Orthodox and Catholic churches with, for good measure, a mosque sandwiched between them and a tomb probably similar to the one used for Lazarus's burial.

When visiting Bethany on one occasion a smiling and friendly Franciscan priest with a pointed beard, Father Augustine, took us all into the church and whilst we were gazing at mosaics reminding us of Jesus's visits to Bethany, he stood in front of the altar and sang 'Ego sum resurrectio' in a powerful voice that resonated around the church and was so beautifully rendered that at the conclusion of the pilgrimage all agreed that it was one of the highlights of the week.

According to John's gospel it was the raising of Lazarus at Bethany that caused the determination of the Jewish authorities to do away with Jesus. And so it was that he went on into Jerusalem for the Passover celebration, the ritual meal that took place in probably a rich person's house where there was space, and hospitality could be assured.

> The day of Unleavened Bread came round, on which the Passover had to be sacrificed, and he sent Peter and John, saying, 'Go and make the preparations for us to eat the Passover.'
>
> They asked him, 'Where do you want us to prepare it?'
>
> He said to them, 'Look, as you go into the city you will meet a man carrying a pitcher of water. Follow him into the house he enters and tell the owner of the house, "The Master says this to you: where is the room for me to eat the Passover with my disciples?" The man will show you a large upper room furnished with couches. Make the preparations there.' They set off and found everything as he had told them and prepared the Passover. (Luke 22:7–13)

It was a large upper room, clearly very comfortably furnished. Frequently Jesus and his group of specially chosen close companions made good use of the generosity of the more affluent members of society.

At this first celebration of the Eucharist, and its institution by Jesus, only the specially selected Apostles were invited, together with some of the women and undoubtedly including Mary, the mother of Jesus. As was the Jewish custom, it was probably she who had the task of ritually lighting the lamps at the beginning of the Passover meal. Today we are experiencing debate and discussion as to who should be invited to share the Eucharist. Changes have taken place in the discipline of all-Christian churches. The imbalance of word and Sacrament experienced in differing degrees in some churches is now being redressed. More non-Catholic churches are realising the importance of Sacrament, whilst we Catholics are giving a greater emphasis to the Word – all signs of the Holy Spirit guiding us. Hopefully this will, in time, lead to a greater openness to all 'who are called to his supper', realising that, as Cardinal Cormac Murphy-O'Connor has said, 'The norms for sacramental sharing flow from our teaching on the close link between the Eucharist and the Church.'

Andrew Ciferni in his book *First Things First* writes, and I quote at length as he explains it so well:

> Hospitality is a hallmark of good liturgy. It is not frivolous or trendy because the way we welcome one another and the stranger is a sign of Christ's welcoming of all God's children. How others perceive Christ to be a welcome host depends upon our ability to provide a safe space for others to express their love of God in common prayer. This means that, as liturgical ministers, we need to avoid drawing attention to ourselves so the Christ may be seen to be the host.
>
> Liturgical hospitality will always be appropriate when its primary concern is to empower the full, active and conscious participation of every member of the assembly. In this sense liturgical hospitality has everything to do with the virtue of domestic hospitality we extend to others in our homes. When we accept others – even others for whom we might not have great affection – into our homes, we accept responsibility for their safety, their comfort, for their very lives.
>
> The place we provide for worship needs to be free and open; a place where the liturgical actions can be easily seen and entered into; where every member's movement will be unimpeded: where every text and melody will be accessible enough to invite our singing and yet be artful enough to proclaim Christ's Cross and Resurrection. The place for liturgy will allow our gifts of bread and wine to stand forth before all other objects, a place where every image will deepen our sense that even the saints are welcomed into our house of prayer and that the mysteries we celebrate are events in our lives today.
>
> Every time we celebrate the Eucharist we proclaim, 'Happy are those who are called to his (Christ's) supper.' The 'those' are all God's children. God's will in Christ is that all human beings should find a place at the table. All – the blind amid the deaf the crippled and the aged, the young and the healthy, the wealthy and those on welfare – should feel welcome. We are more aware than ever that what we do at worship should stretch us so that every child of God can feel welcomed by Christ in the way they are invited to and drawn into gathering as a people, listening to God's Word and responding in procession and song, in eating the Bread of Life and taking up the Cup of Salvation.

A former superior-general of the Jesuits, Pedro Arrupe, wrote in 1974:

> If there is hunger anywhere in the world then our celebration of the Eucharist is somehow incomplete everywhere in the world. He comes to us not alone, but with the poor, the oppressed, the starving of the Earth. Through Him they are looking to us for help, for justice, for love expressed in action. Therefore we cannot properly receive the Bread of Life unless at the same time we give bread for life to those in need, wherever, whoever they may be.

The first Eucharist was marked by the cross which cast its shadow with the struggle of two of the Apostles for first position, the forthcoming denial by Peter (Matthew 26:34–35) and the betrayal of Judas (Matthew 26:20–25), and no doubt Jesus had all this in mind as well as his own crucifixion and the many future disasters that would befall Jerusalem, when he wept over the city (Luke 19:41–44).

On the slopes of the Mount of Olives is the delightful little chapel of Dominus Flevit, the reputed site where this occurred. A Byzantine chapel had for long marked this place. In 1955 it was rebuilt, and that genius of an architect, Antonio Barluzzi, who has been responsible for so many of the beautiful churches in the Holy Land, and who has been so little recognised for his work, by a real stroke of genius, placed the altar of this little church on the downhill side, and behind the altar he put a large semi-circular window. Thus a priest saying Mass there with the people behind him has, as a sort of backcloth, one of the most interesting and impressive views of the old city of Jerusalem that it's possible to find anywhere. Directly above the crucifix on the altar, and in perfect alignment with it, is not as some would think and some picture postcards show, the great golden Dome of the Rock Mosque, but the less significant dark dome of the church of the Holy Sepulchre, marking the tomb of Christ and the place of his resurrection.

The latter is, as St John points out in his gospel, 'at the place where he had been crucified', and so both places are now venerated beneath the same roof in Constantine's Basilica. The first of many occasions of celebrating Mass at the place of Calvary is memorable. I have never had to celebrate the Eucharist with such a background of noise. It probably seemed worse as I had anticipated a quiet contemplative half hour with the Lord. Less than six feet away another priest was saying Mass in a deep guttural German voice with a group of pilgrims around him and merging in with my own group. At the Coptic altar on a lower level a Mass was being sung. All around workmen were hammering and chiselling at the walls, replacing the worn stonework, whilst just outside a Muslim was calling for prayer. This cacophony of sound seemed to reach a crescendo as I reached the consecration – and then the thought crossed my mind that it must have been a little like that when Jesus was crucified. It certainly hadn't been quiet and peaceful with people jeering, the soldiers mocking, the earth trembling and the thunder clapping and rumbling. Calvary is as real today as it was then. Christ is risen, but we have to find him in his life and death in the world around us today.

Some fifty days after Jesus's death and resurrection the Jews celebrated the feast of Pentecost. It usually fell at the beginning of June, and by then conditions for travelling were good, and so Jews would congregate in Jerusalem from all over the known world. It was a great international gathering, which commemorated both the giving of the law to Moses and a thanksgiving to God for the harvest. It was a great national holiday and one can imagine that every household would be filled with guests from near and far. Many were influenced and affected by what they saw of Peter and the other Apostles and the remarkable witness they gave of the power of God's love. This witness was shown in both extraordinary as well as very ordinary ways throughout the centuries.

To celebrate the Millennium there were many great gatherings of Christians throughout the country at Pentecost 2000 – but I was reminded of another 'celebratory' gathering a few years previously. It was the annual balloon festival in the extensive park opposite the cathedral of Northampton. People from a wide area of the country came to launch their hot air balloons and to enjoy a weekend of festivity. On one particular occasion I had been invited to give a short talk about my involvement with the Missionaries of the Poor in Jamaica. Don Maclean was to interview me on the stage at the festival, and it would then be broadcast on Radio 2. The previous day I was invited to dinner with the BBC crew, producer and others. There were about twelve of us in all and a large table had been reserved in the middle of a hotel dining room, which, being a Friday evening, was full of people. Just before we were seated, one of the group turned to me and said, 'Father Ken, would you lead us in the grace?' Immediately everyone joined hands, and most of the other people in the restaurant stopped talking, aware of something possibly unusual occurring at our table. To see a group of ordinary people witnessing to their faith and proceeding to enjoy an evening meal together must have been challenging to some who were there.

The initial sacramental welcome into the Christian community is, of course, through baptism. This is why it should always be celebrated in the midst of the community. Such was certainly the case at a baptism I witnessed in the Greek Orthodox church on the island of Samos. I arrived during the long litany of blessing the water. The font was a sizeable metal container, a little like an inverted bell, standing in the middle of the church. A number of family and friends were there, the godmother was holding the baby, there was a great box of white clothes on the side, and a nicely decorated baptismal candle. Soon after we arrived the litany ended and a lady came forward (probably the priest's wife) to pin back his vestments. The sense of expectancy developed, oil was poured into the water, the baby was stripped naked, and then held over the font and wetted all over. The priest then took the baby in both hands and very dramatically immersed her three times in the water. As this happened there was a real sense of drama and excitement amongst those gathered round the font, and to our utter amazement, not a murmur from the child who seemed to be taking it all in her stride – she must have been about five or six months old. Shortly after the actual baptism the godmother, still holding the baby in one arm, was given the Easter candle to hold in the other hand, and she, together with the priest holding the Gospel book, processed round the font three times. The Gospel book was then placed over the child's head and the priest read a passage from it. Doubtless we can learn something from the drama and symbolism of such liturgy.

The witness to Christ is linked to and depends a great deal on the gift of hospitality. St Paul found this, as did the other disciples who set out from Jerusalem on their missionary journeys. Paul himself was a great traveller, even before he became a Christian. He was on the way to Damascus when he was converted, and was welcomed into the house of Ananias where he came to know other followers of Christ and grew in knowledge and love of the Lord (Acts 9:10–25).

Unfortunately my own journey to Damascus did not involve a similar welcome. In fact it was the reverse. On a particular occasion in 1967 a group of us, pilgrims from Cyprus to the Holy Land, had flown to Beirut and the plan was then to travel in a convoy of diesel-driven Mercedes taxis (this was before the days of air-conditioned coaches) to Damascus for one night before going on to Jerusalem. However, on arrival at Beirut one hour later we were informed that it might be necessary to put on our skis in order to get to Damascus. There was deep snow over the Lebanon mountains, and it was still falling. As a result we had to make a five-hour detour in our cavalcade of eight taxis and it was already nearly sunset when we arrived at Baalbeck, hardly in a state to appreciate the magnificence of the great stone columns of the ancient temple of Baal. As night fell we stopped at a restaurant for our 'lunch', where we enjoyed to the full a good meal. During the meal I happened to glance down at the shoes of one of our group. They were completely covered in mud extending to halfway up his trousers. He had been in one of the other taxis, which had stopped for a few minutes with a puncture. John had taken the opportunity to disappear behind a tree in a field just below the snowline. To his horror and bewilderment the tree had appeared suddenly to be growing rapidly upwards, and before he could do anything about it, he had sunk a foot or so into mud.

A child in one of our cars kept up a flow of questions and comments throughout the journey, 'Mammy, take away those clouds; take away the snow; take away the dark; get the sunshine!' We could all echo that hope as we pursued our way towards the Syrian frontier, many hours behind schedule. It was after 11 p.m.

when we at last arrived high in the mountains and were surrounded by snow and ice; and then our real trouble started.

Seated at the passport office desk was a man of Chestertonian proportions but that, unfortunately, was as far as the likeness went. He was, at first, glum and expressionless as he inspected each passport in turn. I had collected them all as directed and presented them to him whilst the group remained in the taxis. Near the end of the pile, he extracted one passport and placed it face down on the desk. For a moment I had a suspicion that it was mine. Completing his inspection, he looked up at me, showed me the passport he'd taken out, and shouted, 'Whose is this?'

To my horror I saw immediately that it was mine. 'That is mine,' I replied, calmly, though wondering nervously what the problem was.

He opened my passport at the page where the Jordanian authorities had stamped it at the exit point to the Mandelbaum gate leading into the Israeli part of Jerusalem. I had been careful at the time some weeks previously to have a second passport for use in Israel, but clearly there must have been some indication of exactly where I was in Jordan when leaving.

'Where did you go then?' and he banged his thumb down on the revealing page of my passport.

'I left Jordan,' I replied.

'Where did you go?' he shouted out again.

'I left Jordan to go elsewhere,' I replied again. He rapidly became red in the face, his surplus greasy fat almost billowed over the edge of his chair, and he thumped the table so hard that my poor offending passport leaped off the desk on to the floor. With difficulty because of his size and fury he reached down for it, waved it in the air, and on repeating his question yet again, I found that it was not in me to tell an outright lie, which would doubtless have been useless anyway, and so I replied, 'I went into Israel.'

At this he threw the passport at me and declared, 'Cannot go into Syria!' I tried to argue with him, but it was clearly to be of no avail.

The Syrian Embassy in Nicosia had given me a visa but this, it was claimed, had been a mistake. I heard later of someone who had had his luggage searched by the customs at this very same frontier point, and on discovering a pair of Marks and Spencer's pyjamas had refused him entry into Syria.

Angry and confused, I explained to the rest of our group, gave instructions to them regarding Damascus, which fortunately Father Carmello, who was also with us, was familiar with, and told them that I hoped to find my own way direct to Jerusalem where I would rejoin them. I waited behind at the frontier, by which time it was well after midnight and extremely cold. Never have I felt so furious with anyone as I was with that bumptious and officious and gloating officer sprawled at his seat in a cold and dismal little office at the Syrian frontier that Easter Monday. Little did I realise at the time, of course, that the tensions in that part of the world were such that in a matter of days there would be a violent air battle over Damascus, and that within a week one of the shortest and most extraordinary wars ever experienced would be fought between Israel and the Arab states.

Over two hours later three of the taxis taking our group to Damascus returned to the frontier. Tired and cold I got into one of them. The Lebanese driver, Whadi, was friendly and courteous and I think was glad of the company on his return journey to Beirut. The sky had cleared and the bright moonlight on the snow gave everything an unreal fairytale appearance. We passed two cars that had overturned off the icy road and which had not been there on our ascent. A bus was on its side with people seemingly unhurt clambering out.

It was 3.30 a.m. and Whadi was clearly getting tired so, after stopping and discussing the situation, one of the other taxi drivers following behind us suggested that we call in at his parents' home in the next village situated just off the road. We approached the village, which was in darkness, and then, to my surprise and amusement, all three taxis sounded their horns loud and long. The lights of houses came on and we stopped at one, and it seemed only a few minutes before we were all welcomed into what turned out to be the family home of one of the drivers, and were seated around a table that became almost miraculously laden with things to eat: there were meat pasties, salads, fruit, hot soup, cups of hot Russian tea, and all the family gathered around us as if it was quite normal to be awakened out of their beds and to welcome strangers in the middle of the night.

It was a Maronite village, and when they discovered I was a Catholic priest, they were even more generous and hospitable. I recalled a somewhat similar incident recounted by Jesus – perhaps it was not altogether uncommon for people to be awakened by travellers at night in that part of the world, as often, though not in our case, it was preferable to travel late in order to avoid the heat of the day:

> He also said to them, 'Suppose one of you has a friend and goes to him in the middle of the night to say, 'My friend, lend me three loaves, because a friend of mine on his travels has just arrived at my house and I have nothing to offer him.' And the man answers from inside the house, 'Do not bother me. The door is bolted now, and my children are with me in bed; I cannot get up to give it to you.' I tell you, if the man does not get up and give it him for friendship's sake, persistence will make him get up and give his friend all he wants. (Luke 11:5–8)

Feeling well fed, comforted and the anxieties of the night behind us, Whadi and I returned to the road again for the last two hours' journey to Beirut. My own morale was higher now and sleep overtook me as we wound our way down to a lower altitude and below the snowline. However, I suddenly became aware that the taxi was turning and swerving and slithering on the still icy road. It was just as the first greyness of the early morning sky was changing to a whiter hue, which would soon give way to the distant redness that warned of the sun's rising. Whadi turned to me, 'Ah, you have been to sleep?'

'Yes,' I replied.

'So have I,' he added. 'The car was going like this,' and he made a side-to-side rolling movement with his arms and body. From that moment I kept very wide awake until we arrived at the outskirts of Beirut, where we drew into a garage. Whadi got out, but instead of filling up with petrol, he went over to a cold water tap at the side of the garage, turned it full on and thrust his head underneath. 'Now I could drive another three hundred miles,' he grinned. I was glad, however, that he didn't need to.

When I finally arrived at the airport, having expressed my gratitude to Whadi, who only reluctantly accepted the sum of money I thrust in his hand, I found that all the planes to Jerusalem or Amman were fully booked. However, unwilling to take the 'no' as definite and final, I waited around, persisted in my request, and eventually managed to find a seat on a flight later the same day, and arrived in Jerusalem four hours ahead of the rest of the group who had travelled by road. I listened to the account of their brief visit to the places in Damascus associated with St Paul and, although regretting having missed this part of our pilgrimage, I nevertheless felt that my own real-life experience had perhaps taught me more about human hatred and hostility between peoples, but also something of the natural warmth, openness and hospitality of the Middle-Eastern mentality. Shortly after this the six-day war occurred.

Returning to St Paul, we found that both he and his fellow evangelists lodged with their first converts in the many towns where they preached the Good News:

On their arrival they assembled the church and gave an account of all that God had done with them, and how he had opened the door of faith to the gentiles. They stayed there with the disciples for some time. (Acts 14:28)

These two spent some time there, and then the brothers wished them peace and they went back to those who had sent them. Paul and Barnabas, however, stayed on in Antioch, and there with many others they taught and proclaimed the good news, the word of the Lord. (Acts 15:33–35)

After Lydia and her household had been baptised she kept urging us, 'If you judge me a true believer in the Lord,' she said, 'come and stay with us.' And she would take no refusal... Afterwards the gaoler took them into his house and gave them a meal, and the whole household celebrated their conversion to belief in God. (Acts 16:15, 34)

Paul went to visit them, and when he found they were tentmakers, of the same trade as himself he lodged with them,

and they worked together. Every Sabbath he used to hold debates in the synagogues, trying to convert Jews as well as Greeks...
(Acts 18:3, 27)

When Apollos thought of crossing over to Achaia, the brothers encouraged him and wrote asking the disciples to welcome him.
(Acts 21:16)

Other examples abound.

Usually these Christian converts would gather on the first day of the week (not the Jewish Sabbath, but the first working day commemorating the resurrection) in one of their houses for the celebration of the Eucharist: Romans 16:23; 1 Corinthians 16:19; Philemon 2. Nowhere do they put up in the local inn. This is doubtless due to the fact that, at that time, they were immoral, dear and dirty. Perhaps this gives even greater poignancy to Jesus's story of the Good Samaritan.

St Paul writes in 1 Timothy 3:1–7:

Here is a saying that you can rely on: to want to be a presiding elder is to desire a noble task. That is why the presiding elder must have an impeccable character. Husband of one wife, he must be temperate, discreet and courteous, hospitable and a good teacher; not a heavy drinker, nor hot-tempered, but gentle and peaceable, not avaricious, a man who manages his own household well and brings his children up to obey him and be well behaved; how can any man who does not understand how to manage his own household take care of the Church of God? He should not be a new convert, in case pride should turn his head and he incurs the same condemnation as the devil. It is also necessary that he be held in good repute by outsiders, so that he never falls into disrepute and into the devil's trap.

William Barclay comments on this passage:

In the ancient world inns were notoriously bad. In one of Aristophanes's plays Heracles asks his companion where they will lodge for the night; and the answer is: 'Where the fleas are fewest.' Plato speaks of the innkeeper being like a pirate who holds his guests to ransom. Inns tended to be dirty and expensive and, above all, immoral. The ancient world had a system of what were called 'Guest Friendships'. Over generations families had arrangements to give each other accommodation and hospitality. Often the members of the families came in the end to be unknown to each other by sight and identified themselves by means of what were called 'tallies'. The stranger seeking accommodation would produce one half of some object; the host would possess the other half of the tally; and when the two halves fitted each other the host knew that he had found his guest, and the guest knew that the host was indeed the ancestral friend of his household.

In the Christian Church there were wandering teachers and preachers who needed hospitality. There were also many slaves with no homes of their own to whom it was a great privilege to have the right of entry to a Christian home. It was of the greatest blessing that Christians should have Christian homes ever open to them in which they could meet people like-minded to themselves. We live in a world where there are still many who are far from home, many who are strangers in a strange place, many who live in conditions where it is hard to be a Christian. The door of the Christian home and the welcome of the Christian heart should be open to all such.

I had occasion to spend a night once in a small hotel in Kavala, known, when Paul, Silas and Luke passed that way, as Neapolis. It was cheap enough and seemed clean, and although in a secluded corner of the town, turned out to be far from quiet. At 6 p.m. there was a calm and contemplative air about the place, but by midnight this was no longer the case. Greek music was blaring forth from a nearby café, and then late in the evening three men brought chairs out on to the edge of the road beneath my window and sat talking in loud and resonant Mediterranean voices, a conversation and sometimes, by the sound of it, an argument which went on well into the night. I noticed elsewhere that it is invariably the men who are sitting at the cafés at night. Perhaps this is the Greek form of family planning!

The next day I sat by the river just north of Philippi, near the great flagstones of the Via Egnatia where Lydia would have been baptised by Paul. She looked after Paul, Silas and Luke while they were staying at Philippi. The place was marked by a lovely little church, but more impressive even were the great stone slabs, reminding me of those uncovered on the Way of the Cross in Jerusalem, which were lining the banks of the little stream. This was the place where the baptism would have taken place. The Jews were a tiny minority at Philippi – in fact it was the smallest Jewish representation of any of the places that Paul had visited – and because they were such a minority they would have had to have worshipped outside the town; and all the pointers were to this particular place.

The ruins of Philippi are quite extensive but more excavations remain to be done. The theatre has been restored, except for the first two or three levels, and I was interested to note that there were several remains of shrines to Egyptian gods. These must have been introduced thanks to the influence of Egyptian travels. There was a great deal of intermingling of the 'godly' influence throughout the known world at that time. There were the remains of a great church situated near what is reputed to be the prison where Paul and Silas and Luke were held captive, and I was intrigued to notice that to the east end there seemed to be the outlines of a square building which looked as if it must have been at one time a baptistry. What is known as Paul's prison is in fact a fifth-century crypt at one end of this enormous basilica. It is quite possible that the prison was, in fact, somewhere there. It would tie in with the rest of the design of the whole town. Beyond the Forum, which is quite clearly delineated with the great paving slabs covering most of the area, is the Agora, which was the market place, and it was here that Paul would have been arrested. Just by it is perhaps one of the most interesting places in ancient Philippi but not mentioned as such in any of the guide books: steep stone steps lead down to the communal toilets which are in an extremely good state of preservation and I am certain that Paul would have made use of them. It was probably often in such situations, as at Ephesus and elsewhere, that he would have got into conversation with people and, knowing him, talked about Jesus.

H V Morton in his book on Paul recaptures well the situation at the time of Jesus and he describes the old town which Philip of Macedon, Alexander the Great's father had founded, climbing up the side of the Acropolis hill.

Its streets were steep, its houses were old and Greek-looking, its temples flashing in the sun were shining landmarks for miles, and the flat land at the foot of the hill was the new Roman colony which Augustus had founded, very Roman, very official, very proud, full of old soldiers or the sons and grandsons of old soldiers. It was in Philippi that Augustus had settled the veterans of the battle in which he defeated the forces of Brutus, and then ten years later after the Battle of Actium he settled there other veterans who had helped to defeat Anthony and Cleopatra – and that was only about eighty years before St Paul visited it – so the grandsons of these veterans were then the middle aged fathers of Philippi.

It struck me more and more in following in the footsteps of St Paul that it was amazing how he tackled the whole problem of spreading the knowledge of Christ in what was not infrequently an unwelcoming environment.

Paul wrote his letter to the Christians at Philippi some years later, reminding them of the true way of Christ, and in it he says:

> We are the true people of the circumcision since we worship by the Spirit of God and make Christ Jesus our only boast, not relying on physical qualifications, although, I myself could rely on these too. If anyone does claim to rely on them, my claim is better. Circumcised on the eighth day of my life. I was born of the race of Israel, of the tribe of Benjamin, a Hebrew born of Hebrew parents. (Philemon 3:3–5)

One evening after my return I was with a small group of parishioners looking at this passage, when one of them suddenly interrupted. It was fifty-three-year-old Barbara who was slightly mentally retarded and spoke with a broad Somerset accent.

'Father,' she said in a loud voice, 'what is circumcision? Does it mean,' she immediately added before I had time to reply, 'does it mean that a man can't have intercourse?'

I looked down, not daring to catch anyone's eye, but I could feel the trickle of amusement going around the group. Then, with a straight face and in as matter of fact way as possible, I replied, 'Barbara, circumcision is the removal of the foreskin of the man's penis, and this was customary amongst Jews as a sign that they were Jewish.' I hoped there would be no further questions, as it was highly likely that Barbara was ignorant of the facts of life. She was married to a man fifteen years younger, who was also mentally retarded.

Christians continued the long tradition of their Jewish, Greek and pagan forebears in which hospitality to the stranger and visiting the sick were of prime importance in their lives. One of the popular tides of the Greek king of the gods, Zeus, was Zeus Xenios. This means Zeus, god of strangers. Arabs today in that same part of the world, on inviting you to a meal, will often punctuate it by pausing, looking at you and saying, 'Ahleha,' which means, 'You are truly welcome.'

One notable exception to the reception given to Paul, however, was when he arrived in Athens. He walked about seeing all around him the stone figures of the many gods and goddesses worshipped by the Greeks. Towering high above him when he addressed the people of Athens was the Parthenon, crowned with the great Doric temple of the Parthenon. This was the symbol of the supposed power of the pagan gods. There, in their shadow, Paul proclaimed Christ, his death and his resurrection. He was immediately misunderstood. His hearers thought he was speaking about another god, Jesus, and a goddess, as the word 'resurrection' is feminine in Greek, and so this they interpreted as the name of another god. Most misunderstood him and laughed at him. There may well be something to be learned today from this. Our method of evangelisation must be, first and foremost, to appreciate where people are and lead them on a step further towards the truth. The 'main course' may well be quite indigestible at first to many of our contemporaries.

Later in life Paul tells leaders in the Church that they must set an example, amongst other things, of hospitality:

> The presiding elder has to be irreproachable since he is God's representative; never arrogant or hot-tempered, nor a heavy drinker or violent, nor avaricious; but hospitable and a lover of goodness; sensible, upright, devout and self-controlled; and he must have a firm grasp of the unchanging message of the tradition, so that he can be counted on both for giving encouragement

in sound doctrine and for refuting those who argue against it. (Titus 1:7–8)

Furthermore, included in a basic requirement in order to be included in the 'Order of Widows' is that the person concerned must not only have brought up children well, but also have received strangers into her home. (1 Timothy 5:10)

Reconciliation, essential in all our lives, can be both aided by the practice of hospitality and can be the result of it. I have found this in many ways in my relationships with Christians of other Churches. One could give many examples of this in recent years in England, but most memorable are two instances from the years spent in Cyprus where Paul and Barnabas also sojourned.

One Easter Monday I visited some friends in one of the Maronite villages to the west of Nicosia. Maronites are in union with us, and had just celebrated their Easter too. Their ceremonies are similar to ours, although the language used is mostly Syriac. After lunch the whole village went to the church, and there we took part in the ceremony of the flowers. This is an Eastern custom. On Good Friday they have a custom of coming up to kiss the cross and everyone brings with them a bunch of flowers, which they place by the body of Christ. These are blessed, and then on Easter Monday, in the course of a benediction service, these flowers are redistributed to the people, who take them back to their houses as we do with the palms on Palm Sunday.

My second celebration of Easter was a week later, and was thanks to the kindness of two Greek Orthodox priest friends, Father Nicolaos Sideras and Father Antonios Xenonos. On the Friday (the Greek Orthodox Good Friday), I went off to the little church of Ayios Yeoryios (St George) by the sea front in Limassol, where Father Nicolaos had been invited to perform the liturgy. As he was the Archimandrite (that is the sort of chief of staff to the bishop), he was frequently invited to different parishes. The ceremony took place in the middle of the church around a bier bearing an ikon of the body of Christ. The bier was beautifully decorated, and at one point in the service we processed around it singing and covering it with rose petals. The central part of the ceremony was the procession through the streets, led by the Archimandrite and myself and several assistants, and followed by bearers carrying the ikon. The people followed on after the ikon, after they had all passed underneath it – symbolic of entering the tomb. At some of the street corners a group of people would meet us, and one would come forward and present Father Nicolaos with grains of incense and perfumed rose water (probably a reminder of the holy women going to anoint the body of Christ, for, as Father Nicolaos explained to me, the tone of the liturgy was already pointing towards the resurrection, as was evidenced by the use of red vestments and the occasional Alleluia in the chants).

Holy Saturday is a busy day for the Greek Orthodox Cypriot. Large quantities of eggs have to be boiled in different dyes, and made ready for the festivities after midnight and the following day. Eggs are a symbol of life and happiness, in other words, of the resurrection – life comes from something that is apparently dead, just as Christ came from the tomb. Late that Holy Saturday evening I went along to Father Antonios's church on the outskirts of Limassol, and again was given the privileged position of being next to the celebrant. This was the real climax of the Orthodox Easter – as it also is for us, of course. They do not have a vigil in quite the same way that we do, but there are certain resemblances. The priest lights a three-pronged candle from the sanctuary lamp, and all rush forward to light their own individual candles from it. The celebrant then reads the words spoken at the tomb, 'What have they done with my Lord?' and all answer, 'He is not here. He is risen, Christ is risen. Christos anesti.' And they all add, 'Alithos anesti. Indeed He is risen.' Easter has come. The fast is over, for most still observe a serious fast for Lent, as well as for other times of the year. From then on for the ensuing weeks, whenever you meet anyone, you greet them with 'Christos anesti' (Christ is risen). After this ceremony, we processed around the church to the accompaniment of fireworks and bonfires and a great deal of singing before going into the church for the first Mass of Easter. After all this the eggs are cracked – each tries to break his neighbour's egg with his own, in order, as it were, to release the life and goodness imprisoned in the egg; and a special sort of Easter bread is eaten.

On Easter morning at 11 a.m. in the cathedral church in Limassol a further ceremony took place. All the clergy from the town came together to read the different accounts of the resurrection, each in a different language. Normally the bishop presided at this but unfortunately that year he had broken his ankle and was unable to. His place was taken by the Archimandrite, who asked me to do the reading in English. It was a splendidly colourful ceremony – the priests wore some of the most beautiful vestments I have ever seen – red and gold and blue and white. It ended with a procession outside in the brilliant and already hot sunshine to the accompaniment of the great bells clanging joyfully and reminding all that 'Christos anesti', Christ is risen. And so ended an ecumenical Easter, a 'double' one, in Cyprus!

By contrast, a different sort of welcome occurred on two other occasions visiting Greek Orthodox monasteries. Both occurred in the 1960s and the first was along the north-east peninsula of Cyprus, known to the British as the panhandle – the outline of Cyprus being the shape of a frying pan. Near the most easterly point is the monastery of St Andreas where the apostle Andrew is reputed to have called in, found water that was needed for the ship, and cured the ship's captain of his blindness. Since then it has become a place of pilgrimage. Two of us set out one day to go there intending to spend a night at this quiet remote part of the island.

On arrival we were shown to a small bare room with an open window looking out on to some scrubland and, beyond, the sea. The caretaker walked away and I then realised that he had failed to tell us where the toilet facilities were, so I set off to search along the line of closed doors giving on to a veranda, but without success. At that point he returned with a doubtfully coloured and stained mattress for the second bed. I conveyed to him by sign language my question. He replied by pointing through the window. I looked again, and then noticed a semi-circle of no doubt rickety wooden chairs with the wicker seat having been removed, each one standing over a hole in the ground. After he had gone, I went out to investigate more closely. There were some eight or nine chairs in this communal toilet, but on approaching it and seeing the flies and mosquitoes and the spikes of broken wicker on each seat, I decided that the comparative privacy, cleanliness and comfort of the natural undergrowth would be preferable.

The other visit was along a rough and precarious road over the Troodos mountains to Kykko Monastery. Hazel Thurston in her excellent little guide to Cyprus, writes:

> As well as being the richest monastery in Cyprus, Kykko enjoys prestige throughout the whole Greek Orthodox Church, the abbot ranking with bishops of the Church. Throughout many centuries, the monastery amassed great and profitable property abroad, largely due to associations with Tsarist Russia. Since the Russian Revolution, Kykko has come to depend solely on its estates and investments inside Cyprus. Fame abroad began with its foundation circa AD 1080 when the Byzantine governor of Cyprus, being grateful for a cure by the local hermit Isaiah, procured from the emperor of Constantinople the miraculous golden icon of the Virgin, which is one of the three reputed to have been painted by St Luke. This precious icon has survived fires, which have several times destroyed the monastery. It is now covered with silver gilt, and by a cloth decorated with seed pearls, and stands in the monastery church in an elaborate shrine of mother of pearl and tortoiseshell. It is especially venerated as a bringer of rain. Processions of pilgrims traditionally gathered to carry rain-working images to curious outdoor thrones or chairs on the mountain slopes. The windswept trees of this exposed ridge can be seen to be permanently bowed as though in respect – a feature which is observed with awe by the crowds who throng to the monastery on its feast day. Ever since medieval times, Kykko Monastery has been regarded as a sanctuary. It fulfilled this function as late as the period of the British occupation, as well as being so actively concerned with EOKA operations that at one time its buildings had to be occupied by Commandos and the Gordon Highlanders (1956). There are two principal courtyards with cloisters, and several ranges of buildings which provide hospice accommodation for a large number of guests.

And this was where a friend, John and I intended to spend the night. We had fortunately lunched that day at Pedhoulas – on steak, which I'm sure was once part of a geriatric horse! Nevertheless, by evening when we arrived at Kykko, the mountain air had made us both quite hungry again. We were given a room and made to understand that supper was at 6.55 p.m. Unfortunately we had failed to ask where. Kykko is a vast rambling place. However, promptly at 6.55 p.m. a bell clanged in the courtyard outside our room and we decided to go out to investigate. Hardly anyone was in sight – in fact there were only four or five other visitors staying that night – but before we had a chance to do anything, two small boys appeared from the far corner of the courtyard, and made towards our room. One was carrying a plate on which were two forks and a hunk of dry bread and the other held a second plate containing three aubergines. They set these on a table in our room. Although they spoke no English (and unfortunately my knowledge of Greek was negligible) they made us understand that this was for the two of us! So we broke the bread, refrained from fighting over the last aubergine, and waited for the next course to arrive. However, there we made a big mistake. There was to be no further course. We waited for three quarters of an hour but we didn't set eyes on the two boys again. Had they consumed our second course in the corner of the courtyard before coming to our room, or was the single plate of aubergines all, in fact, that was destined for visitors that evening? We shall never know. Anyway it wasn't much to worry about, and caused a good laugh later on. As, however, there had been not even a glass of water with our meagre repast, we decided to walk over to the little café opposite the monastery to have a drink. No sooner had we got outside than who should we see sitting outside the café but the whole of the monastic community of Kykko! I immediately wondered if they too had to endure the same menu as us that evening. We sat down at a table, ordered a large Nescafé and began chatting to some of the priests. One of them, who turned out to be a deacon, was charming and friendly. However, not many minutes had passed when an enormous Ford car drew up and out stepped a venerable elderly bearded priest. Silence suddenly descended on all outside the café and everyone stood up.

'Who is this?' I whispered to our friend the deacon.

'It's Father Abbot,' he whispered back.

Now the Abbot of Kykko was one of the most influential

people in Cyprus. He had been abbot for more than thirty years and had known Makarios, who was at that time the president, as a novice. The monks delight in recounting that he had at one time even had to punish the president – Archbishop Makarios. This I did not find difficult to believe!

The abbot came over and stood by a table adjoining ours and immediately all there approached, greeted him and kissed his hand. John and I decided to follow suit, and he seemed duly pleased, and after seating himself, one of the priests explained to him that we were English and that I was a Catholic priest. From then on he addressed the odd remark to us in English. Then the conversation clearly took on a different tone. Up to then I gathered that the abbot was describing to the rest a visit he had made that day to Nicosia. But then it was evident that a problem had arisen! The abbot himself seemed somewhat concerned. A bustling and a running here and there occurred on the part of the married couple who ran the little café. The table was carefully wiped, a cloth spread over it, and some bread, local goat's cheese, a plate of grapes, other delicacies and a glass of water placed in front of the abbot. The latter immediately set to, and with considerable gusto for an elderly gentleman. He then made a most gracious and kindly gesture. Out of all the people there, he invited us to share his simple meal by offering some of the grapes.

'You are very welcome,' he said. 'Very welcome.'

We stayed the night, were relieved to find that the blankets, unlike those in some monasteries, were not as stiff as cardboard, and we did not suffer from night starvation.

Not only abbots in their monasteries but also bishops in their houses should be specialists in hospitality. I found this to be the case when my father and I in the later years, together with our entire household at the cathedral were invited regularly to have lunch with our bishop; and it became an excellent terrain for discussion and ever-deepening friendship.

Towards the end of the second century, Justin Martyr describes the wealthier members of the Christian community as contributing to the needs of the less wealthy and the president of the assembly having a duty 'to succour the orphans and widows, and those who through sickness or any other cause are in want, and those who are in bonds, and the strangers sojourning amongst us'.

Barclay summarises this:

> In the early church the Christian home was the place of the open door and the loving welcome. There can be few nobler works than to give a stranger the right of entry to a Christian home. The Christian family circle should always be wide enough to have a place for the stranger, no matter where he comes from or what his colour.

One of the clearest instructions on the fundamental importance of being open and welcoming comes in the first papal encyclical:

> The end of all things is near, so keep your minds calm and sober for prayer. Above all preserve an intense love for each other, since love covers over many a sin. Welcome each other into your houses without grumbling. Each one of you has received a special grace, so, like good stewards responsible for all these varied graces of God, put it at the service of others. If anyone is a speaker, let it be as the words of God, if anyone serves, let it be as in strength granted by God; so that in everything God may receive the glory, through Jesus Christ, since to him alone belong all glory and power. For ever and ever. Amen. (1 Peter 4:9–10)

Moreover we find the youngest of the Apostles putting all this into effect when, in obedience to the Lord's dying request, he took on the responsibility of looking after the mother of Jesus (John 19:27). Perhaps this is one of the clearest indications in scripture that Mary had no other children.

However, the last story told by Jesus just before his passion remains the most vivid and poignant:

> When the Son of man comes in his glory, escorted by all the angels, then he will take his seat on his throne of glory. All nations will be assembled before him and he will separate people one from another as the shepherd separates sheep from goats. He will place the sheep on his right hand and the goats on his left. Then the King will say to those on his right hand, 'Come, you whom my Father has blessed take as your heritage the kingdom

prepared for you since the foundation of the world. For I was hungry and you gave me food, I was thirsty and you gave me drink, I was a stranger and you made me welcome, lacking clothes and you clothed me, sick and you visited me, in prison and you came to see me.' Then the upright will say to him in reply, 'Lord, when did we see you hungry and feed you, or thirsty and give you drink? When did we see you a stranger and make you welcome, lacking clothes and clothe you? When did we find you sick or in prison and go to see you?' And the King will answer, 'In truth I tell you, in so far as you did this to one of the least of these brothers of mine, you did it to me.' Then he will say to those on his left hand, 'Go away from me, with your curse upon you, to the eternal fire prepared for the devil and his angels. For I was hungry and you never gave me food, I was thirsty and you never gave me anything to drink, I was a stranger and you never made me welcome, lacking clothes and you never clothed me, sick and in prison and you never visited me.' Then it will be their turn to ask, 'Lord, when did we see you hungry or thirsty, a stranger or lacking clothes, sick or in prison, and did not come to your help?' Then he will answer, 'In truth I tell you, in so far as you neglected to do this to one of the least of these, you neglected to do it to me.' And they will go away to eternal punishment, and the upright to eternal life. (Matthew 25:31–46)

To see one of the many ways this is being lived out in today's world remains for me the most memorable of experiences, which must now be recounted.

Chapter V

THE POOREST OF THE POOR: JAMAICA

> If anyone gives so much as a cup of cold water to one of these little ones because he is a disciple, then in truth I tell you he will most certainly not go without his reward.

> Matthew 10:42

The seeds had been sown; the teaching and example of Christ, the early Christians, and my own more recent experiences, all enabled me to realise the fundamental importance of hospitality, not only to be a good Christian, but, indeed to be fully human. Furthermore, the opening of one's heart and hearth to those really in need was clearly the most important way of showing Christian love. This I found most of all through my experiences in the centres for the destitute in Jamaica. But first, a word about Jamaica itself.

Its history has been particularly traumatic from the time of its discovery by Christopher Columbus at the end of the fifteenth century, through the Spanish occupation, the capture by the British, and the granting of independence in 1962. Subsequent to this, the two main political parties – The People's National Party (PNP) until recently led by Manley, and the Jamaica Labour Party (JLP) led by Seaga – oscillated between being the power and opposition. The JLP came into power at the same time as Reagan was elected in Washington, and the Conservatives there saw it, despite its misleading name, as a good opportunity to test 'Reagonomics' in the Caribbean, and prove that capitalism was the path to prosperity in the Third World.

Tourism brings in some income to the country, but there still has to be enormous borrowing from the IMF. Corruption is rife and this aggravates the antagonism between the different ghetto strongholds supporting either the PNP or the JLP. Added to all this, drug-taking is rampant and the spread of Aids a rapidly growing problem. Unemployment with no government aid or 'benefits' all result in over half the population of Kingston living in slums, or, for some, on the streets. On the road from the airport there is a signpost, which reads 'Downtown Kingston – 5 miles', and from then on the houses on the main road and, even more, on the side roads, reveal a style of building which speaks of former middle-class comfort and stability. Now they are dilapidated and half in ruins. With corruption amongst officialdom and in the police, it is a seedbed for violence and crime.

However, a light in this mass of misery is Father Richard Ho Lung, the Jamaican priest I had already met in Bedford, who was born of Chinese parents who had emigrated to Jamaica. Father Richard, as a young man, had excelled in his studies, been ordained priest in the Jesuit order and spent some years lecturing and teaching – until the sight of the increasing poverty and deprivation of the people in Kingston caused him to leave the Jesuits, become a diocesan priest and, together with two others, begin what was to become his great work for the poorest of the poor. Thus it was that in 1981 the Missionaries of the Poor, a religious community of men, a few priests but mostly brothers, had its beginning. It is now a recognised religious congregation numbering over a hundred brothers coming from India, the Philippines, America, Uganda and the Caribbean. There are communities in India, the Philippines, Haiti, Uganda and Jamaica. In Kingston alone, there are now four centres caring for over three hundred and fifty homeless people, physically or mentally disabled of all ages. A fifth centre, under construction, will cater for street children. Each week there is a 'food line' to distribute food to some two hundred families. The brothers have built and repaired houses for the poor, and generally worked to stem violence in the slums.

As has already been mentioned, Father Richard is a gifted composer, having written over three hundred religious songs and several musicals. The last of these, Jesus 2000, to celebrate the millennium, reached audiences numbering over thirty thousand in Kingston. An ecumenical music group of volunteers, both professionals and amateurs, are involved in the productions and all the proceeds go to the furthering of the work for the poor.

The roads in downtown Kingston, and especially in the slum areas, are punctuated with great potholes and piles of refuse which curious and greedy pigs, dogs, goats, cats and other livestock peck and grovel at. In the daytime most people seem to live in the streets, talking or trying to sell their wares at small shanty stalls scattered at random on the roadside. Most of the people, known as 'yardies' live in small rooms, which can house a whole family, although in the vast majority it would seem that the man of the house is absent and the woman is left to bring up any children. Many, too, are old and alone, and these are the ones who mostly come to the food line, run each week by the Brothers. It was in the capacity of temporary helpers that Judith, Stephen, Lee and I went to Jamaica. Judith, who was in charge of physiotherapy at St Andrew's Hospital in Northampton, spent nearly seven weeks there, Stephen, a surveyor, three weeks and Lee stayed for over six months supervising some of the building work. I was there for a month and tried to help in any way possible.

Prior to my arrival in Jamaica I had heard that Kingston airport was the only one in the world where they had an answering machine and whenever you phoned up or a flight was approaching, the answering machine would apologise that there was no one there at the moment, as they were all down on the beach! Judith actually faxed me warning me to be well prepared for lots of mosquitoes, considerable heat and sleeping in a dormitory.

When I arrived, Father Richard and some twenty-three of the Brothers all assembled in the dining area to welcome me and were introduced to me individually by name. More than half were Indian and the remainder from the West Indies, so all were varying shades of dark brown or black! How was I to remember all their names?

During my first morning Father Richard took Lee and myself with one of the Brothers to show us the three centres, all situated in the heart of the ghetto area. There was Faith Centre to begin with and there I saw Judith in action. Everything was very primitive and most of the occupants were mentally or physically handicapped. Richard had the idea that each centre should be of mixed ages so that it becomes more like a family unit, with those of some ability helping those with less, and there's a certain complimentarity of talents and disabilities. This seemed to be a good principle although it often caused some problems. We then went to the Good Shepherd Centre where Stephen was working. I was most impressed by what Judith and Stephen were already doing; Stephen actually picked up a small child, Jason, whose face was completely distorted by a massive cancerous growth but who had, nevertheless, a lovely smile. Stephen told me that he probably hadn't got very long to live. There were others there in a most appalling state of health with sores, and the smell of urine from those who were incontinent was something I had anticipated, but was nonetheless still unpleasant to encounter. I had really not seen people in such an appalling state before, and yet they were in conditions which were so much better than those from which they'd been rescued in this vast slum area.

There were some eight hundred thousand people destitute and without proper housing in Kingston, just about half its population. There was garbage and human excrement in the streets; there was violence and killings nearly every day – a lot of it due to political differences, and aggravated immensely by drugs and, of course, unemployment. Indeed the day before we arrived there had been the funeral in the cathedral of a priest, Father Pieter, who'd been running a parish in part of Kingston and who had mysteriously disappeared the previous week. After five days his body was found with a bullet wound through his chest and another through his head. He'd apparently refused to divulge the whereabouts of one gang to another, and had met with his death at the age of thirty-nine.

We also visited Jacob's Well, the third centre that Richard runs, all on similar lines, and each accommodating about eighty residents. Finally, we looked at the considerable area of ground where a new centre, the Lord's House, was beginning to be built. It was there that Lee would be working. In a way I suppose little of what I saw was a surprise in view of the video that I'd already seen. However, the reality of it struck me more deeply, and increasingly I found that the human suffering was outweighed by the joy and happiness that permeated the centres.

As we were entering one of the centres a man rushed up to Richard and begged him to come and visit his mother who had an elderly woman in the room next to her, and who'd been beaten up two days previously and who since couldn't speak or communicate in any way. We went there and this was an opportunity to actually look into two of these slum dwellings. It really was a horrifying sight. The woman concerned probably had very severe concussion, and after a little discussion Richard decided to take her in to give her a bed in one of his centres. We looked in one or two other tiny rooms where whole families lived, with cardboard or corrugated iron walls, blackened by smoke from tiny wood fires used for boiling the rice or soya beans. The government is being given some help in the way of aid from abroad, but it is corrupt and the money is not being spent on the purpose for which it was given.

There followed three very eventful and extraordinary days. I felt I was beginning to get used to the heat and, slowly, to adjust to the situation. However, if Judith and Stephen and Lee hadn't been there, I think I would have investigated changing my return ticket to the next day! There would have been really no one to laugh with very much about it. The Brothers, of course, had got used to so many things and, being of a different culture, they were not struck by some of the events and happenings that nearly bowled me over. We were all taken down to one or other of the three centres each morning shortly after 8 a.m. Lee went separately to the building site in a lorry. We travelled in one of the Brothers' two minibuses.

I experienced a baptism of fire on my first morning as I'd no sooner arrived than the Brother in charge of Faith Centre, to which I was allocated, asked me to wash down a man, Kelly (not an Irishman in spite of his name), who had only one leg. His other had been cut off just below the knee. Kelly was about seventy years of age and a little simple. He insisted on collecting small stones and pieces of paper and rubbish and stuffing them in his T-shirt. He was in a wheelchair and I soon realised that he was also incontinent. The stones, much to his displeasure, had first of all to be disposed of. I discovered that he was able to stand up on his own by holding the wall and then I had to hose him down as the shower didn't shoot out much water. When I attached the hose, I discovered by his cries of alarm that he didn't like water! Then of course he had to be washed thoroughly with a flannel and soap. After this I wheeled him into a corner of shade in the yard and shaved him. Both these were 'firsts' in my life, and I told him that he was in fact running a great risk in allowing me to shave him as I hadn't shaved anybody else ever before and not even myself for the past twenty-five years since I had grown a beard. Fortunately I managed it without causing blood to flow. I then moved on and shaved about a dozen other men who were incapable of doing it themselves. In the end I felt I wanted to start a movement to promote the growing of beards!

The event of the afternoon was getting some of the younger members of the centre to have a shower. They were all stripped naked and huddled up one end of the shower area, which was terribly primitive. They were put under the shower, but to augment its effectiveness, I had to hold a hosepipe and squeeze it so that a very strong jet of water came out and this was directed at all parts of their anatomy, accompanied by shouts from the Brother who was doing some of the sponging down: 'Bend down; clean your bottom; turn around; back to the wall; rub your head', and so on. In the evening I sat and chatted with Stephen, Judith and Lee. This unwinding and talking and laughing about the events of the day for each of us was important.

On my second day I gave Kenneth a shave. Kenneth was known as a 'madman', of which there were some one thousand-odd wandering around the countryside and towns in Jamaica. He'd been found by one of the Brothers a few months previously, lying in the gutter, and his head was just a mass of maggots. The smell he exuded could be detected some forty yards away. I saw the photograph of him as he had been. It appeared, looking down on his head, exactly like the crown of thorns. Kenneth sometimes was very bad tempered and aggressive. When I told him I shared the same name with him I think it gave me a good start. He wanted a shave, and decided he wanted most of his beard off but asked me to leave his moustache. I think I managed to do it fairly well. He was still wearing a complete head bandage but for the last two days had been fairly quiet. I then spent a little time tearing up old sheets and making them into rolls of bandages. Every single thing was made use of. Nothing was wasted.

That afternoon we waited from 1 p.m. onwards for two coffins to arrive as there was to be a funeral service in the chapel. Father Arthur, the seventy-eight-year old priest was to do the double funeral. Finally, at 2.20 p.m. the coffins arrived, both jammed into the fortunately copious boot of an undertaker's old car; they were slid out, or bumped out would be a more accurate way to describe it, and put on a couple of trolleys at the back of the chapel. Some five or six of the residents came into the church. The two men in the coffins had both been at Faith Centre as residents but not for very long. Father Arthur, in a somewhat haphazard way, conducted the service, but it was punctuated with instructions in a loud voice to the undertakers to push the coffin here or pull it there or turn it round, and at one point he cried out, 'Mind the dog.' A stray had wandered into the church and was lying in the way! Then there were a couple of dirges going by the name of hymns, which were sung. It was good that there were no relatives because it would have been very upsetting for them. In fact, in view of what happened a little later, it would have been utterly appalling if there had been.

We journeyed to the cemetery, Father Arthur and myself in a car, which led the way, although Father had argued with the undertaker that the hearse should go first. And then a Brother brought up the rear behind the hearse in the minibus filled with some of the residents. We got to the outskirts of Kingston on the west side and turned into the cemetery, stopping at the little office near the gate. There was nobody there. We hooted and waited, and hooted again and waited. Finally, a man appeared out of the bushes nearby and went into the office. He took out a pile of forms, which were clipped together and looked through them.

'What were the names of the two men in the coffins?'

Father Arthur hastily looked at the scrap of paper that he was carrying. 'Wilfred Brown and Wilfred Llewellyn,' he said.

The man in the office looked through the forms – quite a thick bundle of them – and shook his head. No, he couldn't see them there at all. We remonstrated with him and he looked through the forms again. I think in the end he must have thumbed through the bundle five or six times, until in exasperation I took the bundle from him and said, 'Let me have a look.' To my amazement I found that the dates of death of the people mentioned on some of the forms were 1990 or 1991.

'These are old forms,' I said. 'It's no good looking as far back as that. These two men both died within the last ten days!'

'Well, they're not here,' he said.

'Have you got two graves dug?' I asked him.

'Yes, oh yes, there are two graves there.'

And I said, rather on the off-chance, 'Well, can't we bury them then?'

'Oh no, you've got to have a form first.'

This didn't really surprise me at all but I thought I'd try it on. Anything seemed possible in Jamaica! We examined the bundle very carefully yet again, as he had admitted that the forms had got mixed up chronologically. This was an understatement. There was also a smaller bundle clipped together which we perused, but still no mention of Wilfred Brown or Wilfred Llewellyn.

'Can't we phone the undertakers?' I asked him.

'Oh no,' he said, 'there's no phone here.'

Eventually, Brother Louima and Father Arthur decided to go back in the undertaker's car to the funeral director's office to see if the problem could be solved. I took charge of the minibus with the residents and remained with them, having parked it in a shady spot. It was mid-afternoon and very hot.

Most of the residents got out and sat around amongst the tombs. There was a madman trying to cook a meal nearby, cooking on a little open fire. However, what he was cooking was something quite indescribable. It looked very much like human excrement. We kept a certain distance from him. After some twenty minutes of waiting, a man we'd not seen before approached the office, holding some pieces of paper in his hand. I went up to him as he looked as if he could be somebody reasonably official and I asked, 'Could I perhaps see those pieces of paper. Are they forms for burial?'

'Yes,' he said, and there immediately my eye caught sight of the two names that we'd been looking for earlier – Wilfred Brown and Wilfred Llewellyn.

'These are the ones we want,' I said.

'Oh no,' he said, 'they are to be buried tomorrow and the next day. Look – 12 January and 13 January.'

He was right; the dates were the following two days. We waited a further five minutes until Father Arthur and Brother Louima returned, and we then persuaded the official, after some more discussion, to let us go and perform the burial in the two holes that had been dug. We drove through the extraordinary rough, dirty and haphazard cemetery with tombstones, a lot of overgrown areas and great concrete slabs with a name and a date just written in with a sharp point of what had been at one time soft concrete. There was an Indian bison and various cows and other forms of livestock wandering around the cemetery eating whatever they could get hold of. Some people living in a shanty-town area near the cemetery regularly come and dig up the coffins just after they've been buried – which is only six inches to one foot deep – empty the body out, lightly cover it with earth again and then reuse the coffin. I rather suspect the one coffin in which one of our two residents had been placed was a second-hand coffin, possibly dug up in this way. It's quite a gruesome spectacle; and I spied several skulls and bones lying in the grass between the graves.

Stephen had some gruesome stories to tell about life at the Good Shepherd Centre where there are quite a number of children, mostly handicapped in some way or another. He caught one of them eating his own excrement. Incontinence and the like is a very common phenomenon everywhere. Poor Stephen was asked to deal with a baby who'd got diarrhoea and was just soaked in the stuff. Judith fortunately came to his rescue as she was better able to deal with these matters. I admired the Brothers for all that they do, and the problems they have had to cope with.

One evening, after being there about five days, I gave the first of a series of talks, which Father Richard had asked me to do. This was really to tell the Brothers a little about myself and my own conversion, and also I decided to go on and talk about the Catholic Church in England today. They were a very attentive audience, considering it was the end of a day which had been pretty tough for everybody, and we were all seated on the terrace just inside the boundary wall, the other side of which was the busy and noisy North Street.

In the streets all around, the rubbish was appalling. Pigs wandered about and all sorts of other semi-wild livestock scavenged amongst the refuse, which was badly contaminated. Children played around these piles of rubbish. One morning early in my stay I woke at about 4.45 a.m. to the sound of a volley of gunshots. I was told this was quite common and there were killings taking place in the ghetto area all the time – some thirty to forty in January alone.

On my third day there I began by turning the mattresses in the centre, shaking the sheets and tidying up in one of the men's dormitories. This was followed by spending a couple of hours or so sorting out the second-hand clothes and getting them into small bundles in plastic bags to be given out at the clothes line that afternoon. I really felt that it would have been better to have put everything out in a large area of the yard and let the people come and take, perhaps, four or five pieces each, one at a time. As it was, many were given bundles of clothing, which certainly would not have fitted them or been suitable for them in any way at all. However, perhaps they could make some sort of exchange later on. Brother Louima said that he'd tried the other system but there were so many fights and squabbles that he thought it would be preferable with the small pre-arranged bundles. Perhaps he was right.

The distribution of the clothes was preceded by a service in church. Brother Louima, in typically Jamaican style although he himself was from nearby Haiti, mentioned this to me halfway through lunch, and he expected me to conduct this half-hour service. I had nothing arranged so it had to be very much off the cuff. I read them the passage about Bartimaeus the blind beggar and went on to talk about sight and seeing Christ around us. This, punctuated with quite a lot of singing, led into a healing-type prayer, which seemed to be well appreciated. There was an atmosphere of prayer in the chapel. Most of the congregation were women, with probably about twenty men, and their singing was really quite fantastic – mostly gospel songs or the old nineteenth-century Moody and Sankey type hymns and songs. I told them they'd have to teach me some of the hymns they sang so well. At the end of the service they clapped and thanked me for such a lovely service and hoped I liked Jamaica and that I'd be seeing them again and would I pray with them again. Several came to see me afterwards just for a private chat about some personal matter, which ranged from the spiritual to how they could procure a pair of shoes! These people coming for the clothes line were all people who came in from the slum neighbourhood just outside, and who mostly came also to Mass in the centre each Sunday. The following day they would be back again for the food line which was a weekly occurrence. After the service and the clothes line I swept out the chapel. It made me think that all the time I'd been a priest I'd never actually cleaned my own church, and here I was sweeping out this chapel.

On Friday, 14 January 1994 I wrote in my diary: 'I've been here just a week. There have been many times when I've been counting the days and I've done a quarter of my stint here. It still feels at times too much.'

The following day, the food line consisted of another half-hour service in the church, most of which comprised singing revivalist type songs which the one hundred and thirty-odd people who came sang with great gusto; and then, still in the church, they came up, row by row, with small plastic bags to receive food. Stephen and Judith gave out split peas and soya granules. I gave out soya beans and two other people distributed tins of swordfish and soap. All the bags were of different sizes and shapes and had been already used many times over. All went well until one person handed me a bag with a hole in it, which I hadn't noticed, and I was surrounded by spilt soya beans, which rolled around on the floor of the church. Another person also had a broken bag and this caused a similar disaster. Others in the queue immediately scrambled to gather up the spilt beans. It was a good distribution of food and I felt that what we were giving them was reasonably nourishing although it would in no way last a week.

One man came up to me and said he'd been in the clothes line yesterday and when he got home he found that the sack we'd given him was full of ladies' clothes, which were no good to him at all! I told him to bring the sack back and we'd see if we could exchange it.

They were a lovely group of people. Most of them were elderly and had great dignity and were so grateful for everything one gave them. Several of them said how much they appreciated me being there, and very much liked the two rather haphazard services that I had conducted for them. It was inspiring to find people living in such appalling conditions nevertheless full of praise for God and thanks for all that He did for them.

At the centre one morning I was given the job of scrubbing the walls of the showers. They were breezeblocks with holes and not very much plaster covering them. This made them highly unsanitary for the walls of a shower. There were quite a number of brown marks to be cleaned off which, when I examined them further, found that they were different shades of hardened shit! I was amazed at this until I remembered that the young lads, some of them Down's syndrome and with various mental disabilities, would huddle naked, waiting for us to shower them down each afternoon, and no doubt this was when the walls became stained! However, it was difficult to think that these hardened marks and lumps had only appeared in the past week. I made a fairly good job of cleaning the showers and realised that it was no good in investing in tiles, which would have been the ideal, as the wall itself was in danger of collapse. There were so many problems of this sort in the organisation and running of the centres.

In the afternoon Stephen and I between us showered down the young men, and just as I was about to rub down one of them with a cloth and soap I found that he was in no light manner peeing over my feet. Another one came in shortly after, but he at least relieved himself into the gully. These were some of the situations that we had to deal with, and it was important to keep a good sense of humour.

Donovan, aged thirty-one, was involved in drugs in London and then ended up in Miami where he was shot, and since then had been paralysed and really unable to do anything himself. He was a big fellow, and his mother, who lived in one small room in the slums, was unable to cope with him and that was the reason why he was at Faith Centre. He was in a wheelchair, and very often this was parked, together with some of the others, inside the chapel. It was cooler there and reasonably pleasant. Donovan was incontinent and so every hour or so a great pool of water would run across the floor of the chapel, coming from beneath Donovan's wheelchair. This also happened with a number of the others and so one was washing them and changing their shorts or trousers quite frequently, or just hoping that it would all dry out in the heat. Donovan's mother came to visit him several times a week and I was chatting to her one day and she told me of her great sorrow and distress at the condition her son was in. He was her only son.

Then there was Eric who had had two strokes. Judith was able to help him take a few steps, and he was also able to turn over in bed on his own. He was so pleased at this. There were quite a number with whom one could have quite a sensible conversation, and the response was often surprising. On one occasion it developed into a discussion on early European history, and the origins of various settlers in pre-Christian Europe. Charlie was about thirty years of age, but both deaf and dumb. He was about the most caring person I have ever encountered. Whenever he saw somebody in need he would be running around trying to help them. When we arrived each morning he had already showered many of the older disabled men who were unable to look after themselves.

One evening in mid-January seven of the Brothers, two of the Sisters and myself went off to the Wyndham Hotel in Kingston. It was a formal banquet at which Father Richard was to receive the Martin Luther King Junior award for the year. The award unfortunately did not involve any money – merely a plaque. It nevertheless highlighted the work that Richard was doing in Jamaica. Only a limited number of free tickets had been given us and I was all for letting another of the Brothers go, rather than myself but Richard insisted that I went. There was only one problem, and that was that I had only working clothes with me – my light cotton trousers and blue shirts – nothing clerical at all. We talked first of my dressing up in one of the Brothers' habits, but this would not have been really quite honest; so in the end, five minutes before leaving, it was decided that I should don my alb and girdle, with my Taizé cross hanging around my neck. It really must have looked somewhat comical when I walked in with the Brothers in their white habits, blue sashes and rosaries, amidst some three hundred people formally dressed, most of the men in dinner jackets and all the ladies in evening dress.

It was a splendid seven-course banquet, although I found it really too much food after the sparse diet I'd got used to. It also bothered me that inevitably in a situation like that there must have been so much waste – waste that I could see now could be so well used in the centres. The whole event was such an incredible contrast to what we had been doing during the day. I was sitting on table number two with Brother Ambrose, and found myself next to Mrs Virginia Loo Farris, the vice-president of the Jamaica–America Society who organised the dinner. Seated opposite me were a Catholic monsignor and an Anglican bishop. The former eyed me up and down, clearly recognising my garb as an alb to be worn at Mass! I drew myself up to my full height and explained that I was the administrator at Northampton Cathedral, and had come out to help Father Ho Lung for a month, and hence had not included clericals in my suitcase! After the award the whole event concluded with Father Richard and his friends singing several of their songs.

Life in the community with the Brothers was also a great contrast to life in England. I was allocated a small cupboard in which to keep the contents of my two suitcases. The Brothers' worldly goods scarcely filled their cupboard space. Mine could hardly be crammed in. It was also strange at first not having a watch (the Brothers weren't allowed one) and one only knew when something was happening by a bell ringing or a car hooting. I also found that we had no need to carry any money around, nor a Lloyd's bankcard, nor a blank cheque. No diary in one's pocket to indicate where one should be in the next few hours or what meeting one should be attending. These omissions from one's life meant the removal of many of the pressures of modern living. Inevitably, in Jamaica everything began late and if someone said they would see you at 4 p.m. it could be any time at all up to

5 p.m. or after. 'Soon come' is the standard phrase.

I had been asked to celebrate the Sunday Mass and just a few minutes before we started I accompanied Father Richard to see a man who was dying in one of the dormitories of Faith Centre. Richard baptised him and conditionally anointed him. We then eventually got round to beginning the Mass with a great deal of singing and affirmation about everything. I enjoyed it, and so, I think, did everyone else. They were a very warm and joyful people in spite of living in the most appalling conditions. One man said that the tears ran down his face while I was talking, as I was reminding them that God loved them and that He'd called each one of us just as He'd called Peter and Andrew and the rest.

That same Sunday evening some of the Brothers said to me with Father Richard within earshot, 'Whatever he asks you, say "Yes".'

I wondered what was up and then laughingly Richard said, 'Do you think we should go out and have an ice cream? That is what they want.'

So immediately I said, 'Oh yes, that would be a very good idea.'

We piled them into the two minibuses and went to a fairly respectable suburb of Kingston, drawing up at the archbishop's residence. I wondered if there was an episcopal supply of ice cream! After ringing the bell quite a few times and hearing dogs barking loudly, the archbishop appeared at the door in slacks and shirtsleeves, looking a little surprised. He was a big man and, on my being introduced to him, he smiled and pointed out that he was an archbishop and inflated his stomach to protrude as an arch, just to prove the point! He was due to retire later in the year, and I only found out afterwards that he was a Jesuit and in fact would have been a contemporary of Father Jim Morgan, a friend of mine in Boston, Massachusetts. He claimed that he hadn't received the invitation to the dinner the previous evening. This was a pity as he would have heard how Richard was highlighted and his work warmly acclaimed by so many outside the Church. He gave us no ice cream and, we went on to a popular kiosk where the lady serving knew the Brothers and gave us each an enormous ice cream cornet, which made up for our usual diet of rice, chickens' feet, pigs' tails and fish heads.

On the Monday morning when we arrived at the centre I was amazed to find that the corpse of the man who had died at 3 p.m. on the Sunday afternoon was still wrapped up in a sheet, lying on the floor of the dormitory. With the heat I was afraid that it would soon begin to smell. Fortunately the undertakers came a little later in the morning, but not before Judith and Stephen had spent some time mopping the floor and trying to avoid the corpse! Normally the undertakers didn't in fact delay so long and this apparently was somewhat exceptional, perhaps because the death had occurred on Sunday afternoon or, more likely, because it was down amongst the poor in the shanty-town area.

I spent the morning scrubbing the wall of the shower again as it had more brown stains and substance clinging to it. I wondered if it was due to the chickens' feet soup that the residents had consumed on Saturday. One of the residents, Frank Thompson, came and chatted to me while I was scrubbing the wall. He was one of the more intelligent and normal residents and always looked fairly smart. In the middle of our chatting, which I was quite pleased about as it meant I could stop scrubbing for a little while, he suddenly turned round to the wall that I was trying to clean and said, 'I just have to wee here because it takes me very suddenly,' and without more ado an avalanche of urine descended over the lower part of the wall. These sort of happenings, and far worse occur much of the time.

In the afternoon Stephen, Judith and I took two of the residents to the Belle View Psychiatry Hospital. There were three thousand residents in the hospital at that time. There was a problem with Kenneth, one of the residents who'd had maggots in his head and who wasn't at all sure of his surname. The psychiatrist, when we finally saw him, asked him if he heard voices, to which he replied 'No' first of all, and then later 'Yes'. When we arrived at the hospital we found Miss Bluberry Well who was one of the helpers at Jacob's Well and who had with her one of the residents from there. Miss Bluberry was quite enormous and must have been at least three foot six inches in diameter around her bottom. She wore a semi-translucent pale green blouse and occupied two seats in the minibus. We decided to call her Twiggy. The three residents, our two from Faith Centre and the one from Jacob's Well, were all given injections. After I'd walked to the far side of the hospital grounds to the dispensary and queued up for prescriptions with Miss Bluberry, I came back and found Stephen and Judith standing guard over our three residents who had by then fallen asleep, lying across the seats in the uncomfortable and derelict-looking waiting area. The chairs in the waiting area were in two lines facing a dirty blank wall, instead of facing out of the window. I felt I would like to reorganise them all! The whole situation was Dickensian and the hospital conditions were appalling.

The next day we had to take a sick resident to Kingston Public Hospital and I noticed somebody lying in the gutter just near where we parked the minibus. It looked at first like a bundle of clothes, but then we saw that it was a man, clearly very ill indeed, destitute. When we came out someone had given him something to drink. At the outpatients' entrance there was a man begging. He had half a plaster on his leg and must have been about mid-fifties. I was very concerned about both of these but particularly the man who was lying in the gutter, only yards from the entrance to the casualty part of the hospital. I discussed the matter with Judith and then, providentially, a nurse came out who introduced herself as Sister Russell. She turned out to be a sort of liaison between the hospital and Father Richard. I spoke to her about both these people and she explained that the one in the gutter had Aids and nobody would really touch him. There was nowhere in Kingston for people with Aids. I said that I thought something had to be done. Should we take him in or perhaps we could get him in with the Sisters of Charity, Mother Teresa's Sisters, as they care for the dying and probably do have patients with Aids? The Sister was concerned also about the other man who was begging at the door and who'd been there some days. He'd picked off half the plaster from his leg and was in quite a bad way. I said to her that I would speak to the Brothers and particularly Father Richard about it. I mentioned it to Brother Louima at lunch, and on our way back from the cemetery we called in at the hospital again. Brother had a chat with Sister Russell, and it ended with us bringing the man who'd been begging back with us to give him a home at Faith

Centre.

The one with Aids about whom I was really more concerned had been moved on to a trolley stretcher in the outpatients area. Apparently he had spent one night in the hospital but they really could not take up a bed for him, Sister Russell explained, as there were other people who had a greater claim on it; and this was why he had left the hospital a few days previously. The tragedy was that he had ended up in the gutter just outside the hospital, too weak to go anywhere else. While we were there sorting things out for the patient we'd brought, the man with Aids partly fell off the trolley which was some four feet high off the ground and ended up with his legs still on the trolley, but his head touching the floor. Nurses and others were passing by and taking no notice. Two other men who were in there for some sort of treatment called out that he had Aids when Brother and I went over to him, and cried to us to keep away! I was wondering whether we ourselves should do something, although there we were in the hospital with nurses and doctors to-ing and fro-ing, and it was in fact their domain. While I was still wondering what to do there was a plonk and the rest of his body fell on the floor. At that one of the nursing staff moved towards him and began to sort him out. The whole situation was like a nightmare, and I wondered if with our own Health Service deteriorating similar happenings could occur in England in the not too distant future.

Most days were very full with washing people, washing mattresses, sorting out the beds, cleaning down cobwebs, shaving, and cleaning out a drain. One afternoon there was a variation on this by, first of all, someone who'd been delivering equipment at the Lord's House smashing two of his fingers. The wind had caught the door and slammed it on his hand. Rather than go to the hospital he had come straight up to Faith Centre, which was fairly near, to see Sister Mary and Judith. Going to the hospital would have meant waiting hours before being attended to.

Then, by about 3.15 p.m., I was sitting on the steps of the church at Faith Centre, which was just inside the main gate, preparing my evening talk to the Brothers, when there was a tremendous volley of gunshots, which sounded as if it was against the iron gate just by me. I stood up and one of the Sisters who was in the church behind me sorting out clothing said, 'Come in, come in.' I went inside for a moment and then the gatekeeper, Birthright, went down to the gate and looked out and I went to join him, and several others came and then the two Sisters, and in the end we were all just standing in the gateway which had been opened, and crowds of people were milling around outside. The victim of the shooting was someone who normally sat on the corner just outside Faith Centre and he had been badly wounded in the chest. A crowd of people were carrying him off, and later I heard an ambulance come. Just a few yards away there was a group of young men with strange little conical things on top of their heads, which looked to me as if they were some sort of gang. As they were standing quite near our open gate, I said very commandingly to the Sisters and to some of the residents who'd by that time gathered there, 'Come inside and close the gate!' I don't think they were used to me being quite so firm, and they complied immediately. Brother Eugene was in the storeroom and hadn't heard anything. He was only told about it some ten minutes later. Brother Louima was out in the minibus, and one or two people in the centre thought when they heard the volley that it was Louima who'd been shot! I heard later that the man had died, that he'd been involved in drugs, and that it was someone in a white car who had shot him.

A group of nine people of varying ages from New Jersey came on Thursday night. They were mostly professionals, one being a doctor who'd already been to Kingston. They had entertained Father Richard's music group the previous year, and it was really as a result of this that a group of them had come over to see for themselves the Brothers and all that they were doing. One of their number had not managed to come on Thursday night but was expected on a flight on Friday evening. I was asked to go to the airport to meet him. He turned out to be a young lawyer, and this was the first time he'd travelled by air and been such a distance away from home. He sat in the back of the car as Brother Edward was navigating, or rather endeavouring to navigate. Four times he directed me wrongly or indicated a turning after I'd passed it. Our American visitor, Stephen, I could feel was becoming very tense.

He had already been waiting for us for nearly thirty minutes, and was wondering what to do if no one met him. Then, when Brother Edward told me on several occasions that I could drive through the red lights as this was quite possible at night if you saw that nothing was coming, I thought that our passenger was going to have a heart attack and he shouted suddenly to me, 'The lights are red!' I was in fact driving quite carefully, that is, for Jamaica. He was a nervous type and I found out later that this same lawyer had insisted on wearing rubber gloves throughout his visit for fear he would contract Aids.

The previous Wednesday, which is the usual day for the food line, we'd only managed to give out a tin of salted fish to each person. No one had moaned, but we'd promised them a more substantial handout on the Friday. The American group joined in the distribution, some handing out dried peas, soya granules and soya beans. I was left to give out about twenty or thirty wrapped sweets as a sort of bonus! The sweets were, in fact, a coagulated mass of about a hundred or so in plastic bags. Each one had started oozing stickiness out of its wrapping. I remarked to the American lady stationed next to me who was distributing the ration of dried peas that there was one thing I could not stand and this was getting my fingers sticky. I inherited it from my father who was the same. Neither of us could cope with even peeling an orange or the like! My American companion did not, however, offer to swap places with me, but just smiled and said, 'My, I guess the Lord's got a great sense of humour!'

There are many Americans who provide invaluable help and support for the Brothers. Don Washington was a retired engineer from the States who for some years had been supervising much of the building work and maintenance at the centres. At the present time he was involved in the construction of the new centre, Lord's House, where Lee had the immediate charge of the gang of local workers. Don's wife, Grace, much younger than her husband, had turned her hand to typing, nursing and innumerable jobs connected with the care of the residents. Between them they constituted the indispensable executive and administrative back-up to Father Richard who provided the vision, the enthusiasm and the impetus to step out in faith.

One morning I got a lift down to Good Shepherd Centre, and Brother Stephen who worked there, took me on a walk-out in the heart of the slums. We called on five different people and I was able to take some discreet photographs. The slums inside were far worse in fact than they appeared from the outside. There was an old lady, Elvira, in the smallest of rooms, blackened with the smoke from a tiny wood fire on which she was boiling some rice. She pointed out to me that most of the walls were just cardboard. I did notice that as she pulled back a pin-up picture (no doubt her son's, who shared the one double bed that nearly filled the room) there, wedged against the cardboard wall, were several unused bullets! I had never seen living conditions so bad before.

However, on the brighter side, we also saw some of the wooden chalets which the Brothers had built in the heart of the slum. These were little more than garden sheds. The Brothers had been given the sections and had put them up themselves, and thus housed quite a number of people in this way. Elsie was another old lady living in a tiny shack some six feet square, again with a tiny fire in the corner, a bed half filling the space, a kerosene lamp and evidence of a considerable quantity of rain having come through the partly non-existent roof. Brother Stephen promised to see what he could do about rehousing her as soon as possible in one of the aforementioned chalets. Elsie was depressed about it all, and before leaving, I offered to pray over her. She was pleased, and I heard that the following day she had cheered up and was sitting outside her poor dwelling, happy and at peace again.

One night I was particularly tired and my mind was racing so I decided to take one of the sleeping tablets that my GP, knowing I might be sleeping in a dormitory, had kindly prescribed for me. I took this shortly after night prayer at about 9.20 p.m., and was just going towards the wash place to clean my teeth before retiring for the night, when a hand touched my arm and one of the younger Brothers, Gregory, asked me in a whisper if he could have a few words with me. Inwardly I groaned, but outwardly I said, 'Yes, of course,' and then I added hopefully, 'Provided it is not against the rules.'

'Oh no,' he said, 'for anything like this it's all right.'

I wondered what was coming next. We went to the other side

of the enclosed area opposite the dormitories and sat on a step in the semi-darkness. The few minutes evolved into about forty minutes, and throughout I was concerned that the sleeping tablet would begin to work. Fortunately all was well, and I kept awake, but when I finally got to my bed well after 10 p.m. I was asleep almost halfway through negotiating the intricacies of the mosquito net.

The following morning I was once again shuttling people to and fro in the van, after which Sammy took Judith and myself to the rubbish tip which I had wanted to visit. This was the other side of Kingston and near the worst slum area. We drove right on to the rubbish tip. The smell almost made me vomit. There were people living in cardboard and corrugated iron shacks actually on top of the rubbish, crowds who were scavenging, and others who were stopping every lorry bringing waste matter in to see if they could get hold of the perks! There were many hundreds of people living there. A diocesan priest had started a school in a little mission station for them. It had, however, run into some difficulty and aroused no little controversy. I took a few photographs when Sammy told me that I was able to. However, he advised me not to show my camera when anybody was looking, and he made quite sure that we locked all the doors of the minibus. Even so, as we were leaving, some people came up to us and started threatening Sammy. They had noticed that we'd not brought any rubbish to be deposited!

Brother Murray, who at the beginning of February took over Faith Centre as Brothers Louima and Eugene were going to Haiti, was telling us at lunch that the previous day when two priests had visited the centres, one of them, the superior of the seminary had been introduced to Charlie, the deaf and dumb lad who had the great gift for caring and sharing. Brother Murray had given him a banana that afternoon as a little reward for some of the things he'd been doing. Charlie had peeled the banana and put it in his far from clean pocket, which also contained, of course, lots of other things that he liked to share. When Charlie saw the seminary superior and realised through lip-reading that Brother Murray was singing his praises, he immediately, with almost sleight of hand, produced the peeled banana from his pocket and popped it into the mouth of the superior who was forced to consume it. Brother Ambrose, who was with the two priests showing them around, quickly added, 'Oh, Charlie likes sharing everything, Father!'

The last few days of my month in Jamaica I made many warm farewells: so many wanted us to stay or wanted us to return soon. It was the same story with the residents, and then later the Brothers, many of whom were praying that we'd come back and some were even praying that I'd become a Brother! I don't think I've ever had such a warm welcome and so much affirmation, nor experienced so much suffering, nor such great joy as I had in that month. In response to a few words from one of the Brothers at dinner I tried inadequately to express my thanks, as did Judith, but it was impossible to put into words all that we had gained from our month there.

On that last morning I took the Brothers and Sisters down to the centres, and then the morning seemed to be pretty well taken up by going from one centre to another, picking up various items as Sammy, who usually drove, was having a day off. Then we heard of a lady dying in Faith Centre and so I had to go back for the oils and return to anoint her. A phone message then came to say that there were five chickens for collection as Rosa had pointed out that there was no food for the evening meal for the Brothers. When I found that the five chickens were frozen solid from the freezer at Faith Centre I thought that this probably wouldn't be very acceptable to Rosa. Anyway, I'd been asked to take them back so I complied. When Rosa, who cooked most days for the Brothers' Community, saw the frozen chickens she literally threw them on the floor and added something unintelligible in Jamaican patois! 'They're no good,' she said. I said that I thought not, but I thought I'd better bring them up as they might be all right for the morrow! I don't know what the Brothers ended up eating that night because there wasn't very much food around, apart from the usual rice. Perhaps they mourned our departure and fasted.

By about 11 a.m. I managed to free myself of driving the van and got my luggage ready, had a shower and sat down to write up a little more of an article I was composing on the month in

Jamaica. However, it was not to be, as within a few minutes Brother Ambrose called me and wanted me to go to Jacob's Well to pick up a resident to take to the hospital. Then Father Richard wanted to have a final chat with me. Midday prayer was a sign to stop the comings and goings, and after this we had lunch and said goodbye to Don and Grace Washington who were such a fantastic couple and so devoted in all that they did for Father Richard and the centres. Judith and I then had about forty minutes before leaving when there was a phone call saying that a driver was urgently needed to pick up things at Faith Centre, and then call at Good Shepherd Centre – I was still the only driver available. I got back from this mission to find that Jacob's Well had phoned, saying that somebody needed to go to Belle View, the mental hospital, and so would I take them. By this time it was 1.40 p.m. and Judith and I should by rights have been at the airport by 2 p.m. Anyway, I performed my mission and got back to North Street by 2 p.m. Father Richard then drove us, together with boxes of coffee to sell in England, to the airport, which is a twenty-minute drive away. Richard was well known at the airport and we went straight into the check-in point and walked straight through. The magic words 'Father Ho Lung' had been uttered and it worked!

When we got on the plane to Miami we found that someone had occupied one of our seats. In fact one might say he had occupied both our seats because he was by far the fattest Jamaican I had ever come across, larger even than Miss Bluberry, and he overflowed on to three quarters of the second seat. He apologised when we pointed out that we should have been sitting there and immediately moved to the row in front which was in fact the one allocated to him.

At Heathrow we decided it would be advisable with so many boxes of Blue Mountain Jamaican coffee piled high on the airport trolley to pass through the 'red' customs exit. Two turban-clad gentlemen, whom I assumed were Sikhs, stood behind the counter. They eyed me sternly. I explained that I was a priest and that we had both been working in a religious community in Jamaica where we had been given the coffee to sell to parishioners in England in aid of the community's work with the poor. They both listened, and there was silence whilst they looked again at the pile of coffee boxes, and then again at Judith and myself. Then, just as I feared they were about to ask us to unpack the 96 lbs of coffee, the senior Sikh, still looking quite severe, motioned with his hand and said, 'All right, go on – and God be with you.'

Thus ended a memorable month. We had been four weeks plunged, as it were, in the heart of the Gospel: a month of prayer and work, of listening to the word of the Lord and of living that out in His power, of service which involved caring for the poor and praying with them, a ministry that was a blend of the practical and the spiritual, of love of the whole person. The 'Mandatum' of Maundy Thursday, when Jesus washed the feet of his Apostles and told them, 'A new commandment I give you, that you love one another as I have loved you,' took on a fuller and deeper meaning, for the poor we have always with us.

For days, on awakening in the morning, I had short phrases repeatedly passing though my mind – expressions of love and friendship on the lips of the poor whom I had left – 'Goodbye and a safe journey. We'll miss you.' 'Why have you got to go?' 'Come back again soon.' 'We love having you here.' 'You've done so much good.' 'Please come back very soon.' 'God be with you and if we don't meet again in this life it'll be in the next.' The warmth and the love were genuine and very moving.

In fact, I was to meet some of them again in this life, as I returned on several subsequent occasions and it was remarkable that many remembered me. However, I found the visits increasingly difficult, although the welcome I was given was so warm and genuine.

Chapter VI

JAMAICA AGAIN – FIVE YEARS LATER

Lord's House was completed in 1995 and housed quite a lot of children, each with unique and special problems. There was Nicholas who had maggots in his mouth. He was eight years old, quite a normal child, and then went to hospital for an injection, which caused him total paralysis from which he had never recovered. He lay back in a cot with his mouth open and it was because of this that flies had settled and laid eggs, which had developed into the maggots. One of the Brothers had already taken about a dozen maggots out of his mouth, but there were still some more, and there was a hole that they had burrowed just behind his front tooth. I found it difficult to cope with this situation although I merely held the lad's head so that he didn't move around while Brother Eugene, with a pair of tweezers and some antiseptic and cotton wool, did the necessary removal of the remaining maggots.

Then there was Sheldon who was always so helpful. He was unable to walk but moved at an incredible rate by half sliding and half hopping along on his knees. Various things were wrong with his innards and he had to wear diapers all the time. For the last year or so he had been looking after Mario who was about the worst case of a hydrocephalus child that I had ever seen. Mario was two years old and his head was at least four times the size of his body. He had been taken to the States to have the fluid drained but it had made very little difference. He was being cared for by Sheldon who used to feed him and see to the faeces that erupted in surprising measure from his backside. I have wondered if I had been asked to deal with it whether I would have been able to. It was horrifying and yet also inspiring to see Sheldon who was so badly handicapped himself, nevertheless quite intelligent and performing these very basic practical tasks for the baby.

At Good Shepherd Centre there was Jack who was far worse than Kenneth five years ago as far as his head was concerned. Maggots had eaten it right away about six months previously and the Brothers had taken about five hours to clean him up and to get rid of the maggots. A volunteer, Dwight, was helping at Good Shepherd and he was bandaging up Jack's head. However, I noticed that he was putting quite a bit of elastoplast on which must have been painful when it had to be renewed. Jack wasn't able to communicate at all.

I spent the whole of one morning at another centre trying to sort out the card index giving details of the eighty or so residents. I noticed that the mental state of most was such that they were unable to communicate verbally, and in some cases their date of birth was unknown and many were nameless.

Returning from the centres to the community house always had to be by means of the minibus. This was for security reasons, passing as we did some of the most dangerous ghetto areas. It was for security rather than safety as invariably twice the permitted number of Brothers piled into the vehicle. We would often pass what I am sure was one of the world's loudest ghetto-blasters. The road itself vibrated as we threaded our way through the narrow uneven and often crowded streets. This, together with the police helicopter which flew low at night lighting up the area with its searchlights, and the frequent concert of loud barking from stray dogs, all created a cacophony of noise designed to prevent very much sleep.

On this second visit to Jamaica I stayed at the new centre for the Brothers, Prince of Peace. However, at that time, it was not fully equipped and there were only three showers and toilets combined for twenty-five of us. To complicate matters a larger bore pipe was being laid into one of the showers, which meant that it was out of action for some days. One morning I had to wait about ten minutes in order to get a shower. This was a problem when the rising bell only sounded fifteen minutes before Mass began at 5.45 a.m. However, when I returned to England, we remedied this by sending money for more showers and toilets to be constructed.

The big topic of conversation in Jamaica on my spring 1999 visit was the rise of the price of gas. When I first heard this I thought it applied to gas as we understand it but, it is of course the American word for petrol and there had been an excessive rise of about thirty-five per cent in the cost of it, which meant an enormous rise in bus fares, the price of food, and many other items. A two-day strike began. Everyone, but most of all the poor, were going to be affected. All around Prince of Peace is what one might call a red-light district and most of the people were on cocaine. Only a month previously a house just the other side of the wall from the Brothers' enclosure had gone up in flames and this was a brothel. Moreover, there was a ruined building immediately next door and at night it was a frequent hideout for dealers in drugs as well as prostitutes. We were thus in a prime location for violence to break out as a result of the rise in the price of gas. And this, in fact, happened.

In the morning after the announcement, roadblocks were put up and each roadblock seemed to have been set fire to so that the whole city was punctuated with clouds of smoke and flames in the middle of the roads. No traffic was possible. We had a phone call from Father Richard who had arrived back at the airport from the States where he had given some talks. Brother Ambrose and another brother tried to go in the car to meet him. However they returned after half an hour, as they were unable to get anywhere and had great difficulty in the end in getting back to the house. After lots of phoning amidst the shooting which seemed to be getting louder, we heard that Father Richard had managed to get some transport with some other people and they were going to try and get through the blocked streets. Meanwhile, the other Brothers had gone down to the centres on foot, as it had been quite impossible to drive the minibus. Within half an hour of Father Richard finally returning, the gunfire increased alarmingly and suddenly there was a gun battle going on right outside our building along North Street. I saw policemen in bullet-proof jackets running hither and thither and firing. A helicopter had been showering tear gas all around and it was total bedlam.

Everybody I spoke to later said that they had never known anything like it at all, even in Jamaica. There had been shootings and problems at election times but nothing as bad as this. The whole island including Montego Bay where the trouble was also bad had ground to a halt as all the roads were blocked. I found it strange hearing the gunfire only yards away and looking at the bright colours of the flowers and trees around Corpus Christi, the bougainvillaea and the deep green palms with fruit hanging from them. So many beautiful things on this island with the sun shining and the wonderfully warm climate; and yet man is out to spoil it all.

The next day I went with Father Richard and Brother Henry to visit the people in some of the slums near us. Father started talking to several of the men there, telling them that there should be a peaceful demonstration: there could be roadblocks but no guns and no fires and no looting. 'Roadblocks, yes,' he said 'but no shooting, men!' Within two minutes there was a crowd of men and women around him listening to what he said and nodding in approval. I must admit I was a little apprehensive as it was just in this area that there had been the gun battle the previous day.

Needless to say the newspapers were full of the story. Several people had been killed, quite a number injured and a lot arrested. Superintendent Hinds from the police force phoned telling us that there were fifty stranded people, women, who had not been able to get back to the country districts where they lived owing to the fact that there was no public transport on account of the roadblocks. These people had been in town on various missions and were just left high and dry. They had already spent two nights in the police station, without sleep, sitting in chairs. Could Father do something about it and accommodate them? Immediately, Father's compassion came to the fore and he said he would see what he could do. We then had a discussion as to whether they could go into any of our centres but decided although there were some spare beds in Lord's Place, this would not be suitable with the babies there and also the Aids patients. We then wondered if we could put some mattresses down in our own dining-cum-sitting-room area and also on the veranda outside but I wasn't too much in favour of this as we had only the three toilets in the whole establishment and with fifty women plus the community of ourselves of some twenty-four of us life would have been impossible. We then considered whether it would be possible to find a parish hall or a convent that could accommodate them. Father asked me to take charge of the problem and to ring round various places and make some enquiries. I did this and finally found the Immaculate Conception Convent where the Sisters agreed to have them.

There were more phone calls between the police and the convent and ourselves and finally the police agreed to give the group of people lunch and then drive them up to the convent where two Brothers and I would meet them. We would then supervise the situation as the Sisters were elderly and not able to cope with doing that. Brother John, Brother Mark and myself took some food with us and found ourselves at a palatial convent where the nuns ran a private fee-paying school with its own swimming pool and all other facilities. It was in the richer part of the town and a totally different world from that of the ghetto. Sister Celia and Sister Maureen put sheets out on the beds and we chatted with them until finally two armed police vans drove up and out stepped a number of women, three children and some men; not the fifty we had anticipated. Sister Celia immediately said very dogmatically that she wasn't having any men. She knew what Jamaican men were like, and with a miscellaneous group of women she foresaw there could be trouble. So the five men were bundled back into the armed police vehicle and I don't know what happened to them – whether they spent yet another night in the police station or slept out somewhere. The women who had landed on us, eventually – in all there were just seventeen plus three young children, one who was only a baby – were tired and bewildered. However, the Brothers and myself got them organised for getting a meal with rice and chicken and then we collected from a nearby bakery two large boxes of doughnuts, which had been donated by someone who had heard of the plight of the group. Fortunately, that particular bakery had escaped the looting that had begun in many parts of the city.

On driving back we ran into a roadblock and had to turn around. Brother John who was driving saw a young lad walking down towards the roadblock. When he saw us he asked if he could have a rosary as he felt he needed to pray.

Brother John said, 'Well, if you'd like to move a bit of that roadblock down there, yes, I'll give you one.'

I'd previously said to Brother John that he shouldn't get out and move it because there could be a gunman lurking somewhere ready to shoot as this seemed to be what was happening whenever the police attempted to move the barriers. We turned round again while the fellow walked towards the block but I was still apprehensive about him and indeed anybody going too near it. Then, quite suddenly, from behind us we heard sounds and a great bulldozer came charging down the road straight towards us clearing some of the blockages. We immediately moved to the side and we saw that it was manned by someone with a gun followed by a police car all with guns at the level. The roadblock was removed in a matter of seconds followed by another one further down the road, which was equally satisfactorily cleared. Finally, we arrived at the convent safely, and all had supper together in a little kitchen on the first floor of the convent and, in talking with our group of refugees, discovered that some had just gone into Kingston for their shopping, others to see friends or relatives, whilst one lady was pregnant and had found two nights on a chair in the police station a terrible trial. They all lived in villages in other parts of the island.

During the night at the convent I woke up and heard in the distance a few gunshots but otherwise things seemed to have quietened down considerably. In the morning, again after a certain amount of telephoning, we were assured that some buses were running. One of the Baptist pastors came up to collect several people who had come from his part of the countryside, and then the police van arrived and took off the rest. Meanwhile, Father Richard and some of the community had been busy during our absence. The media, radio, TV and leaders of other local churches were all to-ing and fro-ing on the telephone in preparation for a great Christian protest that was to take place that afternoon. Immediately after lunch Father Richard, several specially designated Brothers and myself went down in the lorry together with chairs and a couple of tables. One of the Pentecostal churches had loaned a very complex amplification system with enormous ghetto-blaster speakers, keyboard and all the other paraphernalia connected with it. A very high platform had been erected which even the most agile had the greatest difficulty clambering on to. However, some tables and chairs were later positioned so that the less able could just about get up to the platform.

Amongst the half a dozen speakers who addressed the crowd, the Pentecostal element amongst them was very much to the fore with a lot of raising of arms, clapping and literally vociferous 'preaching'. Father Richard, whose idea it was to have a Christian demonstration, tried to emphasise rightly that it was a moral issue that they were concerned with, because the outrageous rise of between thirty and forty per cent tax on gas was immediately affecting first of all the poor. (I read in one of the Jamaican papers a few days later that people were recommended to shop around and buy food in quantity, which would be much cheaper. But this and various other ideas that were floated showed a total lack of understanding that the poor live hand to mouth and most of them haven't even money for their basic daily requirements let alone for stocking up.) The rally, which had only been organised at the very last minute that morning, attracted some two to three hundred people and lasted about two hours. It was on an open piece of ground, which was politely called a park and the sun, although it was beating down on us, was tempered by a pleasant breeze. Winston, one of the singers in the ecumenical group who perform in Father Richard's concerts, proclaimed that the Church was a sleeping giant, which should wake up and start being active.

The press and radio and television were almost continually on the phone and on Saturday, Father Richard was interviewed over the telephone by BBC radio. Towards the end of the day I took two visiting English journalists around the centres, as they wanted to do a write-up on the disturbances, and they became intrigued by the work of the Brothers. They met Mario, the very bad hydrocephalus child, and Jack, whose scalp had been eaten by maggots, and Rasheen, the three-year-old child with Aids, whose mother's dying wish – she also had Aids – was that the Brothers should look after her child. Our journalist visitors were utterly staggered by all that they saw.

The following morning, my last on that particular visit, at the end of my second class with some of the Brothers, one of them announced to me that he had something to say. I was a little surprised, and he then proceeded to say that he felt that it was quite important that I didn't return to England on Sunday but that I stayed in Jamaica and continued to teach them. Several of the other Brothers, including Father Ambrose and Father Richard, had spoken to me in a similar vein about spending a year in Jamaica helping generally, teaching, but perhaps most important, as an older person giving help by my supposed wisdom and encouragement. In many ways a decision such as this would be out of my hands, but I did not feel I could cope with a lengthy stay. Perhaps I had become too attached to my own comforts and way of life.

However, the inner call to return, again for a short stay, came early the following year. It coincided with a visit by Don and Grace Washington with whom I was able to share some of my thoughts and concerns. One of these concerned the proposed setting up of a further centre, this time for street children in Kingston. This would pose problems as it would need very special supervision and, whereas a few of the Brothers were being singled out for studies for the priesthood, none seemed to be specialising in social work or basic nursing skills.

On my first day the novices were having a day of recollection and so I was asked to make up the numbers to go down to the centres, as they would be short staffed. I was designated to help at Lord's House and on arrival Brother Carmello asked me to help him wash the Aids patients. Inwardly, I revolted at the idea. It included both men and women; several had badly messed themselves, one had some diapers, which were completely full of excrement, and one man had enormous testicles and a penis that extended down between his legs and almost to his knees. I suppose it must have been some sort of growth. We had to get warm water from the kitchen as washing such residents with cold water would lower their pulse rate and this could be dangerous. We rubbed them down thoroughly with soap and then rinsed them with bowls of water. It was no use using the showers as the water would have been too cold, so it all had to be done with small bowls of water thrown over the body. After drying them we then smeared oil over them as in most cases their skin was dry, sometimes flaky and with rashes. Some pretty inadequate clean clothing was then put on them. One lady – who looked quite old but probably wasn't – named Paulette, and who had only a short while to live, was very frail indeed. Even I could lift her without help into the wheelchair, which had a hole in the base so that the whole of the body could be washed. Then there was Derek, who had a glass eye, which he kept pushing round and asking if it was looking out in the right direction. Derek had been there quite a while but was gradually deteriorating. He used to be a scuba diver and took tourists on expeditions off the north coast of Jamaica. He spoke quite openly about his failings and this was so with quite a number of those with Aids.

Then I had to wash down two men with Aids who had just arrived but who were also suffering from scabies. After giving them a good shower I then had to rub the whole of their bodies with some special oil designed to cure the scabies. One of them found it quite painful but the other didn't seem to worry at all. By the following afternoon I was getting more used to rubbing down human bodies and dealing with some of the messy things. I was also able gradually to minister to them more and more, not only physically but spiritually, as they all seemed to be grateful to be prayed with, prayed over, blessed, whatever, and they also had a thirst for knowing more about the Lord. There was a profound simplicity and joy in the majority and this was a lesson to those of us who have a comparatively comfortable life in the Western world. In the midst of helping with their physical needs, basic questions about God's love for them, the reality of the next life and the meaning of a line in one of the psalms all poured out, and had to be answered.

Brother Ninian asked me if I would take a group of the older people for catechism. It was just 1.45 p.m. when he asked me and I replied, 'What do you want me to talk about? And for how long?'

To which he replied, 'Well, make sure they can make the sign of the cross and a few basic things like that in preparation for baptism and you have from now until four o'clock!'

Slowly over the next ten minutes or so they gathered and altogether there were about twenty, several of whom were blind, others a little deaf, and just three or four who were Catholic, one of whom fortunately responded a little and was able to lead some singing. I gave a sort of lesson punctuated with singing and prayer. It seemed to go down well, although it wasn't easy doing it completely off the cuff without forewarning, but that was the way things invariably happened.

Over the next few weeks or so the numbers had almost doubled and quite a few of the younger residents came as well. Most, being handicapped in some way or other, had been 'throw-outs' of society and had had no opportunity to be baptised. It was suggested that after a few more sessions with them I should hold a baptismal service in about a couple of weeks.

On Sunday I was celebrating Mass at Faith Centre with residents and many who had come in from neighbouring slums. It seemed to go well, and my homily was received with lots of 'Praise the Lords' and 'Amens' and nodding of heads. After Mass one lady came up to me and asked me to bless her eye, which was giving trouble. This I did, and immediately someone else came up with another pain and I prayed over her. In no time at all there was a queue of probably about forty people who wanted to be prayed over. I was standing outside the church by this time as one of the Brothers was taking a catechism class inside. They all came up to me explaining what was wrong and wanting to be prayed over. It was a moving experience. I didn't realise until afterwards that Brother Max and several other Brothers were very patiently waiting for me in the car. I apologised and Brother Max said, 'Well, it's all right as long as it doesn't happen every Sunday!'

Derek Pelham had Aids and had also had some sort of a stroke as he had lost the use of his right leg and arm and was in a bad way and unable to move from his wheelchair to the bed or vice versa without considerable help. Brother Carmello and I between us managed to get him undressed and seated on the wheelchair, which has a seat with a hole in it, and is used for putting people under the shower. Lifting is a problem, and many of the Brothers develop bad backs. After the shower we had to put diapers on him, laying him on the bed in order to do it, and while we were trying to fasten them Brother Carmello looked at me and said, 'I have never done this before.' I was far from expert but it seemed fairly straightforward, and I think we managed reasonably well between us. Then Derek wanted to go to the loo. He was a dead weight, unable to move of his own accord and he was bleeding quite a bit from the back passage, which wasn't a good sign. Somehow we managed, and then finally got him back on his bed. I then somewhat hesitantly asked one of the other Aids patients if I could take a photograph. To my surprise he seemed very pleased and then suggested taking one of Derek as well. Derek then wanted me to sit on the bed by him while the other man took a photograph of both of us. Then there was Paulette who was still dying but conscious and I was able to pray over her again, and Marianne who could not read and wanted to know more about the Gospel and Christ and asked me to explain the meaning of one of the psalms to her. She also started talking about her fears at night if she wanted to go to the loo. She felt there was a power of evil about the place and that it was in some way haunted. All this had to be dealt with.

Finally, the number to be baptised was thirty-five. Many of these were mentally retarded, Down's syndrome, and young people who had just been thrown out from society and would have almost certainly not been baptised in infancy. I arrived at Faith Centre on the morning arranged for the baptisms. The first job was to wash faces and hands and get them all assembled in the central area. This was finally more or less achieved with just a few occasionally staggering up and weaving their way round to the toilet although one or two with Down's syndrome and others were not particularly well house-trained and tended to relieve themselves wherever they happened to be! Brother Jacob then unexpectedly produced a quantity of new white T-shirts, which had been donated, and it was decided after most of them had already put on a clean shirt, to take that off and put the T-shirts on. It would really have been better to have put the T-shirts on them after the baptism. However, after about an hour and a half of 'getting ready' we started the service, punctuated with the inevitable semi-Pentecostal songs, which the Jamaicans love. After rejecting the idea of using a hosepipe, I blessed a good half-bucket of water, which one of the Brothers carried and I made sure that each one was properly baptised with a considerable quantity of water poured over them. The little celebratory treat afterwards was to give them each a rosary and a dollop of ice cream, the latter having to be spooned out into a mug.

On my final morning I was celebrating the Mass and I noticed at the end that Father Ambrose had disappeared although I distinctly remembered giving him communion. He related afterwards at breakfast that someone had come in to fetch him, as just outside the gate there was a man in a pool of blood having been badly stabbed. The police had come and taken him to hospital, but it seemed he was fatally wounded.

The farewells, not only from the residents, but also from the community of Brothers moved me almost to tears, and made me, in spite of the difficulties of the life there, wish that I was staying for much longer. The needs are enormous. However, the totally different way of life, culture, food and spirituality would be increasingly difficult to sustain.

Interspersed between the visits to Jamaica, I received several of the Brothers here in England for periods of time varying from one to three days whilst they were waiting for connecting flights to or from India. There was also one occasion when the four Indian Sisters who had been helping the community in Kingston were returning to their own community near Hyderabad. They planned to spend a few days en route in England and then in Rome. By arrangement with the son of a friend of mine, they were met at Heathrow and arrived at midnight in two very heavily loaded cars. Their large suitcases numbered well into double figures, contained all but the kitchen sink and a library of books, and completely filled one of the front rooms of Cathedral House. Two of the Sisters stayed with Judith and two with me.

Joe, who had spent nearly a year with the Brothers, knew the Sisters quite well and was able to show them some of the sites in London and elsewhere. However, their planned visit to Rome had to be cancelled as they had failed to make arrangements for accommodation. One of them had known another Sister who was studying somewhere in Rome, but had not brought her address or phone number with her. Furthermore, they had no visa for Italy!

On their day of departure, Judith, Gareth – a seminarian staying with me – and I set off at 3.30 a.m. for Heathrow. There, after collecting their new tickets avoiding the stay in Rome, together with the tickets for the further journey from Bombay to Hyderabad, we were told at the Alitalia check-in that they would nevertheless need a transit visa for Italy even though they were only going to be in the transit lounge for a couple of hours! This, after our good early morning journey down on the motorway, which had taken only an hour and ten minutes, and all else going quite smoothly, was bad news indeed. The transit visa apparently could only be got at the consulate in central London, Eaton Square, later in the day, by which time of course they would have missed their flight. There was no other flight by Alitalia with vacant seats for a further five days! Furthermore, their tickets on Alitalia were not endorsable. We did our utmost to sort out the problem with various officials, and by phone to the travel agent. The Sisters themselves, exhausted by the waiting about and the bulk of their luggage, agreed that they had best get fresh tickets on a flight which we found was available by Air India direct to Bombay and which had seats and was leaving in a few hours' time on that same day. However, the cost was considerable but the alternative would have been nearly another week in England, with the purchase of a visa, taking them up to London to get this and all the other necessary hassles. They clearly wanted to get back to India as soon as possible and were by this time suffering from the cold as our spell of fine weather had exhausted itself. Judith and I went from one terminal to another, attempting to sort things out with various forms of officialdom. I was glad that Gareth had accompanied us as he was a great help with the lifting of luggage and looking after the Sisters whilst Judith and I chased around to various officials. They needed some supervision in the unfamiliar environment of Heathrow. At one point Sister Prakeesh was attempting to steer one of the heavily laden trolleys down a ramp between two of the terminals and failed to listen to Judith's advice to pull up the green part of the handle which served as a brake. The result was that she ran at an ever-increasing speed, veil flying and skirts billowing, clutching at the trolley. There was a clash of metal against metal at the bottom. Sister managed to keep her balance and was unhurt, but the barrier at the foot of the ramp suffered a permanent indentation.

Finally at a mind-boggling cost to Judith's Barclaycard, we purchased the four Air India tickets. However, our problems were not over for there was still the excessive quantity of luggage to be dealt with. I foresaw problems and was not mistaken. Sister Mary Rose had argued with me that all would be well because American Airlines in Jamaica had accepted their luggage. However, their regulations differ from most other airlines. At the checkout we were not allowed to go right up to it with the Sisters. We stayed there looking on as if at a sideshow for nearly fifty minutes whilst they seemed to be bargaining, as in a Jamaican market, with two checkout girls, the supervisor and another official, all standing around joining in. Eventually, they gained a small allowance free of charge, but still had to pay between one hundred and one hundred and fifty pounds sterling for the extra luggage. This they paid themselves as somebody had given them two hundred dollars before leaving Jamaica. In all we spent five hours in endeavouring to sort out the good Sisters. I later suggested that when members of any of the communities were leaving Jamaica it was essential that all necessary visas were obtained and luggage was kept within allowable limits!

A different and less traumatic visit occurred when the ecumenical music group who perform many of Father Richard's religious songs and musicals spent ten days with us. Their stay began with the slight complication of meeting fifteen of them who were arriving on seven different flights at two different airports and spread over four separate days. They stayed with several families in Northampton who had agreed to host them, but whenever they gathered at the cathedral for a practice or at a rendezvous prior to giving a concert in London, Birmingham, Walsingham or Bedford, the cathedral house kitchen was raided for food and gallons of pure orange juice were consumed. Audiences were good, the performances were excellent, but there was no need for the expensive amplification equipment that they had asked us to hire for them.

Shortly after this, one of Father Richard's musicals, *The Rock*, based on the story of St Peter, was performed in a theatre in Kingston. For one of the performances as many as possible of the residents of the centres were taken to it. One scene depicted Jesus meeting the Samaritan woman by the well, and part of the props for this was a big earthenware container used for carrying the water. Whilst the singers were singing an appropriate song, 'Give us living water', the earthenware pot was placed near the side of the stage. At this point, one of the residents in the front row, twenty-six-year-old Jack, suffering from Down's syndrome and of no mean proportions, together with Junior, who was always smiling, leapt up on to the stage and urinated into the pot. The electrician controlling the lights was unable to see what was happening, but decided that whatever action was taking place at the side of the stage needed highlighting, so he proceeded to direct a full beam of light on Jack and Junior. Jack must have really enjoyed this as he was always a showman. Father Richard was backstage at the time and realised that something unusual was going on. He sent a helper out to see, who immediately grabbed at the earthenware pot, marched off the stage, exclaiming, 'It has liquid in it, and it's warm!' The singers came off as soon as they could and collapsed in a rolling heap of laughter.

Jamaicans have good voices and use them to even greater effect than those from some countries around the Mediterranean. Is it something to do with the heat, or maybe the fact that much of the time one is meeting and talking with people in the open air and hence the need to project the voice? Just a year after my first visit to Jamaica, Judith received a letter from Grace Washington. 'You cannot imagine', she wrote, 'how much we all remember you. You moved among us so quietly and gently: it is a kind of presence I treasure. I remember Father Ken's question: "Why does everyone shout, even the Sisters?"'

And so, with many laughs and countless tragedies, joy shines out as the work of welcoming and caring for the poorest of the poor continues. The Brothers' commitment and enthusiasm for their work is a tangible sign of the action of the Holy Spirit. Apart from visits to help the Brothers, we try to support them materially and financially and to spread the good and inspiring news of their great work. A Third World experience and dimension is an important part of our Christianity, and welcoming works both ways.

Chapter VII

ATTEMPTS AT HOME HOSPITALITY: 56, HIGH STREET, AYLESBURY

> I came as a stranger; you received me as a guest; and now I am
> departing as a friend.
>
> Tagore

Before moving on to other warm climes and continents, I must
relate just a few of the experiences of reaching out and opening
the sometimes uninviting doors of a presbytery to others.

At Aylesbury the High Street presbytery clung to one side of
the long, narrow church and, considering it was originally built
towards the end of the nineteenth century for just one priest, had
a surprising number of rooms. There was a second floor that was
beneath a steep sloping roof. This already had several rooms, but
with space and possibility of others, which in due course were
constructed. In appearance it was somewhat forbidding, and I
recalled again the words of Henri Nouwen:

> Even in our technically more advanced countries, presbyteries are
> seldom experienced as places where you are welcome at any time
> with any problem. Some people fear priests and ministers; others
> feel hostile or bitter towards them; many simply don't expect
> much real help from them; and only very few feel free to knock at
> their door without uneasiness. In the eyes and feelings of many
> who suffer, church buildings are perceived more as houses of
> power than as houses of hospitality.

Nouwen goes on to state that, if we are truly poor, then we can be
a good host. Poverty makes a good host.

> Poverty is the inner disposition that allows us to take away our defences and convert our enemies into friends. We can only perceive the stranger as an enemy as long as we have something to defend. But when we say 'Please enter; my house is your house, my joy is your joy, my sadness is your sadness and my life is your life' we have nothing to defend, since we have nothing to lose but all to give.

Aylesbury is the story of the success and failure of this.

Jimmy was a dosser who often called and stayed. He was in his mid-fifties and had been promoted from the dossers' hut in the backyard to reside on the put-you-up in the parish hall. However, every month or so he would go on the bottle with the inevitable consequences. We had been trying to help him, and he in return was a good worker, when sober, and did a number of odd jobs about the place.

One year the annual Passover Supper for Christians took place shortly before Easter. All tickets were sold, the parish hall was full, and there was just the one empty place set at the table for Elijah. Towards the end of the meal, at the fourth pouring of wine laid down in the ritual, I as the 'father' of the family, had to pour out an extra glass for Elijah. Jews still await the return of Elijah, and so a place has to be kept for him, and one of those present has, at the appointed moment, to go to the door to see if Elijah is there. The person so designated opened the door and in lurched Jimmy, showing evidence of having consumed a considerable quantity of alcohol. He immediately sank down at the vacant place left for Elijah, consumed the glass of wine, and was quite at home. Most of the people there thought that it was all pre-arranged as the staging and the timing were perfect. I, for my part, wondered exactly what the Lord was telling us – it was easy to see the hand of God in Jimmy when he was sober, but more difficult when drunk.

I answered the door one day at about 5 p.m. and, to my amazement, there was Father Andy on the doorstep. Andy was a Capuchin priest from Ethiopia who had lived with us for a year and had travelled into Oxford to follow a course at an English Language School. He had returned, this time staying at Greyfriars in Oxford, and was doing further studies in English. He looked fatter in the face, with a longer beard, and I commented that this was perhaps not a very good advertisement for the famine for which we were collecting in Ethiopia. Andy had been taken by the guerrillas about a year previously and had been taken to the Sudan as a prisoner, together with a group of others including some English people. There he had been a prisoner for about three months. The situation in Ethiopia was complex. He explained to me that there were three political groups of people – all of them Communist – there was an extreme Communist group which followed an unadulterated Marxist/Lenin doctrine; then there was the middle group which was the group in power as government; and then there was another group, also Communist, who were the guerrillas. Each group was at war with the others. Those who were not Communist had no representation at all and were not organised. We talked about the situation in Ethiopia and about the famine relief being organised. Cardinal Hume had just visited some of the worst areas, but Andy was telling me that the people who were being helped, the people who were being given food, thought that it was due to the government. 'What a good government this is – much better than we had thought, bringing us this food, or enabling others to bring it to us.' The other danger was that the food did not get to those who were starving but was used to feed the army. I asked Andy to speak about this at our Rich World/Poor World Supper that was being organised by the young people early in December.

I had known Easter Woodcock since I first went to Aylesbury and had been taking her Holy Communion every week until she moved to an old people's home in Wendover. She was a wonderful person and used to be an operatic singer. Any event in life that I'd recount to her, any situation, any human emotion, invariably brought forth the comment, 'Ah that is just like so-and-so or such an event in such and such an opera.' She would then proceed to sing an aria from the appropriate opera. Even in her late eighties and early nineties she was able to sing and remember many of the great operatic arias. A happy person, with a great humour and tremendous warmth and affection. We all loved her. When she was living in Aylesbury we sometimes had her in the presbytery for a fortnight whilst her daughter and son-in-law, with whom she lived, were away. When she moved to an old people's home we would fetch her for a day – and Mary also living in the presbytery would get her a nice lunch and she'd pay a visit to the church and to our little bookshop. I heard one day that she was not at all well and so I went over to see her and found her indeed very poorly. She had had two enemas, and while I was with her, talking with her, praying with her, praying over her, the enema started working and we had a rather upsetting little incident which took me back to the problems we had with my own mother in an almost identical situation. I rang for the nurse – twice – and nothing happened, so having tried to sort things out a little myself I then went down to see where I could get help. Apparently the bell was not working. Later that evening, Sarah, her granddaughter who lived nearby, phoned me to say that her grandmother had died early that evening – just after we'd been praying for her at Mass.

A young man named Walter arrived one evening from Yugoslavia. He was a member of Servas, which is an international organisation to which I belonged. Through Servas you can agree to host anyone for two nights, or longer by arrangement, and they can stay with you free of charge. This is reminiscent of the rules of hospitality in the desert, where a guest is also entitled to protection. This, as we have already seen, is exemplified in the story of Abraham (Genesis 18). However they have to be willing, if necessary, to help in some way, such as preparing a meal, or doing some cleaning, gardening or repair work. You in your turn, of course, can travel to other countries on the same conditions, staying two nights here, two nights there. It would be possible to do a world tour in this way. In the summer of 1984 we had several Americans come over. One family was from Taiwan – six of them came – too many for the house at that time as we were already fairly full, so I put them in the Parish Room with mattresses on the floor. There were a husband and wife, three late teenage youngsters and the husband's elderly mother, in her seventies. She, in fact, was really more active than the rest of the family; a wonderful old soul who'd run a farm in Taiwan for many years. This, her son explained to me, had made her tough!

The young man from Yugoslavia spent most of the suppertime telling us, in some detail, of the situation in his country. He himself was Catholic, but it was clear that there was a considerable lack of freedom, although – as he pointed out – we in the West are also restricted in some ways in our freedom. Walter explained that there were only a few Servas members in Yugoslavia (this was before the death of Tito), and in order to leave the country on holiday it cost nothing for the first time, but it would be ten pounds for each successive visit. However, at the end of the year, that money was refunded, but it had diminished considerably because of the enormous rate of inflation and so it was really a deterrent to people leaving. Ten pounds, of course, meant a great deal more to someone in Yugoslavia than it does to us here, both then, and of course today. Walter had studied Economics at university and he had recently completed a year's military service. When he returned after his holiday he was going to look for a job which was not at all easy because there was a great deal of unemployment in Yugoslavia and it was very difficult for young people to find work. We discussed the problem of Albania as he had spent several holidays in the southern part of Yugoslavia adjacent to Albania and was interested to learn that I had driven up from Greece in 1968 near the Albanian frontier, and along the west coast of Yugoslavia. Albania, of course, had for many years severed all connection with other countries, apart from a tenuous link with Italy. This tiny country, surrounded by mountains, had quarrelled successively with Yugoslavia, Russia and China and was almost alone in the world. However, its problems, brought about by estrangement, were increased by its rapidly increasing population – the average number of children per family in Albania being about eight.

Not all the guests who come through Servas are so pleasant. One strange fellow stayed with us and as 'voluntary work' offered to prepare the supper on his second evening in the presbytery. He insisted on putting unpeeled and unwashed carrots, parsnips, onions and potatoes all in the pot together to be boiled up. I was quite unpopular when I announced to the others that I had already arranged to go out that evening, others followed suit and it ended up with just Gerry New having to sit down and make some attempt at consuming the resulting dubious brew.

Some years later several of us reminisced about some of our visitors and recalled how we knocked a hole through the chimney to make an extra bedroom on the second floor, which in the end was my bedroom, as my father took over my own after Mother died. Then there was Billy who'd lived in the house and robbed us of various things, another who'd lived in the cellar and decided he wanted to destroy some personal papers and we suddenly discovered smoke coming through the floorboards of the kitchen. This resulted in the hut at the back being made into a little dormitory with three beds, but this developed into a dosshouse for drug addicts, alcoholics, and possibly prostitutes as well. We then reduced it to one bed although I'm not sure whether that made much difference! They were good days, and the house was very open and friendly.

One cold November evening I had a phone call from the Samaritans at Milton Keynes. They asked if I could put up a lady who was apparently a very fervent and devout Catholic, and who was in a desperate situation having just left her alcoholic husband. I enquired why it was that they should have phoned us, 'Wasn't there someone – somewhere else where she could stay in Milton Keynes?'

The good Samaritan voice replied, 'No, nowhere at all there, and you are on the Samaritans' list.'

This was probably because of the dossers' hut we had. However, this was clearly a case of someone who could not use the dossers' hut. I replied that if there was nowhere else she could come along and we could put her up in a spare room. She was going to phone back the Samaritans in an hour's time, and they would put her on to us. She came for the night and then went on to relations nearby.

I was reminded that it was just a year ago, on bonfire night, that I was called out to deal with another lady who was in dire straits through having taken an overdose, and I took Angela, a nurse living in the house with me. We found the woman rolling about on the floor of her living room, and Angela trying to get her to vomit up the overdose of pills she'd taken; and then in the middle of it, the next-door neighbours who had been out at the bonfire, and children, all rushing in together with the doctor who got her off to the hospital.

The Catholic Church does not welcome to its fold any one particular race, culture, educational or social background. Like its founder, Jesus, it welcomes all. However, in doing so there are inevitable hazards. On a certain Sunday the principal Mass was musically disastrous owing to the presence of 'the pineapple lady'. This was a poor woman who had a mental illness. We called her the 'pineapple lady' because she once brought me a pineapple when I was in bed with flu. Since then she regularly came with fruit and honey and all sorts of other things to give to me. I always tried to refuse as I felt she hadn't much money. She lived with her aged mother, but would never take no for an answer, and always insisted that she loved coming to church and loved singing. The disaster and chaos were caused that particular Sunday by her trying to sing at a different pace and on different notes, louder and more discordant than usual, in a voice that could be heard at the other end of the High Street. The following day I suggested to our local chemist that his pills didn't seem to be as potent as they used to be!

I returned home late one evening to find that another member of our household had given shelter to a young woman who was homeless for the night. She was, in fact, someone known to me. Her parents lived nearby. She was the result of a Polish–Italian marriage – and she, Amy, had given her parents a great deal of trouble over the past years. She had three children from different men and had recently divorced her husband and gone to live in Slough. She had returned early that particular morning, thinking she could take refuge there, but her parents had thrown her out. I was fully aware that she had behaved badly, but I still felt that her parents were wrong in not sheltering their offspring, and showing compassion when help was needed. So I rang up the father and expressed my anger with him over the phone. I asked him where his Christianity lay. How many times was he prepared to forgive his daughter? Was there a limit to the number of times, and how could he say to me that I should turn her out and hand her over to the police? If a mother and father are unforgiving, the hang-ups are multiplied, the inhibitions, the terrible traumas, fears and anxieties the offspring must live throughout their lives, are deep wounds to be healed.

When I arrived back Amy was asleep upstairs. In the morning she left, but turned up again after a few nights having spent the previous night with her parents but once again they had turned her out. She had applied to our local Carr-Gomm house, but in view of what I knew of her I could not countenance her admission there even for one night, as it was for single lonely people.

It is appropriate to mention here the origins of the Carr-Gomm Society. Richard Carr-Gomm was a charismatic figure, who during World War Two was an officer in the Grenadier Guards and continued in his regiment in peacetime. He then finally came to retirement, was asked to go with the Kabaka of Buganda to accompany him on his return from exile. However, he declined this as he had increasingly felt a need to help people who were lonely. He then did an extraordinary thing: he applied for a job as home help in Bermondsey and spent his time visiting lonely people, scrubbing floors, doing housework, cooking and all the other menial jobs a home help is called upon to do. It was this great desire to work among people in need – the old, the handicapped, but especially the lonely – that led him to this, and as a result of that, shortly afterwards in 1956 to form the Abbeyfield Society together with some friends, who catered in a homely situation for elderly, lonely people. The name Abbeyfield came from the road in which Richard was living at the time. Six years later, after many such houses had been opened all over the country, there were divisions in the leadership between those who wanted to concentrate more on the material and the practical, and those who felt that the human and emotional and the spiritual were, if anything, more important. As a result of Richard Carr-Gomm opting for the latter attitude, he was dismissed from the Abbeyfield Committee by a vote of eighteen to seventeen – he, who had founded it, was rejected from it! He then turned his attention to Africa and spent some time in Africa but still maintaining his ideal to help the lonely. At the end of 1964 he was back in London and started up what came to be known as the Carr-Gomm Society. It was decided to adopt his name for the society, as various other titles were found to be either in use already, or for various reasons undesirable. The new Carr-Gomm Society was not limited to the elderly, but extended to the lonely of all ages, who came to live in houses with a housekeeper in charge of each. Since then, in the last twenty years, Carr-Gomm houses have spread throughout the country. Richard Carr-Gomm himself was reconciled with the Abbeyfield Society, and subsequently also set up the Morpeth Society, which is primarily for lonely gentlefolk and centred in London.

The Carr-Gomm house in Aylesbury, which I was instrumental in starting – in spite of a certain amount of opposition by people who did not think there was a need in Aylesbury for such a house – was situated not far from the High Street, on the Tring Road. It was an eight-bedroomed house, with a small flat for Jane Boothroyd who was appointed the first housekeeper. Within a few weeks we had filled it. Some mistakes were at first made in the allocation of rooms, but we learned through experience. It was an old house in a very bad state of repair, which had to be renovated and some of the rooms divided up. We had it very pleasantly decorated and furnished, as we felt that a new clean and tidy atmosphere would help raise the general tone of the residents.

Thus it was that I considered Amy's past history regarding her relationships with men would make it highly undesirable to have her in such a house. I said I would rather have her in the presbytery for one more night. Samantha who was a seventeen-year-old girl staying on in Aylesbury to complete her exams (her parents moved at Easter to a farm in Devon) was in the room next to the one I gave Amy and I discerned that she was a little nervous. However, I think I reassured her and spent some embarrassing moments trying to find a key to fit her door, but without success. Anyway it was all part of her education – she came from a very good family and life in the presbytery opened her eyes to some of the problems in the world.

Most town-centre presbyteries are busy places, and even more so when it is known that there is invariably an open door to all. There are rarely quiet days. Prayer-time had to be the first priority early in the morning before the phone began to clamour for attention and the day's post is dealt with, although, increasingly, a greater proportion of this is junk mail, precious trees which go into the bin. One such day, the first caller at 9 a.m. was the correspondent to the governors of the local Catholic school. There had been a particularly traumatic meeting the previous evening, and he wished to discuss with me several problems that had arisen.

By 9.15 a.m., another ring at the bell: the headmistress of the lower school, Susan Saunders, had just had a talk with the deputy education officer, and Susan, who was quite emotional and volatile, wanted to tell me of her meeting with him. After discussing business with him she had commented in her open and sometimes slightly naive way how calm he always seemed to be, no matter how many pressures he had on him. The secret, he divulged to Susan, was that every morning he would spend some time reading a passage from the Bible and praying, and he felt that if he didn't do that he couldn't really cope with the day ahead. It was good to hear of a Christian layman being committed in this way.

After Mass I received, by appointment, Mrs Fins, who wanted to talk to me about the organisation CRUSE, a branch of which she was hoping to start in Aylesbury. This is designed to help in any way possible those who are widowed, and something which I wished to support and encourage. Maria, who is Greek Orthodox and from time to time has spurts of devotion and attendance at Mass, called in order to collect some of our Easter Draw tickets, which she hoped to sell. Maria was widowed, lonely and very difficult to understand because of her foreign accent. However, she was overflowing with goodwill and enthusiasm. Two other callers then came in quick succession in order to arrange for Masses to be said – and this usually involves conversation and discussion about death or bereavement. It was my turn to cook on that particular day so I spent twenty minutes in the kitchen preparing a few tasty items before having my snack lunch. Father Bob Bulk then called. He obviously wanted to chat, and over-flowed with some of his grumbles about the diocese – bishop, priests and situations. Bob was a heavily built, six foot four inches, a good priest beneath an eccentric and slightly off-putting veneer. His eccentricities and abruptness became considerably more noticeable and forbidding in later years after his falling into his cellar and crashing his head on the stone floor. This resulted in brain injury, although he persevered in running his parish for a number of years afterwards.

Whilst Bob was unburdening himself, the lower school head-mistress phoned again as the builders who were constructing some houses bordering on the school property had begun to stake out a part of the playground. On checking with the authorities, I discovered that whereas asphalt playgrounds are church property, the grass areas belong to the County Council. The area in question turned out to be council property and their responsibil-ity. No sooner had I clarified this when the door bell rang and it was Louise who had an appointment with me for confession and spiritual direction. Bob left, only to be followed by Maria returning the counterfoils of no less than thirty books she had sold since the morning, followed by Patricia informing me that she would be happy to help with the junior youth group we were about to form. As she left the house Stephen Finn arrived for his regular monthly tutorial in preparation for the permanent diaconate. This left just fifteen minutes to sort out the final steps of preparing the supper for the rest of the household – seven of us resident at the time. After evening prayer I chaired the local Carr-Gomm meeting and subsequent to the meeting, which was in our parish hall, I discussed with the deputy chairman, Nathan, some of the problems we were experiencing with relationships on the committee. Nathan finally left at 11.30 pm. I noted in my journal at about that time that in order to do justice to those who came to see me, I would need to create space between the many and varied happenings of the day, especially when, as not infrequently occurs, a couple comes regarding a baptism or marriage, filled with the joy of the forthcoming event, only to be followed by a family who are in mourning and want to arrange the funeral of a close relative. The immediate switch of emotion can be taxing and tiring.

One's greatest joys as well as trials are in dealing with people and their problems. A man came to be interviewed for admission to the Carr-Gomm house. He was Pakistani but not yet eighteen years of age. We had a strict rule not to admit anyone under the age of eighteen, so prior to asking him in to the interview I went outside to see him and explained the situation to him. The community relations officer had already telephoned me and had spent half an hour pleading with me to accept him. However, we really could not bend the rules to this extent, and anyway it would need the consent of the rest of the committee, so I quickly sized him up and decided that as he was homeless that evening we ought to have him in the presbytery. He had lived with his parents in Scotland until 1979 and then they had gone back to Pakistan. About three weeks before, he had come over to England by himself to stay with a friend of his father's living in Aylesbury. Initially this friend, Mr Bottram, was living in private accommodation, but a few days previously had moved into a council house, and the council officials were coming to inspect the house to see what furnishings were needed. It was imperative that Mr Bottram should not be seen to have a tenant on his threshold, so Aziz, the young man in question, had to leave. He seemed a good lad, intelligent, and had applied to the McDonald's restaurant just up the High Street for a job. Having lived the last few years in Pakistan, his stomach was accustomed only to Oriental food, and unfortunately on the night he arrived he was quite ill after having eaten some of our boiled vegetables and a few other unspiced items of food, which for us were normal fare. I told him he could stay for a week or so until he could find something else. Once again we had a Muslim in the house.

I was late down to breakfast one morning and just after going into the kitchen Loretta walked in. Loretta had been working in the presbytery in the mornings for the past five years or so – keeping the dust moving! She had been quite seriously mentally ill, her husband left her, as did her four children, and when she first came to us she attempted several times to take her life and was in and out of the local mental hospital. However, she improved and lived in group accommodation under the auspices of the hospital until she was well enough to take on her own flat. Loretta's first words that morning, accompanied by a relaxed smile and in her usual slow and somewhat mournful voice, were,

'I nearly lost my cat down the loo last night. He clambered up round the rim of the loo and then slipped in.' The cat's name was Sammy and was, in fact, only a kitten. My father, who was also having breakfast at the time, immediately said, 'Had you just been?' but fortunately she hadn't and the kitten was easily fished out.

On another later occasion Loretta, who had ten days previously, met Colin, who was also slightly mentally handicapped, asked my advice. She had known Colin for just ten days and he had proposed marriage to her no less than five times. Should she accept? I advised her to give it just a little longer! Meanwhile, Anna, by contrast an attractive Italian blonde, widowed and who, as we shall see later, was staying with us for a while, heard of Loretta's supposed predicament and exclaimed, 'Good God, here have I been looking for a husband for five years and she has five proposals in ten days!'

One of the difficulties of the ever open door and the constant welcome to all and sundry was the drain on one's emotional resources and the limitations of one's space, both physical and psychological. Kahil Gibran said that in a marriage there should be spaces in one's togetherness. This is even more important in the less binding relationships of a community or in living together beneath the same roof. The continual change of most of the occupants of the house also added to the difficulties.

Gerry from Switzerland came with a six-month visa, but failed at the appointed time to renew it with the result that at the local police station, instead of arranging for him to be immediately escorted to Heathrow, he was kindly given seven days' grace and thus spared us any possible scandal. Just two hours after he left, Habib, a friend of Sherif's in Cairo, phoned asking if he could stay until he found work in a hospital. It was about the same time that a Belgian lady married to a Pole came to the door with her son, Pascal, aged twenty-seven and a qualified architect. He was to start work for the local authority, but this was to be his first experience of living away from home, and away from what I quickly discovered was a very domineering mother. Fortunately, he settled in well and was joined by Eddie, who was pursuing a course at the nearby Rocket Propulsion Centre. Both these young men had been pretty desperate for accommodation. Eddie had spent a few nights in the hostel in Bicester Road which was for lorry drivers and some of the dossers who leave from the hut at the back of our garden. I felt it was impossible to have empty rooms in the house when there was such a need. On the other hand there were times when I wished the house were quieter and emptier.

One day the doorbell rang, and who should be waiting outside but Keith Burnwell, the lad who set fire to the church three years previously. On that occasion, I had just returned from some visits and was parking the car at the rear of the house. It was about 5.30 p.m., and as I got out I saw smoke ascending through the tiles of the church roof. I rushed into the house and, before even investigating what had happened, dialled 999. At the same moment, fire engines screeched to a halt outside. The church was ablaze. Someone in a shop opposite had already seen the smoke and phoned for the fire brigade. In all, seven fire engines blocked the High Street in the afternoon rush hour, but happily the conflagration was brought under control and, apart from the appalling mess only a third of the roof was destroyed. Whilst the firemen were in action, I insisted that everyone in the house continue with their regular 6 p.m. supper. This included my parents, whom I did not wish to alarm. We were, of course, at some risk, as there was only a single door between the church and the house.

The police got to work and within a couple of days had arrested a young boy of fourteen who, the psychiatrist claimed when the case was later heard, had had a bad day at school and on his way home had entered the church, which was always kept open for private prayer, and set fire to the blue curtains behind the tabernacle. The curtain stretched from floor to ceiling, and thus it was that the roof caught the worst of it. However, the heat generated was considerable, and whilst the whole veil over the tabernacle vanished in the flames, when, after several hours, everything had cooled down, I was able to open the tabernacle, I found the white coverings inside completely unharmed and the Blessed Sacrament untouched.

Keith, who had caused it all, was nearly eighteen when he

called again at the door. He was tall and dishevelled and still looking rather peculiar. Apart from the occasion when he came immediately subsequent to the fire with his father in order to apologise, I had only seen him twice before that occasion. The first was two hours before the bishop came on 21 November 1983 for the blessing of the restored parts of the church, and on that occasion Keith turned up on some pretext or other. He then turned up a year later on the anniversary of the fire. I think I was out on that occasion, and Mary answered the door. And then on this particular evening just a few days before yet another anniversary of the fire, he had appeared. He explained that he was a disc jockey and had quite a lot of money now, and in the course of conversation asked if I minded if he came to church here sometimes. I replied, 'Of course not,' and then looking him straight in the face added, 'Provided you don't set fire to it!' There was no reaction – which seemed odd. He merely asked to borrow one of the church microphones, as his had broken. I refused, at the same time hoping that it would not be the catalyst for another conflagration.

One day there was a phone call from Stoke Mandeville Hospital asking for help. It was not the customary expected sick call. A young lad from Italy had arrived in the paraplegic ward. He had been diving off the rocks on the coast just north-west of Rome, had hit a submerged rock and ended up partly paralysed from the waist down. His mother, Anna Berti, who had lost her husband in a plane crash a few years previously, had arranged for her son to have treatment in England as she had heard of the fine reputation of Stoke Mandeville. Anna had come over with the son, Pierfrancesco, and because the stay in Stoke Mandeville Hospital promised to be at least for some weeks, she herself was looking for some accommodation – initially for a few nights until she could find something suitable. I told the hospital that if she contacted me direct, we could put her up at least for a short time.

Anna arrived, an attractive middle-aged blonde with an outgoing personality, clearly dampened by the tragedy of her son's accident. We all immediately warmed to her and she to us, with the result that she stayed for several months, during which her daughter and her maid also filled two other spare rooms. At that time each of us took it in turns to prepare the evening meal. Anna, when her turn came round, generally set to in the afternoon to make pasta, rolling out the ingredients on the kitchen table. The final result was delicious, accompanied as it invariably was by bottles of Valpolicella wine.

During this time, Pierfrancesco made great progress at the hospital, occasionally visited us in the house, until one day he walked in, using just one remaining stick to help him. He stood in the doorway of the dining room, called to all within earshot for attention, and threw the stick across the room. 'Look,' he cried, 'I can walk without it now!' It was a great moment for him, his mother, and all of us. Anna returned to Italy a few days later, very grateful for her stay with us, but we, I feel, had gained the most.

We continued to correspond, Pierfrancesco continued to make progress, but tragedy hit the family again. Eleven years later whilst staying in Rome, I took the train to Orbetello. It was quite a slow train but this I didn't mind. Italians on a train start up a conversation with complete strangers. Regardless of age or nationality, somehow conversation springs up. In England we have got out of the way of this, that is if we ever had the habit. This maybe is partly due to temperament and partly, in more recent years, due to the bombardment of the media, especially the television, which has killed the art of conversation. I arrived at the station to find a bus just outside. It was only a couple of kilometres or so into Orbetello itself where I found I had to change to another bus to get to Porto Ercole. As we were descending the steep hill into Porto Ercole I just happened to notice the name of Anna's road as we passed the end of it. She lived in a flat with not a particularly pleasant outlook as there were other flats blocking the view of the harbour and the bay. But far worse than that, she was confined to sitting in a chair most of the time and had put on over forty kilos in weight, so that I hardly recognised her. She was paralysed down her left side through the vein that burst in her brain and Pierfrancesco seemed to be more incapacitated than when he had left Aylesbury. Perhaps he had not persevered with some of the physiotherapy and exercises he had been prescribed. He was about twenty-six, and Anna reminded me that she stayed for about five months in Aylesbury as long ago as 1980. She had someone come in every day to cook the midday meal and then return for an hour every evening to wash and undress her. She had certainly been the mind behind the fabulous meal that we enjoyed – with many courses and which went on to well into the afternoon. Her daughter, Teresa, had been staying with her in America where Anna had gone soon after the stroke to have further physiotherapy and treatment which she was unable to get in Italy. Teresa had come back to Italy and then one day was driving to the airport to meet her mother when she had a fatal car crash involving a lorry and a trailer which didn't have a proper signalling system. She was killed outright. Anna went to live with her aunt at Porto Ercole but this aunt had become quite senile and started doing quite ridiculous and somewhat dangerous things such as putting washing-up liquid into the frying pan to fry the potatoes, so she had to go to a clinic in Rome. Anna was thus on her own most of the time. We had a good chat and a few laughs, and I think it was good for her to think back on Aylesbury days. She asked after everybody, most of whom she remembered by name. Her doctor had told her to think back on the best moments of her life and ponder on them, and she told me that she regarded her stay in Aylesbury as one of the happiest times of her whole life. Because of this she wanted to load me with gifts of bottles and all sorts of things, which I had, I hope without too much discourtesy, to decline. I saw for the first time photos of her husband, and one with Pope Pius XII. Anna's mother was distantly related to Pius XII – a sort of second cousin. It was heart-rending to see Anna whom I had remembered so full of life and energy and goodness being reduced to a life where she was unable to go out and had little to occupy her mind.

Supper at Aylesbury was always at 6 p.m., and whoever was in the house was expected to join us at the round table set in the not over-spacious kitchen. One evening the doorbell rang. Someone at the table answered it and returned to tell me that a lady was enquiring about a prayer group in the parish. I decided to go to see who it was, and was met with a lady in her thirties with dark hair and moderately plain clothes who spoke with a foreign accent. I replied that we did have a prayer group to which she was welcome to come to, not realising at that point that she was in fact a religious. It then turned out that she was also, in fact, looking for accommodation. She was staying temporarily with a teacher from the high school where she had just been appointed French Assistante for the year. It so happened that we had at that moment an empty room and so Françoise came to live in the presbytery and rapidly became a most useful person in the parish, and over the year she was with us was a considerable help to many people.

Some years later I visited her in her convent in an industrial part of north-eastern France. I and another priest piled into her car and she drove us to Arras and then on to the War Memorial at Vimy. I'd been there before with Françoise, and it's always a very tragic place to visit, a very sad place. Just after we got into the car we were talking a little about Françoise's work with the young, those who were HIV positive or suffering from Aids, and the importance of understanding the real-life problems and tragedies of today's youth. These continue to be ongoing issues for the Church as a whole. There must be an ideal form of behaviour at which to aim, but, on the other hand, there must also be allowances made according to the circumstances.

Michael came down from the Carr-Gomm house to patch up part of the roof of the dossers' hut where it had been leaking badly. Michael was about twenty years of age, with spiky black hair, tight jeans and a rather scruffy punk-like appearance, but he had a good smile and an open expression and was, I am sure, basically a good lad. Anyway, he did the roof and then we sat chatting for a few minutes over a cup of coffee. Michael told me that he had been in court that morning, and he had been put on eighteen months' probation and given a two hundred pound fine for robbery, but he added, 'I didn't do it. In actual fact it was my friend who did it; I was slightly linked with him, but it was he who did the robbery, but if he had gone to court (because he's got previous convictions) he would have been put in prison right away. So,' said Michael, 'I went to court and as it's my first conviction they just gave me eighteen months' probation and I admitted having done it. But it was jolly difficult,' he added, 'because I've had to keep on talking about something that I didn't actually do – an event that I wasn't actually part of.'

I was quite astounded by the generosity of this lad, to say before the court that he'd done something which he really had not done just in order that his friend should not be put in prison. There was a generosity, a kindness that it's difficult to find in a lot of people. Joyce from Carr-Gomm came down to see me later on about something else and I asked her, and she said, 'Oh yes, I went to court with him, and I do believe it's true. He didn't do the burglary; it was his friend.'

He who lays down his life for his friend...

The list of those who found a home at the High Street presbytery would have filled many chapters. Not least of them being my parents, my mother who died there, my father who continued for many years after her death to find a home there and, later, in Cathedral House in Northampton. There were many occasions when all of us seemed to form a community. However, nearly all who came had a particular need of a roof over their head combined possibly with the need of friendship. I felt, however, that a common purpose was often lacking. On reflection, if there had been more emphasis on prayer together combined with some minimal form of pastoral activity, some of the inevitable difficulties and dangers of an open house might have been avoided. Nevertheless it proved to have been a good and memorable growth experience for nearly all of us.

Chapter VIII

FURTHER ATTEMPTS: CATHEDRAL HOUSE

After eleven years at Aylesbury, having experienced the joys and pains of the many and varied guests who had filled the house as well as the hut in the garden, I was ready to move on. My mother had died three years previously after residing in the presbytery for the last eight months of her life, but my father continued to live with me as a member of our very fluid and uncommitted community. We were both sad to leave behind associations with so many good people. However, the next thirteen years, which were to be at Cathedral House in Northampton, where it was not possible to create quite the same open house situation, nevertheless turned out to be a busy and varied ministry as the cathedral was a magnet for so many.

In the nineteenth century, Northampton harboured a little-known lady, Caroline Chisholm, born there and who was inspired by her parents' example, when they, a Protestant family, welcomed into their home a stranger. Mary Hoban, in her biography of Caroline Chisholm, writes:

> One day as the family sat down to dinner they heard a great hullabaloo out in the village and her father went to see the cause. He found people shouting abuse and throwing mud and stones at an old man of foreign appearance. Seizing one fellow by the shoulder, he enquired the reason. 'He's a Romish priest' was the reply. 'We'll send him hurrying out of here right soon.'
>
> But when Mr Jones called a halt they listened to him at once. The old man, he reminded them, though not of their persuasion, was still a man of God.
>
> Taking the stranger by the arm, he led him home, and when the mud had been wiped off and the priest had regained his

composure, he was invited to the family dinner table and asked to remain in the house as a guest. He explained that he was one of those hundreds of French priests, the émigrés who had found refuge in England after the Revolution. Many had now returned to their homeland, but some continued to do pastoral work in England. He was travelling on foot from one Catholic centre to another. William Jones, who respected his cloth, welcomed him also as an outcast of Napoleon's regime. His patriotic feelings ran high, and he had been a generous contributor to the Voluntary Fund.

The old priest warmed to the kindness shown him. There was not much he could do to repay it, but he could help to entertain the little girl who, though only five years old, seemed to be eagerly intelligent and so receptive to good. At times her busy mother had to put her firmly out of the kitchen – then they would sit together and he would tell her of the French homeland he had had to leave, and of other lands he had visited, answering all her childish questions with slow and careful English.

He remained as an honoured guest for several weeks. William Jones was the object of some unfavourable comment, yet when the time came for the old priest to go, he farewelled him with cheerful ceremony at the dinner table, proposing a toast to his health. The abbé rose to reply. He thanked from his heart the family Jones for all their kindness to him. Here he had found true Christian feeling, and he prayed God to bless all in this house, 'and especially this child,' he added, placing his hand on the head of his little friend, for of course her place was beside his.

Caroline later became a Catholic and went with her husband to Australia where she immediately tried to alleviate the appalling situation of many of the young girls, immigrants from England and Ireland. She invited them into her home, set up hostels for them and enabled them to find work with the families of settlers. She also was the first woman to address a standing committee of the British government, pointing out the disgusting conditions that prevailed on the British ships transporting the girls to Australia. So great and lasting was the social work she accomplished, that until recently her head appeared on the five-dollar note in Australia. She and her husband eventually came back to England and she was buried in a Northampton cemetery not far from her birthplace. The inscription on her grave is 'The

Immigrants' Friend'.

Most Northamptonians are unaware of Caroline's worth and fame. However, when I invited a choir from Sydney to give a concert in the cathedral, before they left, after their overnight stay, they asked to go to Caroline's grave and venerate the memory of someone who had done such great work for the abandoned, lonely and bewildered young girls arriving in Sydney. It was a bright and clear sunny July morning, and we all encircled the grave, prayed and sang a hymn in thanksgiving for a great English lady.

Social problems also abounded in the twentieth century in Northampton, not only through an unexpected ring at the door, but often by the telephone. It could be an urgent call to the General Hospital or someone who was overburdened with an anxiety, which they wished to discuss. Either could take an unplanned hour or more.

On one occasion when I was visiting the General Hospital, the ward sister asked me if I would have a word with a certain James O'Reilly who was suffering from a broken skull which needed to be treated in one of the Oxford hospitals. He was refusing to move and threatening to discharge himself. I went over to his bed. There was something familiar about him that I couldn't quite identify. He was lying in bed with a great mop of ginger hair and beard and dried coagulated blood on both his head and beard. After chatting for a few minutes I did my best to persuade him to allow himself to be taken to Oxford, but to no avail. All he wanted was to discharge himself and claim his dole money in order, clearly, to obtain more booze! I reported back to the sister and she was not particularly surprised. Shortly after my visit he discharged himself and then some weeks later I read in the paper that this same James O'Reilly had been found dead in a deserted house in Northampton. It was not known at that stage whether foul play was involved or not. I also discovered that he was one of a partnership – O'Reilly and Hennessy – who intermittently over the past years had raided the boxes and done general petty damage in the cathedral. I had in fact seen them once furtively looking through the doors of the cathedral to see if anybody was about, and on another occasion they had attempted to break into St Patrick's Hall, setting off the alarm system in the middle of the night. Hennessy was the younger partner, in his mid to late twenties, and whether he had anything to do with the broken skull and the eventual death of O'Reilly, I never discovered. All the clientele of the local soup kitchen knew O'Reilly. He was popular and they all turned up in full force for his funeral. Just prior to this, at 2.30 a.m., the telephone awakened me. I leapt up thinking it would be a call to the hospital. A female voice at the other end of the phone, slightly hesitant said, 'Is that Father Payne?' The voice then continued, 'I've been reading the paper and I can't stop thinking about this man who was found dead. Could I talk to you about it, Father?'

It was someone probably mentally ill or who had been drinking, so I immediately replied, looking at the clock as I did so, and registering that it was 2.30 a.m., 'Well, I think there are plenty of times tomorrow when you could come and see me and talk about it but I'm not prepared to discuss it now over the phone at two thirty in the morning. Did you realise the time?'

'Oh yes, were you in bed?' was the reply.

To which I said, 'Yes, and I think you ought to be as well, and I suggest you go to bed and go to sleep. Good night and God bless you,' and I put the phone down. Later, I reflected on the humour of the situation as my homily the previous day had been on the Advent theme of staying awake!

The telephone can be at times an obtrusive and unwelcome means of communication, as on another occasion I was awakened at 1.30 a.m. to hear a voice at the other end of the line asking, 'Do you want some blankets for Romania?'

'No,' I very curtly replied, 'but if you contact me at a more civilised hour I will tell you where you can take them.'

'Oh, you don't want to help the Romanians! I thought a Catholic priest should always want to help others,' and the phone was slammed down.

May Hayes was a wonderful old lady, originally from Ireland. She had retained all her Irish ways, including her expertise at making soda bread. She had the key of the cathedral as she invariably got up early and liked to walk from her flat a quarter of a mile away to say her prayers before Mass at 9.30 a.m. However, she would punctuate her rosaries with a cigarette outside.

'Coming to church to pray,' she once informed me, 'saves money as I can't smoke in the cathedral!' Her prayers were also interrupted by her going through to the kitchen where, with great regularity, my father would by 8 a.m. be having his breakfast. May would get his tea, with a cup for herself as well, and ply him with her home-made soda bread. They got on well with this daily ritual.

Religious rituals can be in very contrasting styles, especially when they concern the 'hatched, matched and dispatched' – the baptisms, weddings and funerals. Travelling people can be the most unpredictable, annoying, but at times the most faith-filled. I celebrated baptisms when crowds of children literally clung to the font, with the hands dipped in the water and the whole group charismatically replying with great enthusiasm to every phrase I uttered. However, their respect for law and order is often non-existent, as when the police arrived at the back of the church to enforce the removal of some dozen or so cars, vans and lorries parked outside on the double yellow lines.

One afternoon, having just been ordered immediately to move off a nearby field where they were illegally camped, a group of travelling folk arrived asking for confession and communion. I welcomed them. Their faith is simple and uncomplicated.

The children, who have no regular schooling, are nevertheless taught their faith by their mothers, but, of course, their practice of certain basic moral values is open to question. After they had gone I went to the cathedral to make sure everything had been put away, and found a pool of wee in front of the Blessed Sacrament Chapel, some sickness on the floor in the porch, and nuts under the front bench.

Then there was the wedding of Danny and Molly Doolan, both with the same surname, which is very common among the travelling folk. I had impressed on them that they must arrive on time at 11.30 a.m., as I had a meeting at Bedford which I should attend at 12.30 p.m., but at least if I could be there for 1 p.m., I'd be happy. However, travelling folk have little idea of time – which in some ways is good – but it can be for the rest of us highly inconvenient. They finally arrived at 12.20 p.m. all with their glittering bangles and rings and cheap smart dresses smelling of body odour, and the breaths of many of the men smelling of drink. There were innumerable children between the ages of about three and twelve, and they provided a background of noise as they ran around the altar, the sanctuary area, the side chapel and everywhere, in fact, where there was space, scattering confetti as they went. This was during the wedding and Mass. When I saw many of the adults carrying on a conversation, I was in two minds about continuing with the Mass and I stopped for some minutes at the offertory waiting for silence, and appealing for them to be quiet, but to no avail.

As the couple walked down the aisle, some of the guests started showering them with more confetti, which later took weeks finally to gather up from the gaps between the floorboards. Two days later a headline in the local newspaper announced that subsequent to a wedding at the Roman Catholic Cathedral, there had been havoc created by young tearaways at the local pub. Police were called when about seventy children aged between eight and ten had removed the bungs from the barrels in the cellar, flooding it with beer, let off fire extinguishers and ripped lavatory fittings from the wall. The pub proprietor had no idea he was hosting a gypsy wedding reception until the guests began to arrive. The person making the booking had given a false address in the town.

At breakfast one morning, Frank Diamond, a retired priest living with us, asked me if I'd heard all the noise at about 11.30 p.m. the previous night. I had heard nothing as I had retired fairly early and gone to sleep. Frank thought there had been a great deal of noise on the landing. At that moment Tom, one of the two assistant priests, came in and burst out, 'Did you hear all the noise last night?' to which I replied, I must admit with some inward satisfaction, 'No.'

It appeared that the doorbell had been rung and Andrew, the other assistant, had answered it. A man had forcefully pushed past him, dashed upstairs stripping off his clothes as he did so. Tom had appeared on the second-floor landing, being just about to go to bed, but the intruder was already outside his door, by this time, stark naked. Tom restrained him as best he could whilst Andrew rang for the police, who appeared within a few minutes. Tom reported that he was completely naked except for his wristwatch. He was from one of the local mental hospitals and had decided to test out the possibility of freedom from its confines.

A more serious invasion of our premises occurred one morning when I was out. A man came wanting a chat about his problems. Gareth, at that time a student for the priesthood, opened the door, invited him in and talked with him. Meanwhile, I had returned and was upstairs in my room talking to an engineer who had come to repair our telephone system. Gareth came up, looking somewhat worried and told me that the man with whom he'd been talking had recently come out of prison, had discovered that whilst he was inside his wife had been having an affair with another man and the police were looking for him as he had threatened to kill his wife, and then himself, and that in the bag he was carrying he had a gun. He seemed, however, agreeable to giving himself up to the police. Gareth was unused to dealing with such situations and asked my advice.

I confessed that for me, too, it was a first. However, I advised him immediately to phone the police. Meanwhile, the man concerned went into the cathedral as he wanted to be quiet and pray. Within minutes the police arrived, some armed, and in no time, the whole cathedral and house were surrounded. The police knew him of old as a very violent man who'd been previously in prison several times. In view of the Dunblane tragedy, when a gunman had opened fire on a class of children, only the previous week, it seemed more than prudent to be very wary of him in case he opened fire.

John Preston, who before he moved to Hereford had been one of our organists, had arrived to practise on the organ at about the same time as the telephone man. He also wanted to have a talk with me as I was otherwise engaged when he arrived. He decided first of all to go to the cathedral to play on the organ. This he was doing when our little drama began. Roy Honeywell who was on house duty was instructed to go and tell him after the police had arrived to carry on playing to give the impression to the man concerned that everything was as normal. John complied, not knowing quite why he had been asked. Meanwhile the police set up an operations HQ in our front room, which had an interior monitor giving a view of the altar area of the cathedral so that we could see something of what was happening inside.

After a while Roy went in to rescue John who stopped playing, whilst our uninvited guest was still wandering around inside the cathedral. From then on the drama intensified and evolved. We found that the whole area of the main road, the cathedral and Semilong to the rear were cordoned off. There were armed police everywhere and no less than four within our own house. They then wanted to evacuate the whole house except for myself; Gareth, Roy, John Preston and the telephone engineer were escorted off under armed guard, the telephone man leaving his van behind, John and Roy both leaving their cars in the car park. The police officer then focused on me and asked, 'Is there anyone else in the house?'

I said, 'Yes, my father, but he's ninety-seven and we certainly can't move him; he hasn't been out for over a year.'

They accepted this for a few minutes and then turned to me again. 'Well, can't we carry him out and take him somewhere?'

I knew there were many people in the parish who would welcome him but it would have nearly killed him to have moved him from his familiar surroundings. He was too old and frail for that to happen. I dug my heels in and said, 'No way, but we can perhaps lock his door when necessary and barricade his room.'

They were clearly afraid of our man who was six foot three inches in height, massive build, highly dangerous, a psychiatric patient as well as ex-prisoner with a record of crime behind him. He could have charged through the sacristy doors into the house and run rampage there. However, I looked around and saw the armed police all around and really felt that my father would nevertheless be safe. I also had to stay around not only because of my father, but it was necessary to be there to guide and inform the police of the ins and outs of the cathedral building, the various light switches, which way the doors opened, and so on.

A team of negotiators then moved into the front room. They used the radio mike from the house through the public address system in the sacristy into the cathedral. The chief negotiator said when he came in, 'Well, give us two hours and we'll have him out.' Their policy was to persuade by word rather than by force and ultimately, although more costly in time and resources, it was the best way. It avoided damage to body and possible loss of life. However, the siege went on to well into the evening and I could see that I would have to care and tend for my father, put him to bed, and I myself, finally after midnight, retired for a little sleep. However, not for very long – although the police did not disturb me, I was in quite a state of tension and unable to relax. I heard the police beneath me in the bookshop, going in and out of the toilet and using the radio mike to communicate with the man still in the cathedral. He had gone into the candle room which led to the organ gallery, and occasionally was heard playing the organ himself and when the police wanted to put a mobile telephone point through a small open window into the candle room they had to make sure that he was sitting at the organ playing while they did so in order to protect themselves.

We still were not quite sure whether or not he did have a gun as no one had seen it. However, later on, as the siege continued, we found that he had appeared on the lower roof of the cathedral. I was mystified by this because I knew for certain that the door from the gallery up to the lower roof was securely locked. We found out later that he had chiselled away the lintel and thus opened the door and got out onto the roof. This was alarming because, if he was armed, he had command of quite a wide area of Barrack Road and the surroundings. For this reason a police sniper was later put into one of the first-floor rooms of Bishop's House next door to keep an eye on our roof. There were also snipers in one of the houses opposite in Langham Place. Many of these houses had been evacuated and a relief centre had been set up at St George's School just outside the cordoned area. By Saturday morning I felt it was necessary for someone to come in to look after my father, and so, after some persuasion, I managed to get permission for our good friend Judith to come. She would be able not only to look after him but also be some support to myself as well as a help in various practical ways. The assistant priest and Gareth who had both slept out with friends on Friday night wanted to return to pick up their belongings in case there was going to be a further night out.

They had a police escort in and it took them three quarters of an hour to get through all the formalities and obstacles of returning to the cathedral. En route, Gareth was diverted in order to be interviewed by a barrage of press and television staff. The other priest picked up his things and went off again, but Gareth decided he would prefer to remain in Cathedral House. This I was very pleased about as with him and Judith, I felt more supported and able to cope with the situation. I spent a great deal of the time in the operations room listening to the police, answering the odd question, and hopefully being of some help.

Being Friday evening and Saturday the traffic congestion in other parts of Northampton with diverted buses, taxis, cars and vans was, I gathered later, quite appalling and the local paper had four pages devoted entirely to the siege, with the national news also giving it considerable mention. The media were continually on the phone but I was advised to divert them to the police press office. I could not praise the police enough in the way that they dealt with the whole situation, nor could I perhaps be critical enough of the media that caused interference and hindrance by bombarding the telephone system with calls – the telephone at that time needed to be used for more urgent matters. I think my father did not quite appreciate the seriousness of the situation, until halfway through the following day when two armed policemen entered his room to ensure that he was all right.

Several times I had to wear a bullet-proof jacket in order to go to a 'danger zone' to show the police where certain locks and switches were located. At one point our 'friend' was clearly seen walking up and down with the gun at his throat. However, in the later hours of Saturday night, he was persuaded to lay it, together with ammunition, on the altar. It was then that the police had to use a megaphone from outside as he had severed all the loud speakers installed in the cathedral and unplugged the telephone that had been put through a window.

Our 'guest' occasionally got almost to the point of responding to the persuasive powers of the police and coming out of the cathedral of his own volition, but it was not until 7.15 a.m. on

Sunday morning, with hands held high, that he appeared through the main door of the cathedral and, at the police's bidding, threw himself flat on his face on the ground whilst he was properly searched with the armed police standing around him. The precautionary measures adopted by the police had been fully justified. If they had entered the cathedral to take him by force, there could so easily have been a gun battle with a disastrous outcome.

Cathedral House gradually quietened down as its weekend visitors packed up to leave. The police had imported great hampers of food with tins of curried beef, which, when opened, after about fifteen minutes, automatically heated up to a piping hot meal. The coffee and tea had flowed continuously, and we had, with the police, almost begun to form a community, welded together by the common predicament and danger.

Outside there had for two and a half days been an unnatural and almost eerie silence with no traffic on the normally busy road.

The police carried out a very thorough inspection of the interior of the cathedral and discovered a small supply of ammunition half-hidden in a candle box as well as a suicide note. The only damage done was a small broken window, a door leading up to the roof had also been broken and the cables to the loud speakers severed. By Sunday afternoon, the barricades had been removed from the surrounding streets, and I was able to celebrate the Sunday evening Mass with relief and thanksgiving and with a small number of people who had heard by bush telegraph that the siege was over. The man who had caused all the trouble, whose name I discovered was Stanley Wapping, had been interrogated and I made arrangements with the police to go and visit him in the lock-up at Campbell Square. He was actually talking with his mother at the time. She offered to leave but I said that she need not unless her son wanted her to; so the three of us remained there in the tiny room with a guard sitting just a yard away. Stanley was at least six foot three inches and took after his mother, who was a good runner-up in height. She was also a very big-framed woman and I could see there was a strong resemblance between them. I did not know how he was going to receive me but I extended a hand of reconciliation and said that I just wanted to thank him for not having done very much damage in the cathedral: just a few superficial items and it could have been so much worse. I also said that I hoped he would respond to and follow the medical and psychiatric advice and medication that he was given, as this would help him to retain his balance in the future and live a reasonable life. We had a short chat and he expressed his sorrow at all the inconvenience and trouble he had caused.

'What happened to the baptisms?' he asked. In part of the interrogation process it had been mentioned to him that there were three baptisms due in the cathedral on Sunday morning, and that he had to get out before that.

I replied that they had been diverted to another church but that normally there would be about eight hundred people coming to Mass in the cathedral, and these had all been diverted elsewhere, so he really had caused quite a lot of inconvenience.

I found in the short time I spoke to him that there was a soft streak in him, and the police officer who had shown me in to whom I made this remark said, 'Yes, perhaps with age he was getting a little softer and mellowing.' However, he had been known to the police for so long and had given them a great deal of trouble and was a tough and dangerous customer. In his better moments, he seemed to have some faith in God and in prayer. This was evidenced by a prayer he'd written in our Memento book in the Blessed Sacrament Chapel.

Throughout the whole operation the police had acted admirably, and I could not praise them highly enough. Gareth became known as the 'rookie priest'; a 'rookie' constable being someone under training and about to hatch out. The bishop, who had been away at the beginning of the siege, returned to his house adjacent to us under close police escort, not realising at first that we were all in danger with a gunman in the cathedral and with him having access to the roof.

Unfortunately, the drama of the siege had little effect on the local red-light area, which was extending its influence along the road near the rear of the cathedral. The police, amongst their many and varied tasks, had only managed to scatter a few prostitutes, two of whom came to our door the next day demanding money to go to Exeter. They met with a refusal: compliance might well have been misinterpreted, although perhaps the Lord would have dealt with them more graciously than I did.

On a different and more 'middle-class' level – for hospitality should operate between all people of whatever class or origin – there were a number of exchanges between members of different churches in Northampton and our twinned town of Poitiers in France. There had for some time been visits by football teams, choral groups and others, and several of us felt that links on a more religious level would be desirable. A catalyst, which helped this exchange of hospitality, was when Bishop Francis Thomas, who was on the pilgrimage I took to the shrines of France, met the bishop of Poitiers during our brief halt there; and also Suzanne Martineau who lived in Poitiers and for many years had been involved with ecumenical work.

As a result, welcome on both sides of the channel was given by and to Baptists, Anglicans, United Reformed Church, Catholics and Methodists, accompanied by a sharing of pastoral concerns and interests. Even this was not without its problems, as when we received a phone call just a few days before the Poitiers group arrived to say that instead of fifty-three people coming, there would be about seventy, for whom accommodation with families had to be found.

On another occasion our inter-church group visiting Poitiers took part in a Mass celebrated by the bishop of Poitiers in his cathedral. He welcomed everyone very particularly highlighting our group from Northampton. The Mass itself, although quite solemn in some ways, had an informal touch to it, without some of the pomp and ceremony that is so often the case elsewhere. The readings and bidding prayers were read in English by some of our own people, and after the post-communion prayer, the bishop said a further word of thanks, so I leapt to the microphone explaining that when we have a Mass in Northampton Cathedral with our own bishop I usually try and have the last word, which I was trying to do now. I then went on to thank all our hosts and say what a wonderful occasion it had been. As I went back to my place at the side of the bishop he took my arm and whispered to me that I couldn't really have quite the last word but he would let me take part in the last gesture.

'Come,' he said, 'and do the blessing with me.' And so I found myself giving the triple blessing. Needless to say, and thankfully, it was not a foretaste of things to come.

Welcoming someone with a problem of any sort was never easy when it occurred in the middle of the night. On one occasion at 4 a.m. it was Frank Upton. Dermot, one of our church students, had very dutifully lifted the receiver. Frank used to serve Mass fairly regularly at 8.30 a.m. on Sundays. He had been encouraged to do this by one of the other priests, although I had had certain reservations due to a mental imbalance and a question regarding his criminal background. He had more recently taken to looking after an old lady in the flat below him, and the social services carers had been told not to come in. Frank, at the other end of the phone, stammered out, 'I've just committed a murder, and I want to go to confession; and I'm on my way to the police station to give myself up!'

I immediately phoned the police, to find that he had in fact just arrived and was admitting to having been the cause of somebody's death. The police were busy questioning him and I left it that they would contact me if he still wanted me to go and see him. However, before this happened the police came to the house to question Dermot and me regarding the details of the phone call. When I did eventually go to the cells to see Frank, I found him looking pretty shattered and he told me that he'd been feeding the old lady on the Saturday night and had slapped her face and then, for some reason which I didn't discover, he had gone down to the flat below, shortly before 4 a.m. to see how she was and had found her dead. He panicked and started beating her chest, which apparently caused broken ribs.

This was the story that he told me, and when the court case came up later on Monday it evolved that she had in fact died of natural causes, but that he had been guilty of grievous bodily harm and in the meantime was on remand in prison at a nearby town. Fortunately, his association with the church did not hit the headlines and cause unnecessary scandal.

Michael Mulligan died rather suddenly one Friday afternoon. He was taken into hospital Friday morning and Rita Bonner who doesn't drive, walked down to see him in medical admissions and found that he was somewhat confused so she knelt down by the bed and, taking his rosary, made the sign of the cross and gave it to him to kiss the crucifix. Halfway through the first 'Our Father' Michael died. She immediately got the hospital to phone for me.

I had known Michael for some years. He had tried his vocation in several religious orders and finally ended up in Northampton helping in the kitchen in the bishop's house. From there he frequently welcomed the men of the road, the unemployed and anyone in need, and thus began the soup kitchen which later moved to St Patrick's Hall, next to our house and then to Oak Street and Ash Street where it became well established. Michael at some point had had the idea of setting up a group of Brothers who could run a soup kitchen for the homeless and needy, but that idea did not come to fruition. However, his energy and vision came to fruition in other ways. He was extremely generous both with his time and resources and was sadly missed in Northampton. He himself was a great little man, an orphan, being brought up by Nazareth House Sisters. He originated in Sligo, but he had friends all over the country and there were even people who came down from Dundee for the funeral – no relatives, just friends, and it was a lovely funeral which Michael would have appreciated – and indeed did appreciate as I'm sure he was aware of all of us gathered around his coffin.

There have been occasions when people have not been made welcome. Mistakes have been made, as when a man aged about thirty came to the door and said he wanted to see a priest. The lady on house duty told him that I might be quite busy at the moment. When I appeared he was waiting just inside the door, a somewhat dilapidated rucksack over his shoulder, and immediately I summed him up as somebody who wanted money, especially when he said, 'Can I see you in private for a moment?' This is the usual opening gambit that I had heard so many times.

I countered it by looking him full in the face and said, 'I'm sorry but we do not give money but we'll give you a cup of tea and a sandwich.'

He reacted angrily and shouted out, 'I came here to discuss getting married.'

I was completely bewildered, but before I could reply he turned away in anger and walked quickly off.

I called out, 'Well, if you would like to wait a few minutes I will see you,' but by then he was striding away and I realised I had made a most awful mistake, although, on reflection, there was still a doubt in my mind, and I did wonder in fact, if he was pulling a fast one.

Then at 9.30 p.m. on the evening of Good Friday, I saw a man seated near the door of the cathedral, with a tightly packed small rucksack and looking somewhat dishevelled. He wanted somewhere to stay for the night. I found it difficult understanding him so I bent down to listen as he repeated his request. It was then that I smelt the alcohol. This always made me react rather firmly and I told him accusingly that he'd been drinking and to be spending money on drink was not the way to be seeking accommodation for the night. He countered this by saying that he'd been given a couple of drinks by a friend. He seemed, however, to be a mild and reasonably polite person. I suspected that he might have been homosexual. My inclination was to have answered his request and given him a bed as he'd left the night shelter when two skinheads had attacked him there the previous night. He pleaded with me that anything at all would be all right. By this time one of the assistant priests was standing nearby listening to the conversation. It was not a cold night and I could have put him in the garage where there was a mattress and he could have covered himself with a blanket and been reasonably comfortable. However, my assistant objected to this as his car was in the garage. He suggested the outside toilet. I was more than unhappy about this, as it was such a small area, too small for the mattress.

However, I was weak and unassertive and did not wish to have a confrontation with my assistant, so I ended up by offering the man the four-foot square area of concrete floor in the toilet. We gave him some rubber matting and a blanket and he ensconced himself gratefully, half-sitting on the floor. I felt mean and very distressed and that Good Friday evening identified our visitor with the Lord. Whether or not he slept much, I will never know, but I was awake most of the night thinking about him and wondering whether I should go out and offer him a place in the house. In the morning I went to see him and I was moved to tears to find the blanket and the other covering that we'd given him neatly folded up in the corner, but of the occupant there was no sign. I thought of the discovery of the empty tomb and the folded linen winding cloths.

As part of the way of life in Cathedral House, we entertained amongst others the bishop, his sister Kathleen and Catherine, the housekeeper, for lunch each Christmas and Easter Sunday. It was, as always, a happy gathering but that particular Easter I was still haunted by remembrance of our friend of the previous day, as well as the many others in Jamaica and elsewhere who lacked our comfortable way of living.

On a brighter note, just after that incident, I received the following letter from someone whom I had no recollection of helping, as so many would come to the door.

Dear Father Payne

Hope you are keeping well. Father, I would like to thank you for your very kind help towards food when I was on the road looking for work between 1983 and 1992. In 1993, I got a cook's job for the summer season. In 1994 the council gave me this lovely house, but it is taking time to furnish properly being on the sick now. At the moment I am waiting for a heart valve operation which I am a little scared, as I have always had a fear of hospitals. Thank you again for your kind help.

God bless you.

Yours very sincerely
Keith

Thank God there are times when one takes exactly the right course of action – 'If anyone gives so much as a cup of cold water…' (Matthew 10:42)

My father was always so appreciative of hospitality that he

continued to receive in Cathedral House. I considered this quite normal anyway, and he made a most important and vital contribution to the whole atmosphere of the house, even up to the moment of his death. He died in his own bed having been confined to it for a few days beforehand just four months before reaching a hundred. Only two years previously he had remarked quite seriously, 'I suppose I have to admit that I'm getting an old man!'

'You can say that again,' I exclaimed.

He told several people in his last months that he did not really want to live to be a hundred. Perhaps if he had, he would have had to admit that he was an old man.

One evening when we were sitting having our evening meal, he suddenly broke a short silence by uttering sounds, which at first I failed to understand. Then I realised he was reciting a number of letters. He continued without interruption and pause. I became alarmed, thinking that perhaps his mind was going.

'What are you trying to say?' I hesitantly asked.

To which he replied, inferring by his tone of voice that I was not really very knowledgeable, 'They are the letters on the typewriter keyboard forwards and backwards.' There was a further short pause and then he said, 'I was thinking earlier today of the different people who lived in our road, Bulwer Street, when I was a child – No. 56, so and so; No. 54 so and so; 52 was where the Thornbacks lived and that was the old lady Thornback with Auntie Totts, Mother's aunt,' and so he went on listing the people for about eight or nine houses away down the road. He came to, I think, No. 44 and said, 'That's where Fatty Gadstone used to live. He was a six-year-old boy, a year or two younger than me, who whenever we saw him pass the house we would remark, "Look, there goes Fatty Gadstone and he's crapping again."' Apparently the poor lad used to crap in his trousers and you could see it running down his legs.

My father's memory was phenomenal. This was doubtless in part due to the fact that, being partially sighted since the age of seventy-three, he would often sit quietly and exercise his mind and memory in this way. Not only was he approaching blindness, but his hearing was also very impaired, and perhaps it was because of this that he was able to contemplate in greater depth whatever he did experience through his senses. I often used to say that he practised what I preached and frequently failed to put into effect in my own life.

As in most Catholic churches, many different sorts of people would drift in and out of the church. Not a few being those who were mentally sick. There was Russell who had once been a brilliant musician but, subsequent to a breakdown, had fallen on hard times, continued to be mentally ill and was living in one of the hostels near to us. Frequently he would come to ask for one pound to buy some cigarettes. I generally refused this, but offered him a 'cuppa' instead, which he would accept with a grin. One day as he walked into the cathedral, with each step towards the bench where he wanted to sit, his trousers would slip down a further three inches or so. As they crumpled on the ground around his feet, I approached him and sternly ordered him to pull them up, which, again with a grin, he proceeded to do. This happened before Mass began.

Sometimes there were incidents during Mass, as when another character, the Count, frequently caused a distraction. We called him 'The Count' as he came from Eastern Europe and claimed to be well connected. He had very little English although he had lived in Northampton for many years.

He was a man in his late sixties who lived in what was more or less a dosshouse not far below us, near the bottom of the hill. He had always professed in a somewhat vague sort of way, to come from a distinguished family although he dressed very shabbily and his body probably saw the water not more than once every three months. Added to this he was, on the quiet, a bit of an alcoholic. Sometimes this wasn't quite so much on the quiet as he was frequently seen by all and sundry during Mass to bury his head under his jacket and take a swig out of a small bottle. He usually sat on the front bench if there was still a seat vacant when he came in, often late. There was one occasion when he was sitting on the gangway on the front bench and I was preaching, standing not more than four feet from him; after picking his nose and fiddling about in his mouth, he gave a loud yawn, audible throughout the cathedral, followed by a plop and a clatter. His false teeth had fallen on the tiled floor in the central gangway. This brought the sermon to an abrupt end as I had to sit down, try not to catch anyone's eye and bury my face in my hands.

Regularly taking exercise by swimming in a public swimming pool can also give rise to disconcerting situations, as when a small boy calls out from the other side of the pool, 'Ooh, there's Father; hello, Father!' Or when at a formal mayor's reception with crowds of people milling around, a lady whom I had frequently seem swimming came up to me and in a loud voice exclaimed, 'Oh, I haven't seen you before with your clothes on!'

We have seen that welcoming others into our lives and into our homes means being ready for humour and tragedy; it means encountering and dealing appropriately with both relatives and friends as well as those who are difficult, daft or dangerous, and the strategy required varies with each one.

Today an increasing number of people live on their own. This isolation in living applies to all strata of society. The elderly live away from their families, who have often disintegrated through divorce and separation. When age and illness makes it no longer possible to live alone, instead of rejoining some of their family, they are left to share a room in an old people's home. Often, by this time, they are too geriatric to worry any longer about preserving their privacy and independence.

This isolation of people, one way or another, is found also amongst the celibate clergy in the Catholic Church. In the past, until, in fact, the latter part of the twentieth century, it was usual in England for most parishes to have two priests living under the same roof with a live-in housekeeper. In the one-man parish, she would be another human being in the house, someone who could call out 'goodnight!' when the priest came in after a long and busy evening, someone with whom, perhaps, he could to some extent share and confide. By contrast, today, most of our parishes are run by a single priest, living on his own, with, if he is fortunate, someone coming in just in the mornings to clean and shop and cook the lunch and leave food for the evening. The house is empty most of the time.

Meetings may be held in the evenings, but after the last person has gone home, all is quiet and empty and with a forlorn, often untidy and uncolourful masculine appearance. The priest is alone. There is no one with whom he can share his thoughts and reactions to the events of the day, no one on whom he can unload his frustrations and irritations, no one who can lend a listening ear, give an encouraging grunt or smile away a difficulty.

It is not good for man to live alone. True, married folk, after the death of a partner have to face this aloneness. For the celibate priest, it is laid down even before he is ordained. Roderick Strange quotes Archbishop Derek Worlock as saying how committed he was to the priesthood, but questioning 'the how of priesthood', the way the ministry is lived (reported in *The Tablet*, 27 September 1997). Is the way of inherent loneliness the answer? Some priests are attracted to living alone, especially after having spent some years living in the same house with another priest where the rapport has been non-existent. However, one may ask whether this attraction has a truly altruistic value. I would suggest that very few, whether clergy or laity, have a genuine calling to living in 'isolation'.

For the possibility of real growth in spiritual values, we need one another, and so we need to explore more widely the case for some clergy to be married; communities of clergy and laity, both married and single; much closer support, in communities, or at least under the same roof, for the single and the widowed. Collaborative ministry will then become more easily a reality rather than something just to be talked about.

The 'bonding', as it were, in this opening out to others, must of course always be prayer, contemplative prayer growing from the Scriptures. Then we will be able to communicate with and 'cash in' on the spirituality of the vast majority of the non-church-going people who believe in God, who sometimes pray and who give flowers when Princess Diana dies, who do not see warfare as the answer to injustice, and who give generously when emergency aid is needed anywhere in the world.

If one gives, one receives back in abundance. The small boy who gave his two barley loaves and five small fish received in return from Jesus a copious quantity of food which was more than enough for the great crowds who were there. This will happen to us if we are willing to welcome others into our hearts and our homes. A few memorable examples of this in the next chapter will help to illustrate this point.

Chapter IX

A HUNDREDFOLD RETURN: FIVE CONTINENTS – AFRICA

> Give and there will be gifts for you: a full measure, pressed down, shaken together, and overflowing will be poured into your lap.
>
> Luke 6:38

It was the summer of 1974 in Bedford when some parishioners asked me if I could find accommodation for a young Egyptian medical student, Sherif Said, who was doing a spell of training at a nearby hospital. He was lodging with them and wanted to stay a further week in Bedford. However, they had arranged to go on holiday the following day, hence their request to me, it being assumed that the parish priest could solve all problems. I had a spare room and as it would have been near impossible to find anywhere at such short notice and in the middle of the holiday season, I agreed to take him in. He was a pleasant young man, a practising Muslim, and very grateful for the hospitality offered. The week extended to two weeks but after he left he corresponded with me and on a number of occasions, stayed with me both in Bedford and, later, in Aylesbury whilst he was working at Stoke Mandeville Hospital.

Sherif's family lived in a suburb of Cairo, Heliopolis, his father being an influential general in the Egyptian army, in charge of logistics.

'You must come to Egypt,' Sherif persuasively said to me on a number of occasions.

It was an attractive proposal and, after some hesitation, John, a priest friend, who also knew Sherif through living in the presbytery at the same time, and I both decided to make the journey to Egypt one summer. However, this, we later realised, was a mistake for not only was it Ramadan, but more disastrously, it was the hottest time of the year.

We decided to travel by Czechoslovak airlines, being the cheapest we could find, although a longer route. It included an overnight stop in Prague, where we arrived on a Tuesday evening and where, to my alarm, at the airport our passports were immediately taken from us. It was several years prior to the lifting of the Iron Curtain, and it caused me no little alarm: in a communist country with no passport and no means of identification. We were made to understand that they would be returned to us on our return to the airport. However, this failed to allay my fears.

Getting on the wrong bus outside the airport, we found ourselves in the centre of Prague, although eventually found our way to the International Hotel where the airline had arranged accommodation. At that time Prague was drab and grey, with ill-kept buildings. Vegetation, where there was any, was overgrown and one had the impression of bad planning – it had few shops, dusty streets and an almost menacing spartan quiet about it. This, perhaps together with the fact that our passports had been taken from us, gave us an insecure and trapped feeling.

When, finally, we arrived at the hotel, one young fellow who'd been travelling with us decided to forego his supper and room and explore Prague. He, in fact, spent the whole night wandering around and reported back to us the following morning that he had to be very careful what he said: police were watching and listening everywhere. John and I decided not to forego our sleep and we had the luxury of breakfast being brought to us in our room at 5.30 a.m., being taken to the airport, thankfully collecting our passports prior to leaving for the plane which should have taken us via Beirut to Cairo but instead went via Athens, owing to the troubles in Beirut at the time. After a short stop at Athens we went on south to Libya and flew over the desert about twenty miles inland along the coast to Cairo. My first sight of the pyramids from the air was amazing. There was a quite sudden demarcation line of yellow to a hazy greeny red between the desert and the Nile valley, and on the edge of the desert the pyramids stood, looking from the air like tiny symmetrical sand castles. Cairo was sprawled out across the fertile band of the Nile valley, covering pretty well the whole span of the valley, the pyramids being on one side, and the airport where we landed on the other.

Landing was something I shall always remember. As we stepped down the gangway from the plane I thought I heard over a loudspeaker the words, 'Mister Ken, Mister Ken.' I was not mistaken. A group of army officers at the bottom of the gangway advanced towards us and, having with some difficulty identified us with a mispronunciation of 'Mister Ken', whisked us both off in a military vehicle printed on the side in large lettering 'VIP Visitors'. I would like to have seen the expression on the faces of the other passengers on the plane for we had up to then merged in with the crowd of tourist class passengers, and they must have been surprised to find that they'd been travelling with such notabilities! I myself was so surprised and bewildered that I only gradually came to as we were being ushered through various barriers, one officer having taken our passports and another our hand luggage, which for each of us comprised somewhat shabby haversacks. We were ushered at great speed through all the officialdom, security and customs to the VIP lounge. I doubt whether the prime minister or the Pope himself could have been given better treatment. In the VIP lounge a group of other special visitors came through, one of whom was in his twenties and who, as he entered, opened a coca-cola can which half exploded over him. He turned to us as he passed and remarked in a cultured English accent, 'There, I'm disgracing them all.' I empathised with him.

General Ali, Sherif's father, awaited us in the brigadier's office attached to the airport and we were driven to a pleasantly cool flat in Heliopolis on what was considered to be a warm afternoon – 38°C. This was Sherif's parents' home. There we were warmly welcomed by the general's wife and daughters. Maha was the eldest daughter, who was engaged to be married to Khaled. Maha means 'beautiful', but I think all of Sherif's three sisters lived up to that description. The other two were Soha and Heba. On arrival we exchanged presents and the general seemed particularly pleased with the framed photo of John's painting of St Joseph's. He presented us with a galabay each. This was the full length garment worn by many Egyptians. The word itself means 'Thanks to God', and I found it a pleasant garment to wear over swimming trunks in such a hot climate. It was 7 July and the temperature was, for the most part, between 35 and 40°C.

After a sumptuous Egyptian dinner, which we sat down to immediately at sundown, Ramadan having already begun, the general took us both to the Sheraton Hotel to meet a great friend of his, General Adley-el-Sherif, who was an expert on Egyptian history. We sat in the cool of the hotel drinking a pleasant fruit drink called Florida, and absorbing the atmosphere and the tempo of this amazing country. General Ali had worked out a detailed plan for our two weeks in Egypt and the first part of that time was destined to be, to a large extent, under the guidance of a Professor George Shellaby, an expert Egyptologist, whose enthusiasm overflowed at every point, and who was to make even the smallest mundane sights of interest to us.

The next day, having passed through the edge of Cairo, an incredible jungle of domes, minarets, ghettos, modern hotels and unspectacular shops, we came to the famous pyramids of Giza. The most important of these is the pyramid of Cheops, 8.6 million tonnes, with a base two hundred and thirty metres square, and one hundred and forty-seven metres high, made from granite transported over one thousand miles and supposedly built in only twenty years. Professor Shellaby believed that these and other achievements, such as the enormous statues at Luxor that we were to see the following week, could not have been built without help from aliens – from another planet? Cheops is in the exact centre of Egypt and also, in some sense, the centre of the world. We stood beneath it for a few minutes and then drove down to another mystery – the Sphinx. The word itself means 'mystery', named by Herodotus in 500 BC. According to some papyrus records, it pre-dates the pyramids by some fourteen thousand years. One legend has it that eighteen thousand years after the Atlantis catastrophe there would be another and the Cheops pyramid would then reveal its secrets. This would be in AD 2012. We had to wait for another day in order to go inside the Cheops pyramid and then we were accompanied by Professor Shellaby's brother, Maher. He was quieter than George, and rather more pedestrian, but still very interesting. According to Maher we learned that the word 'pyramid' came from two words: 'pyra' meaning 'house' and 'mid' meaning 'of the dead'. The shape was devised because in the *Book of the Dead* it said that to be reincarnated, the soul of the king must look from its mummy and focus on the sun. Indeed the pharaoh is a ray of the sun who took the form of a human in order to bring about the 'word', and then returned to the sun. The words 'the Word became flesh' apparently appear in this *Book of the Dead* – three thousand years before Christ.

We were led into the heart of the pyramid by an old Arab who had to keep pausing to catch his breath. It became very humid and we traversed some three hundred and fifty feet in order to reach the burial room and a large granite sarcophagus in the very centre of the pyramid. The granite walls of the chamber were smooth with fine joints and in the centre was a twenty-foot hole with a stone plug next to it where presumably the treasure had been placed. Some more recent books about the mystery of the pyramids link them with the Orion constellation of stars. Whether or not our planet earth played host to beings from 'outer space' we may never know. Certain it is, however, that both the construction and situation of the pyramids, especially that of Cheops, raise many mysterious questions.

Our main destination on that first day in Egypt with Professor Shellaby was Sakkara. Italians had found on papyrus drawings there an aeroplane. This dated from about four thousand and four hundred years ago. Could it be that people of that time had contact with those from other planets? Professor Shellaby voiced the opinion that if they did not visit us now it was because we were so bad, and this view seemed to be expressed on the papyrus. We passed three pyramids at Abu Shir, and also a temple, but there had been no excavations there because of the scorpions and cobras. Nearby at Memphis, the one time capital of Egypt, we saw under a canopy a huge four hundred-ton statue of Rameses I, and the city itself lay under many feet of silt and sand upon which we stood. Hardly any of it had been excavated. However, further on at Sakkara over 127,000 tombs have so far been discovered, and in the course of visiting a few of them George Shellaby explained some of the carvings and pictures on the walls. The monkey is always a significant carving because the time of day was calculated by the number of times a monkey urinated, that is, hourly. In one small room there was a version of the Ten Commandments on the wall in an affirmative form, and they pre-dated the Ten Commandments as we know them: 'I have not killed', 'I have honoured my father and my mother', and so on. These carvings were forty-eight centuries old. I found the pyramid of Teti particularly interesting. In an upper room there was the complete *Book of the Dead*. In some of the oldest carvings we saw we were told that there was symbolism and meaning to the colours used. Black meant joy, though no one yet knows why this is so; red = men; yellow = women; green and blue = osiris, heaven; and white = mourning. The smell of eucalyptus trees along the roads made the return drive a pleasant one. Eucalyptus trees are used to keep away mosquitoes and the juice of the leaves have other mainly medical uses.

Back in Cairo itself, the traffic was unbelievable. It was quite the worst I had ever witnessed. The continuous noise of hooting accompanied people everywhere, cars all but mowing down pedestrians when they attempted to dodge between the traffic. There is, in fact, an underground train system and one might have been tempted to retreat to this for safety, but for most of its meandering route it ploughed its way above ground down the middle of the streets with concern for no one. To drive, or even to walk, in Cairo demanded great courage and quick reactions.

Our hosts and guides all insisted that we should eat at midday, and drink beer, while they, to our embarrassment, sat at the same table eating and drinking nothing at all, not even a glass of water, which for me would have been an absolute necessity given the hot climate. After the main meal of the evening, begun at the point of sunset during Ramadan, most of the population seemed to resort to the streets, which became crowded until well after midnight, everyone in this hot climate moving slowly, and frequently stopping for a drink at one of the cafés or stalls. However, the drinks were entirely non-alcoholic, in the form of a modern aphrodisiac – coca-cola or Pepsi. The mosques were crowded, mostly with men chanting and moving rhythmically: this is a traditional Ramadan custom. Most Muslims carry a set of beads, somewhat like our rosaries, only with thirty-three beads. The full set is with ninety-nine and on each one is recited one of the ninety-nine names for Allah. We saw in many of the shops beautiful framed plaques with the name of Allah, rather like the one I had noticed in great prominence in the general's office on my first morning.

At the Egyptian Museum, George Shellaby explained to us the cult of reincarnation. When a body was mummified only the heart was left in it – the brain, the liver, the kidneys and so on were kept in four separate bottles. The heart was the centre: it was the very essence of man. In order to be mummified the body was washed in date wine and left in natrum (a kind of salt) for sixty days. This turned the body brown. It was then washed again and wrapped in linen with amulets to guard against evil and illness. A person then had to pass through various levels of both hell and heaven, being tested at the different stages. Fortunately, when he reached the seventh heaven he could either live there for ever or be reincarnated. In the museum we saw findings dating back to 9000 BC. There were vases of incredible symmetry, made of stone no longer to be found, and some items made of twenty-four carat gold; there was linen, mummified animals and beautiful jewellery. It was still a mystery how they had such knowledge and art eleven thousand years ago!

We also visited the Islamic Museum – at least John did – I fell asleep on a bench in the entrance hall as I had been quite unwell with a strange infection in my gums. The general had taken me to the army doctor who had given me some antibiotic tablets. However, in the evening I was still far from well and unable to do justice to a splendid meal at the Sheraton Hotel, so by 10.30 p.m. we were on our way to see Egypt's top dentist, the one who tended President Sadat, and he diagnosed an infection of the salivary glands. I ended by being on a course of six different tablets, which fortunately in a couple of days cleared up the problem.

In the Coptic quarter, of course, we visited the famous hanging church built on the side of a fortress. Both there and in the Coptic Museum, we noted that the early Coptics did not wish to sever their links with their Egyptian ancestors and so the old gods and symbols took on a new meaning. An ikon of Peter and Mark, who brought Christianity to Egypt, was given the head of Anubis, the god of mummies who gave new life. Iris became Mary and Osiris became Peter. Some carvings were made capable of different interpretations, because of the danger of persecution: the Holy Spirit was made to look like a falcon which was the symbol of Upper Egypt. The oldest church in the world, St Sergius, was built in AD 182 on a grotto where the Holy Family were supposed to have stayed in their flight to Egypt. It was flooded, despite recent attempts by British experts to drain it, and the church was a former tavern. There is a Coptic belief that Jesus was brought up in Egypt. The first known ikons are here in this church.

It was on the occasion of a day out from Cairo to visit the Suez Canal that I had my experience of driving in the general's chauffeur driven car, flag flying and with escort in the front and to the rear. It was a veritable VIP outing and we were greeted at the headquarters of the 3rd Egyptian Army by the general in charge, his aides, and a photographer who darted to and fro taking flashlight photographs of me attempting to keep up an intelligent conversation on the Lebanese crisis, the British attitude in the Middle East and various other topics that I didn't really know a great deal about! At the Suez tunnel we were given a detailed tour of the control room and after having traversed the mile-long tunnel and driven along the edge of the Sinai desert we arrived at a point almost opposite the town of Suez and near the entrance to the canal. Here there were trenches, gun posts and burnt-out tanks: the remains of the Israeli occupation in 1967–73. The photographer continued to take his pictures of us although the 3rd Army general had not accompanied us this far.

We then turned off into the desert in search of Moses's Eye. I was not very clear as to what this was. Neither, it appeared, was our guide, Colonel Sisi. At the first oasis we came to we picked up a local Bedouin who took us to another small oasis and showed us a dried up hollow. None of us thought much of this, and Colonel Sisi clearly told him so, so he then led us across a desert track to a spout of water from an old iron pipe set in concrete. It could, I suppose, if one had a very perceptive imagination, have once been a spring from ancient times, which had helped Moses and the Israelites on their journey across the desert.

We finally left Cairo and went to Alexandria for a few days, travelling there by train in a comfortable first-class compartment, with Colonel Sisi accompanying us. We were met at the station at Alexandria and a Captain Tamar joined us. I think he mistook our priorities for he escorted us immediately to the beach for a swim and sunbathing. However, the water was rough and only a few square yards available for swimming. Later, in the evening, we walked, or rather struggled to walk, along the streets and promenade of Alexandria. I found it difficult here to recapture the history of this ancient city, Cleopatra's city. It had changed so much. It was still during the Islamic Ramadan and we found the place so populated and people so anxious to take the air after their evening meal that London's Oxford Street during the sales would be a desert in comparison. One of the busiest squares in Alexandria is the small Saad Zagloul Square. From near there two obelisks were taken in the nineteenth century, one to New York and the other to London, the latter known as Cleopatra's Needle, now blackened in its site on the Embankment.

One night we witnessed dancers outside one of the mosques. This was an extraordinary experience: about thirty men and a few children were dancing vigorously, seemingly in a semi-trance, and chanting to Allah. We were told they were getting rid of their sin. The music and the dancing had a very hypnotic effect even on the spectator. However, this was only part of the tremendous sense of festivity, uninduced by any form of alcohol, that we witnessed each night during our stay.

In one of the fairly new mosques we visited in Alexandria a young man, a complete stranger, came up to Captain Tamar and said he'd like to get to know him better and be his friend! I wondered if there was much of this sort of thing in the Middle East. The colonel and the captain – the former who understood very little English but the latter who spoke it quite well – both insisted on accompanying us again to the beach in the afternoon – perhaps for fear that other young men might approach us. We felt rather like prisoners with two guards.

Not far out of Alexandria is the site of Nelson's victory over

Napoleon. We climbed the slight rise at the side of the road, which ended in a cul-de-sac, the defence port and a pleasant calm bay with yachts spread out before us. This was where the final battle took place. However, one could hardly describe it as a final battle, as we had no sooner poised ourselves to take photos when men suddenly sprang up from nowhere and surrounded the car and ourselves. Photography was apparently forbidden, although the colonel and captain both insisted that we were not pointing our cameras towards any form of military defence. This was of no avail, the men surrounding us became very heated, and no less so did Colonel Sisi and Captain Tamar. A verbal battle ensued, but our escort, like Napoleon, finally lost, got into the car and swung round back to Alexandria – not, however, before I managed to take a quick photo through the car window as we drove off!

We had travelled to Alexandria by train, as General Ali had thought it would be safer. However, after much discussion and because he had arranged for us to travel later to Upper Egypt, it was decided that we should risk the road back to Cairo. The highway, at first rather like a motorway, turned out to be an unfortunate confusion of alternating fast dual carriageway sections and country lanes. Heavy lorries, many laden with bales of new cotton, fast cars, like our own Peugeot 504, rickety donkey and cart, women with water pitchers on their heads, cyclists, unexpectedly parked vehicles, small groups of cows meandering obliviously along the side, or even, more dangerously, on the central reservation – all these obstacles had to be negotiated, and our driver insisted on doing it at great speed! Every bit of land in this delta region was irrigated and cultivated – Egypt has four crops a year – and one realised the vital importance of Egypt's main artery and lifeline, the Nile.

That same night saw us once again travelling, this time south from Cairo, on the night train to Luxor. A different climate and diet often plays havoc with a person's inner mechanisms! I had in fact suffered from constipation for nearly a week, but then chose that particular evening as we were driving from Heliopolis to the station in Cairo to have an overwhelming need. The army officials who greeted us at the station were unable to show me to a toilet, which I gathered anyway was the reverse of a show piece and was in a filthy state, and I was unable to make them understand that it didn't matter as my need was desperate. They insisted that I waited until the train came in. I was in utter agony for over ten minutes, until the train appeared. I left John with our luggage and could not be concerned with finding our correct coach and reserved place, but dashed into the first open door I could find, pushing past a guard, and found myself in a first-class carriage, the first toilet being locked, but one further along was vacant. The train was still standing in the station, but I was unconcerned. Then I realised that no paper was provided and so had to improvise with my pocket handkerchief. I later joined John established in a compartment further back, and asked the attendant, with some difficulty, making him understand that I needed toilet paper for further needs which I had already sensed were imminent. But no, after three attempts of making my request, I realised that such things were not provided, so John, having primly declined the use of the pages of his diary, gave me part of an old green towel which had to be cut up for use during the rest of the journey. The Scout motto 'Be prepared' is advised for such contingencies.

I travelled from Dunkerque many years ago on my first ever visit abroad on the completely unpadded wooden slats of the night train to Munster in Germany. I've 'slept' on the top bunk of the night train from Paris to Bordeaux in winter, with snow and hail hitting the roof just above me, and then getting out of the train with my body covered in enormous flea bites, so that my friends, when I arrived, put me straight in the bath and dealt with my clothes! However, the night train from Cairo to Luxor was far worse than either of these experiences. Never, anywhere, have I experienced rolling stock that not only rolled, but swayed and creaked and banged and groaned so much. It was one of the old French wagon-lits, probably discarded by the SNCF at the beginning of the century. The air conditioning was virtually non-existent. There were two bunks and the top one had no guardrail, so with the precarious movement of the train it was too dangerous to use, for in the unlikely chance of dozing off, one would almost certainly fall off. John, in truly heroic style, put the one-inch thick mattress on the floor. It was an eleven-hour journey. Perhaps sleep did overtake us for a few isolated minutes. However, I was seldom so pleased to be awake just after 5 a.m. when I saw the sun rising above the desert horizon, shedding its first rays on palm trees and fields irrigated from the nearby Nile, villagers setting off to work on foot or donkey, and in some cases illuminating a still sleeping Arab lying on his bed out of doors. The night temperature was about 27°C.

Punctually, at 6 a.m., itself a minor miracle in Egypt, the train drew into the station at Luxor. Arab porters and drivers of quaint little pony drawn cabs waiting to attract custom, swarmed around us. Having refused all offers of transport, as we were being met by one of the general's officers, we then experienced the only breakdown of the logistics of the whole wonderful fortnight: over an hour's wait, as the message from Cairo had mentioned our arrival at 8 a.m.! However, it was an experience to watch the town awaken. A notice outside the station warned tourists that redevelopment was in progress. This excused the local populace for their bad roads, driving, which had no respect for right or left, and seemed also to have little respect for life itself.

We were taken to a spacious chalet built on the edge of the Nile and reserved for relaxation by Egyptian army generals! It was surrounded by luxuriant foliage, including several jasmine trees, the scent of which pervaded the whole atmosphere. There were ten concrete steps from the veranda down to the water's edge. A sociable soldier called Nasser attended to our needs. After only a short rest we went with Colonel Ibraham and his daughter, who had both accompanied us from Cairo, to the temples of Karnack and Luxor. We were fortunate to be guided around by a young Egyptian officer, Gemma, who had a degree in Egyptology. The temple at Karnack is said to be the biggest religious building in the world. It is dedicated to Amun, and includes a fine roofed temple built by Tuthmoses III, and another used as a church. There are some early Christian paintings still on some of the pillars. Best of all, however, was the hypostyle hall, an oblong enclosed space filled with enormous pillars, one hundred and thirty-six in all, and each one over forty feet high. Some had capitals, large enough, it is said, for one hundred men to stand on. Only a mile and a half from Karnack is the temple of Luxor, and the two are connected by a row of sphinxes, which still survive at the Luxor end. It is smaller than Karnack, but in some ways more beautiful. I was overwhelmed by the age and the splendour of these pagan temples, and how the ancient Egyptians had planned and carried out the transportation of the stone through many hundreds of miles, probably making use of the River Nile.

That afternoon was fortunately unplanned and gave us time for a much needed siesta, although the temperature in the afternoon was over 40°C. Sitting reading on the terrace and watching the incredible sweep of red sky as the sun set over the Nile and the distant desert, was indeed a memorable experience. It was completed by a visit to the Son et Lumière at Karnack where we were fortunate enough to have an English commentary. This superb presentation of the history of Egypt and in particular that of Karnack, with effective background music and well-qualified actors and actresses taking part, helped to situate in its context all that we were seeing. The theme throughout was strongly theistic, built around the glory of Amun. Our guide did not join us as he was still endeavouring to arrange for our return journey to Cairo. Looking back on this day, I wonder how we survived it so well, following as it did on the night journey, the intense heat and the sightseeing.

However, the following morning we were not allowed to sleep it off as we were already at 5.30 a.m. setting off to take the ferry across the Nile to see the Valley of the Kings. Our guide explained that it was essential to go early in the morning as it was far too hot later on and we also noticed that he himself began to weaken and droop during the morning. Fasting for Ramadan also involved abstinence even from all liquids including water. The Valley of the Kings contains the tomb of Tutankhamun, which was found intact in 1922. Many books have been written about all that we saw and experienced on the west bank of the Nile. It was all highly interesting, impressive and exhausting both physically and mentally.

On returning to Luxor I finally found something I had been looking for for a long time – a fairly long walking stick! In fact, it was second-hand – probably left behind by a shepherd or by somebody visiting, but clearly Egyptian, hand carved, and exactly what I wanted. After bargaining I was delighted to get it for less than two pounds. Later that day we sat by the Nile, reading, writing and attempting to fish – needless to say without catching anything – and then had a short dip in the river, which I discovered afterwards was a foolish thing to have done as one could easily have contracted a skin disease which is very common in that part of the world and particularly derived from the waters of the Nile.

The night train back to Cairo was less uncomfortable than the journey there, and as we travelled northwards the following morning, approaching Cairo we witnessed the beginning of the celebrations for the end of Ramadan. Ibraham and his daughter changed into brighter clothes on the train and when we arrived back at General Ali's flat various relations appeared in still subdued but evidently happy mood. It was very like Christmas Day and Boxing Day combined into one, particularly when we all sat down to a splendid celebration meal, no longer waiting for the sun to disappear gently below the horizon; and Ali explained that it was better not to eat too much at first, but gradually to grow out of the Ramadan fast over a period of two or three days. However, this hardly applied to us as we had not observed it.

We flew back to England the following day, not without a slight mishap as we had failed to check by telephone on the time of the return flight which, according to our tickets, was scheduled for 5.50 a.m. We arrived at the airport at 4.45 a.m. and in leisurely Egyptian fashion were ushered into the VIP lounge. General Ali, encountering various friends he knew, began chatting to them and introducing them to us one by one. After a while I noticed on wandering outside for a moment that the indicator board was already flashing the flight departure for our 5.50 a.m. Czechoslovakian flight, the time having been changed to 5.15 a.m. It took me several minutes to convince the general that there was considerable urgency, as our luggage had not been weighed in. Thus by the time we had assembled our luggage and ourselves at the passport barrier, we were informed by the Czechoslovak airline that it was too late for us to board the plane. The general suddenly became very active, flew from one office to another, from one official to another, flashing his identity card as he was not at that moment in uniform. He did everything possible to get us on the plane, but without success, and I remember the horrible sensation standing there in the middle of the terminal between passport control and departure and seeing the plane take off some forty minutes before the scheduled time and without us on it. However, without too much difficulty, Ali managed to arrange for us to go on Egyptair, which eventually arrived in London two hours before the other flight would have done.

One of the most interesting memories of the two weeks in Egypt was the experience of living for most of the time in a Muslim household where members of the family, particularly General Ali and his wife, practised their religion very seriously and conscientiously. I noticed that Ali and his wife were faithful to their prayer five times a day, and it not infrequently happened that one or the other would leave the meal table, the television viewing or the conversation or whatever was going on at the time in order to go to a small alcove where they would kneel and prostrate in prayer for a few minutes. Ali himself would frequently be seated in silence and prayer at his office desk for some minutes before welcoming anyone in, or before speaking or making a decision. For the Muslim the most important duties are prayer, alms giving, fasting and pilgrimage. The times of prayer are laid down and he may, if he wishes, after some of the prayers, recite the 256th verse of Chapter Two of the Koran, then repeating thirty-three times 'the perfection of God', thirty-three times 'praise be to God' and thirty-three times 'God is most great'. These, with other short prayers in between, are counted on his beads, called the 'Subhah'. God – Allah – was an ever-present reality in their lives, and so although we clearly differed in certain ways, we felt to a great extent 'at home', and there was no problem or conflict in continuing our own particular prayer life, with Mass in one of their rooms, such was their incredibly generous and understanding hospitality.

An Anglican vicar in a nearby parish, Colin Wake, informed me that he had a Catholic seminarian from Mauritius coming to stay with him for a few weeks and would I like also to have him for a short while. This seemed a reasonable idea to which I agreed. Colin and his wife had visited Mauritius several years previously and a Catholic priest they had met there had contacted him regarding the seminarian, Sylvio. My own one link with Mauritius was through a good family, John and Paula Lebon, whom I had known in Aylesbury who had been thinking, on retirement, of returning to their roots.

Sylvio had just completed his third year at seminary in Nantes. He was a tall man in his early thirties and had been a primary school teacher. He had African features – unlike John and Paula who were more European. Mauritius is a very cosmopolitan island, as I was to find out in due course; for four years later Sylvio invited me to go to Mauritius for his ordination, and John and Paula, who had by then just returned and settled there, invited me to stay with them. Thus it was that I set out to visit what is sometimes known as the island of hospitality.

The plane from Paris was due to touch down in the Seychelles, just south of the equator, en route for Mauritius, but on descending for the touchdown at Victoria on the Seychelles it ran into clouds which developed into a very heavy dense mist. At one point I caught a glimpse through the cloud and the mist and saw the sea quite close below. We spent about twenty-five minutes circling around, attempting to land but without any success. I found it quite alarming as most of the time when I looked out through the window I could hardly see as far as the wing tip, so thick was the mist. Then I noticed that the flaps were down and we were rising again and an announcement came through to say that the pilot had decided that he was unable to land because of the mist, and so with apologies to those who were hoping to get off in the Seychelles we would nevertheless go on to Mauritius.

The sequel to this was that on the return flight, several weeks later, I was talking with a passenger seated next to me, a Mauritian living in Edinburgh, and whose work at Edinburgh University took him back to Mauritius several times a year. I mentioned the experience on the outward flight of being unable to land on the Seychelles when he countered it by telling me that his colleague had been on the same plane, had fallen asleep and didn't realise the problems as we were trying to land in the Seychelles. Finally, when we got to Mauritius he got out and went straight to the transit lounge thinking that he was in transit in the Seychelles. He waited in the transit lounge for about three hours and then enquired why the plane wasn't going on to Mauritius to be told that he was there in Mauritius at that very moment.

Awaking on my first morning south of the equator was a strange experience for one who always likes to be aware of his geographical orientation – which way a house faces, where the prevailing wind comes from, and the alignment of the bed. On that first morning I realised that my bedroom window faced west, and yet the sun seemed to be in the north – until it occurred to me that it would be strange if this were not so, south of the equator. However, it was a disorientating and disconcerting feeling.

John and Paula had had a beautiful house built very near the country and with a view of the sea albeit some distance away. The house was not yet finished, but quite habitable. They had moved in just two weeks previously. The builders were still pottering around outside and there was a double balcony which still had to have a balustrade fixed, as well as a number of other lesser works. It was quiet and peaceful, at least until the builders moved in each morning at about 8 a.m. One could also often hear the distant sound of the muezzin chanting the early morning prayer for the Muslims. There were a number of mosques, almost as many as there are churches in Mauritius. Its population at the time was a little over a million and some said that only a third were Catholic with over a half being Hindu, making it a truly multi-racial and multi-religious society in which peaceful coexistence was the hallmark.

Much of the island reminded me of the Mediterranean with a touch of Jamaica thrown in. The temperature varied between about 18 and 25°C throughout the year, akin to an English summer, and I noticed a remarkable lack of pollution in most parts. There are at least three different climatic regions, there being parts of this tiny island where it rains most of the time, whilst there are other areas where the rain falls only at certain times of the year.

Most of the Catholic parishes in Mauritius comprise active groups of people, churches are full and young people take a lead. I concelebrated one Sunday mass with a Père Souchon, a seventy-year-old priest, cousin of the former Archbishop of Birmingham, Maurice Couve de Murville. Père Souchon was an enthusiastic and energetic man who had a very well-organised parish in which young people were particularly active. Apart from taking a lead in the Mass, they arranged each Sunday evening a simple service of prayer and readings for a group of *clochards*, people for the most part unemployed or homeless. The service was followed by the distribution of a hot meal on the steps of the church. Père Souchon who was there wandering around explained that this was really a couple of hours each week when they tried to show love and concern and care for this particular group of people, not many of whom exist in Mauritius, as there was hardly any unemployment. The whole exercise of organising the service in the church and the meal afterwards was done by several groups of young people, mostly sixth formers and students, and this exercise was really seen to be as much beneficial to them as to the poor themselves.

It was a different scenario from what I had experienced in Jamaica. We took one little old lady back home in the car and she had her sister there and had a very clean, although tiny, room with a bed and a little stove and several chairs. However, she rented this for quite a considerable sum of money each month from the proprietor of the building. This rent left hardly any money from her pension for the necessities of life. The distribution of food also included a regular distribution of clothing to those who needed it. I found them all very polite and quite a few of them came to me to be prayed over and for a blessing, but none asked me for money.

Later in the evening the young people, together with Père Souchon, John, Paula and myself adjourned to the garden of the presbytery where we sat around for an hour or so whilst each group of young people reported back on their activities, discussions they'd had during the week, work they were engaged in and work they were about to do, including their rota for the Sunday evening distribution of food to the dossers. Père Souchon was clearly a great character, well loved, and an inspiration to many, especially the young.

One of the main purposes of my visit to Mauritius was to attend Sylvio's ordination. Sylvio was the fifth in a family of ten. His father had died earlier that year and shortly after this his mother had suffered a stroke, which had left her disabled. She was a dear soul, although when I met her at her home near Pamplemousse, I found it quite difficult to understand her, not so much on account of the stroke but because the Mauritian version of French, interlaced with the local Creole, resulted in an unfamiliar blend of sounds. I found that this made communication difficult with a number of people there.

The casual way of the Mauritian culture, common to most countries of a warmer clime than our own, demands greater trust than we more regimented races normally have. However, I did notice that during Sylvio's ordination a hitherto clear sky clouded over and the heavens opened. Quite suddenly hundreds of umbrellas and parasols also opened up. Some ninety priests concelebrated with the bishop and a crowd of over twenty thousand. The altar was at the shrine of 'Marie Reine de la Paix', halfway up a hill on the outskirts of Port Louis. The music of the ordination was superb. The gospel, which was the marriage feast at Cana, was sung by a priest in Creole and punctuated with a Creole refrain 'Do what ever He tells you'. It was very moving.

One of the great qualities of Mauritian people is their hospitality. A French couple with whom I was chatting who had come over especially for the ordination and also for a holiday remarked to me that they had never, in their travels all over Europe, encountered such openness and such hospitality as they had since they'd been in Mauritius. The welcome that I too had received was memorable. Paula was one of an extensive and widespread family in Mauritius, and I met many of them and the encounter would invariably also involve a substantial meal. This would frequently be accompanied by a serious turn of conversation such as discussing the previous Sunday's sermon and, on one occasion at the end of a meal, a young wife, niece of Paula, burst spontaneously into a song of prayer and praise to God. It is rightly said that Mauritians are totally committed to three things only: their religion, food and eating, and the sea.

Before leaving Mauritius I visited the shrine of Père Laval

This is the tomb of the saintly priest of the mid-nineteenth century who did so much work in Mauritius for the black people. He was born in France, in Normandy in 1803, qualified as a doctor and settled into a very comfortable and social way of life in a practice not far from his home village. However, an idea took root in his mind that he should become a priest and he started living a strict and ascetic life before finally entering the seminary of St Sulpice in Paris and at the age of thirty-six being ordained a priest. The further idea took root in his mind of spreading the faith in some mission country, and a series of events led him to the island of Mauritius in the Indian Ocean, where he ministered to the most oppressed and disadvantaged people on the island. 'This unfortunate colony,' he wrote, 'is in a pitiful state. There are some eighty thousand blacks on the island and I am alone to care for them.' He died in 1864, just seven years before Archbishop Scarisbrick (possibly a distant relative of mine) came to Mauritius. He had become known and loved by all strata of society in Mauritius, but particularly by the black population, most of whom had come at some time or other from Africa. In 1979, shortly before Pope John Paul made a pilgrimage to Mauritius, he was declared 'Blessed'.

Many graces and favours have been granted and his tomb is situated in the grounds of a church which in the 1960s was knocked down by a cyclone and in its place a new one built: an impressive and spacious building. The tomb is situated in the grounds of the church and there is a small museum and tiny piety stall. Every Friday and on certain big feasts thousands of people flock to his tomb. When I visited the shrine there were just seven or eight other people praying. There was a sense of prayer, both at the tomb and in the church itself. Some more people arrived and I noticed them coming and touching the tomb, placing a candle on it and then taking it away, touching it with a bunch of flowers before taking them away. This was faith, although at times it could seem to border on superstition. However, I reminded myself, as I sat there contemplating the scene, that touch was important and found a place in our incarnational theology. God's love shows itself in so many different and varied ways, and there, in Mauritius through the intercession of this holy priest, and perhaps it was something to do with his saintly example that I found that Mauritius lived up to its reputation of being an island of hospitality.

Chapter X

FIVE CONTINENTS CONTINUED: SOUTH AMERICA, AUSTRALIA, EUROPE AND ASIA

A third journey, of quite a different genre to the Indian Ocean, was to Brazil. I had felt somewhat run down after the death of my father, and had agreed with the bishop to have a break – a 'mini sabbatical'. I looked at various courses available on spirituality, but had not made up my mind exactly what to do when within ten days I received three invitations. The first was a persuasive phone call from Jamaica asking me to return, the second was a letter from Sister Katy, a friend working in a very poor part of Brazil, inviting me to visit her and see at first hand the work she was engaged in; and then, on a visit to Hengrave, an ecumenical community in Suffolk, I met Sister Regina, an Assumptionist nun who had been Provincial in Rio de Janeiro, and she, too, invited me to Brazil. I thus felt that the Lord was pointing in a very clear direction.

Rio de Janeiro is a unique and amazing city, sometimes called the city of the hidden hills. The biggest urban forest in the world descends right into the heart of this city of some seven million people. A considerable number of these live in the favellas, the slum dwellings which are like dark shadows extending in streaks up the steep hillsides and cowering as it were between the high modern blocks of flats, offices and hotels. The thirty-metre high statue of Christ, the Redeemer, set on one of the hills, is visible from afar and seems to be saying that God loves all people, no matter what their earthly condition might be.

The Portuguese colonised Brazil in the sixteenth century. They landed at first on the north-east coast, which now happens to be the poorest area of the country. They then gradually moved on towards the south of what is now a country more extensive than the whole of Europe, renaming towns as they did so according to the month or feast day on which they arrived. Hence the names Rio de Janeiro (January), Sao Paulo (St Paul) and so on. Today Brazilians are far less concerned, as are most others, about giving truly Christian names to places and people. This results sometimes in quite unusual combinations of sounds. I heard of one person who had been named 'Medinusa'. This was not, I discovered, the name of a little known Greek god, but something the parents had seen in a shop, marked on the neck of a shirt, 'Made in USA'.

Whilst I was in Rio, three experiences especially struck me. There was the visit to a small community of Salesian Sisters who lived in one of the many slum areas, Coelho Neto, to the north of Rio. The underground train which took Sister Regina and me there was spotlessly clean, air-conditioned and well organised, in stark contrast to the situation we were to find at our destination. One of the Sisters, Gabriella, spent some time telling us of her work in the favela. The community had been there for about fifteen years. There was no priest resident in the area: most seemed to be afraid to work in the slums. A young priest ordained just eighteen months before came out as a matter of duty just to celebrate Mass. He arrived a few moments before Mass was due to begin, usually criticised the liturgy that had been organised, and then made off as quickly as he could. This seems to be typical of the attitude of a number of newly ordained clergy in many countries today.

During the time the Sisters had been there they had organised health, education and religious instruction for the whole slum area. Their aim had been to train the local people to help themselves and so the four health centres were now organised by the people. Much of what they did stemmed from reflecting on the Gospel and realising how to put it into practice. From this arose the eight base communities that now existed in the parish and it was these communities that gave rise to the provision of other needs, such as education in personal hygiene, religion and so on. The members of the base communities were involved in visiting the whole area. As far as the health centres were concerned there were some doctors who worked on a semi-voluntary basis, but this demanded money from the Sisters and so they themselves used to organise various events to raise the money. There was a general return in Brazil to natural forms of medicine and I noticed later in the morning in visiting one of the health centres that about half the medications available were natural.

As far as education was concerned there were classes for young people, teaching them to read and write and then leading into television courses from which they would perhaps get a qualifying certificate. It was important to keep people busy as the greatest worry was drug trafficking, which was very common. Drugs, arms and prostitution were rampant, so it was important for the young to be occupied and to work. There were three hundred young people learning to work on computers and these were being trained by other young people who had started it off. A small fee was charged and half went to the upkeep of the teaching centre. Many of the young people were then able to go off afterwards to get a job.

In the parish community there was a bakery run by several people, men, women and children and a three-month course in bakery. The profit from this was divided amongst those working in it and approximately one thousand loaves a day were made. In one base community there was also a broom factory. They had also started an ice-cream factory but this had to be closed, as they found that in selling ice cream you could easily sell drugs as well. Many who came to the computer training were also into drug trafficking, but they were in no way excluded from the training because of this.

On the pastoral scene, many came for baptism, and the previous Sunday there had been as many as fifty baptisms. In each case the godfather was invariably a leading drug trafficker. I did not discover what happened at weddings, but often when a man died there would be several widows at the funeral. All baptisms, marriages and funerals were performed by the laity, mainly because there were very few priests, religious or diocesan, who accepted the style of life that was necessary living amongst the slums.

The law against rape and theft was very strict. Thus it behoved the drug traffickers not to break this law otherwise it would attract police attention and the drug trafficking would be uncovered. Hence the slum area was the safest from the point of view of rape and theft! Fortunately, the church building was still regarded as a sacred place and was sometimes used as a refuge. Just a few days previously a young man had been accused by a girl of rape. In fact, it wasn't him, but he ran off and took shelter in the church. A gang pursued him but did not go into the church out of respect. Later, after he had remained in the church for quite a long time, the girl admitted that he was not the man who had raped her. The gang then turned on the girl and beat her up. Rape is really considered the worst possible crime that can be committed.

We walked out of the little dwelling in which the Sisters lived and through part of the slum area and down to the river. There by the side of a very murky looking river about twenty metres wide, were tiny wooden dwellings in a tumbledown state. There were pigs and other doubtful breeds of animals moving around in the mess and rubbish that was everywhere mixed with the mud. In the middle of this I saw one little hut, which was one of the four health centres. Visiting one of the centres, which seemed to be very well equipped I saw a dentist at work. He was doing it partly as a voluntary service and partly paid. The volunteer helper there commented that if you were paid for everything you couldn't do it for love. 'Otherwise how can you show love if everything is for money?' This was her logic.

In the midst of the squalor I saw a number of quite acceptable tiny flatlets but these were the exception. Many were made of bricks or breezeblocks and apparently it would take years for the occupants to buy enough bricks for a complete dwelling, so many of them were just half built, and situated as they were on steep hillsides, previously common land, where it was almost impossible to build roads. To live and work amidst what little of the conditions I had been able to witness demanded a very special call, but I could see that Sister Gabriella was a very happy person. Of the other three Sisters living there one was involved completely in parish work, another a teacher and therefore earned an income and a third Sister was on a pension, and so all in all the community was self-sufficient.

Very close to the convent where I was staying there was an extensive group of favellas, and one evening after supper I accompanied Sister Regina to a 'base community meeting' being held there. We clambered down the steep and twisting pathways between the broken down dwellings of hundreds of Rio's inhabitants. We ended in one tiny abode of just two rooms housing a whole family. Christians from the neighbouring favellas had gathered in one small room in which there was just a settee and a couple of upright chairs. There were already a dozen or so people there, mostly seated on the floor. Someone insisted that Sister and I occupied the settee. I would have been happy sitting on the floor, in fact happier as it turned out, but they insisted. After half an hour I began to find it a most uncomfortable experience. The springs were coming through and it was impossible to find the right position to protect one's posterior, and the back of the settee seemed to be lurching sideways.

Fortunately, much of this discomfort was forgotten when the group got under way. Soon, not only was the small room packed with people, but through the open door and non-existent window there must have been another dozen or so leaning in and straining to hear what was being said. Sister Regina whispered mini-translations to me, as my Portuguese was practically non-existent. From this I discovered that these base communities were following, very broadly, the 'see, judge, act' principle, to which they added 'evaluation' and 'celebration'. They would look at a particular situation or event in their lives, link it with a passage from the Gospel, and then discern what action could and should be taken. The particular themes, in this case for Lent, were suggested by the Brazilian bishops, so that communities throughout the country were looking at similar topics. In the group that evening, serious discussion was interspersed with prayer and songs, led by a talented guitarist who was seated in a corner of the room. He also happened to be a great talker, and I suspected that sometimes a song was suggested in order to shut him up! The topic for study ranged from problems of education, housing, street children, land problems, to that of unemployment which was the subject for that year, and one was reminded of this by the sight of posters and signs proclaiming, 'No work – why?'

The particular group I had been welcomed into had started in that favella because eleven years ago a big company wanted to run a high-voltage line across the favella. They protested and meetings were held at the nearby convent. There was mention of it on radio and TV and finally some of the members of the favella received a letter from the boss of the company in Brasilia who had decided to put the power lines elsewhere. The people then realised from this that there was strength in numbers and in putting on a united front. From this had grown their regular meetings together and the formation of a real community centred on the Gospel.

Father Mario, an Italian priest who acted as chaplain at the convent, was also present, and there was some heated discussion at one point regarding the forthcoming Good Friday Way of the Cross. Father Mario had suggested starting at the bottom of the steeply sloping hill, whilst most of the people wanted to begin at the top. Finally, when Father Mario gave in, there was a great cheer. The Way of the Cross was to be in the open on the hillside and the different stations to be held in different people's houses in the favella. I guessed it would be an appropriately difficult Way of the Cross owing to the manner in which the dwellings were built, almost one on top of another on the very steep hillside. I was most impressed by the participation of everyone of all ages and the children who were so very well behaved as well as some of the young people taking part in the discussion. Most of the favella Christian communities are fairly stable. People lived there for a long time. Sometimes if someone moved the new occupant paid rent to the original occupant who may even have built the dwelling, but no one generally owned the land.

For me, the Way of the Cross was the following day when Father Mario drove Sister Regina and myself to the outskirts of Rio to a centre for street children run by Father Renato Chiera. We wound our way throughout the suburbs and I very quickly discerned that Mario was not the safest of drivers to be with. He scarcely ever kept to any particular lane but seemed to wander all over the road with cars hooting at him and then, without warning, deciding to do a U-turn in the middle of fast-moving traffic. Regina was sitting in the front on the outward journey and I took over the front seat on the way back. Regina was also unhappy about the driving and I commented to her that there was one thing worse than Brazilian driving and that was an Italian priest driving in Brazil!

Finally we got there after having caused traffic congestion in a number of places whilst Mario stopped several times in the middle of the road and shouted to some people to ask directions to the boys' home and to Father Renato. When we arrived we were told that Father Renato was away in Europe promulgating a book he had written on his work. It was already translated into French but not English. We met his deputy and a volunteer helper who were most helpful, showing us around and explaining the set up. This was not without difficulties as the phone seemed at one point to be ringing continuously. There were eight houses, each for about fifteen children. They were spread out in a fairly small suburb of Rio. Most of the roads were not made up and had enormous potholes. The whole area was very run down, hot, dusty and noisy. None of the buildings looked very substantial. At least this was the case until we came to two of the centres, which had been kept in a good state of repair.

Father Renato had been working there for twelve years with the street children and it had all started when he was parish priest in the town and had found several children sleeping in his doorway. He became uneasy about this when he went to bed at night – he who had his own bed to sleep in and there were children out there on his very doorstep. He challenged the local parish, asking them how they could look after the children. Firstly, a young girl took up the challenge and then several others began accommodating some of the children on church property. This was first of all in the daytime, but then the children still had nowhere to go at night. A married couple had two spare rooms in their house and they offered to have the children in with them. By Christmas 1986 some relatives of Renato sent him some money to help build a house for the children. The children started calling it home, Casa Renata. Gradually the whole work developed according to the needs, and more land was bought, and more money came in.

One four-year-old girl said one day to Father Renato, 'You're my father but I want a mother.' There was a need for a feminine influence. From this came the idea of homes run by a couple with one other adult to be a sort of educator. The children began to grow and then one had to ask what was the future for them? How were they to earn money differently, apart from drugs? The idea then developed of training them towards some sort of trade.

Many of the children being admitted had already become drug addicts. Evil then reared its head as the drug pushers did not want the reform of the children, and in revenge, one of the houses was partly destroyed. The locals said it was dangerous to have the children in homes when the drug dealers were becoming violent about it, so some of the young people were moved further away where they could not be followed by the drug traffickers. For the older ones there were now workshops for them to learn a trade – carpentry, metalwork, computers and needlework. Many of the items made by the young people were sold to raise money. There were small profits but they were slowly increasing. After the young people had attained the age of eighteen, if they didn't have any family to go to as was the case with most of them, they were supervised in small groups for the next three years.

We visited the reception house where children from the streets come for up to the first six months. They were then sent to a home and we visited one of these and chatted for a little to the couple running it. This couple had three children of their own and were finding that the street children needed a lot more care and attention than their own and this was giving them consider-able problems. There were nineteen living in the house altogether. I rapidly came to the conclusion that it was again a very special and demanding vocation looking after one of the homes. These devoted people were truly practising the Gospel: 'Let the little children come to me; do not stop them.' (Mark 10:14)

The south of Brazil is more cosmopolitan with different nationalities, many of them, for example the Poles, not even bothering to learn Portuguese and having their own industries and there is much less poverty there. The north-east is the worst area from the point of view of poverty. The Portuguese had gradually drifted down from the north and, as previously mentioned, they had named many places according to the month of the year or the feast on which they first arrived. It was a little like the house numbering which I found completely confusing at first, for it is done by measuring the metres from the beginning of the road so that you might leap from house number 43 to house number 51 and you wonder where the others are, but of course they aren't anywhere!

Since 1960 the newly constructed city of Brasilia, situated inland, has replaced Rio as the capital. I was given a whistle-stop American-style tour of the city, on my way up to Palmas, by the Assumptionist Provincial, Sister Rachel. Brasilia is planned and built in the shape of an aeroplane, the central buildings, administration and cathedral are all in, what might be called, the fuselage. It reminded me of a very much larger and more grotesque version of Milton Keynes. After a substantial lunch in the convent, which was clearly an open house to many different visitors, I was hurried back to the airport for the TAM airline flight to Palmas, my destination for the next two weeks.

In the departure lounge I was amazed to find that we were only a handful of people and I failed to see how the plane could be running at any sort of a profit. However, the mystery was solved when we approached what was certainly the smallest plane I have ever been up in. We were handed a small plastic box containing fruit juice and a few snacks and then crawled into the plane where there were just twelve seats, two wings and a propeller. The pilot and co-pilot helped me adjust a rather unusual safety strap and then explained, I suppose, what would happen if the plane crashed. I didn't dare think with just a comparatively small propeller in the middle of the fuselage. It looked more like a dinky toy standing alone near the runway. My hand luggage was taken from me before I got in and this was hardly surprising as there was no room for anything else apart from the twelve bodies on the plane. However, it made a prompt start and exactly to the minute we were airborne, and, of course, flying at a comparatively low altitude so that one could see quite a lot of the countryside which I noticed was very green and seemed to be totally unpopulated. There was an irregular pattern of green fields and forests punctuated here and there by long, brown, winding rivers extending to the distance. The plane seemed to zigzag occasionally in order to avoid a rather heavy cloud and just as we were coming down to Palmas I noticed very thick black clouds not far away and very soon after there was lightning streaking across the sky just before dark. It was near the end of the rainy season.

Katy met me and drove me to the bungalow where she lived. She is a St Louis Sister who had been a great help to me years previously in Aylesbury. The land round where she was in Palmas was fairly flat, quite overgrown with green shrubs and all sorts of plants and areas which had been carved out of the scrubland for the building of very simple dwellings. Some of the settlers had been there since about 1989 and they were in more established areas with concrete roads quite pleasantly laid out. However, most of the people were unemployed and had come in from all over Brazil in order to find work. Very often they began in wooden plastic huts and then gradually improved their situation by gathering together enough bricks to build some sort of a dwelling. But much of the land was still divided up by earth roads, which after a shower of rain became soft with mud. The Sisters' bungalow was situated between a Pentecostal church and a café, Bunny's Bar, which seemed continually to be polluting the atmosphere with a very loud ghetto-blaster. I had no sooner had a quick bite to eat when we went off to a Penitential service, which was run by two of the priests from the parish. The parish was divided into eleven communities, each community living in a designated area in what was until recently shrubland. The service was led by lay people while two priests heard confessions outside the very rough and primitive hut which passed for a church.

The next morning, Palm Sunday, we were up (as every morning) early and joined the procession which began at 7.30 a.m. when the temperature was already nearly 30°C. We wound our way through several of the Christian communities, waving palms and branches from the undergrowth, singing, pausing to listen to passages read from the Passion of Jesus, and gathering up more people at each stop. We passed dwellings of varying degrees of dereliction and poverty until we finally ended beneath a lean-to roof on the side of a school building. I remained amongst the congregation whilst Padre Pedro, a long-haired

Brazilian priest in his thirties, together with two others, prepared to continue the celebration of the Mass.

Then, to my amazement, I realised that Padre Pedro was beckoning to me to come up to the altar and join him in concelebrating. With some hesitation, I complied, and no one seemed to worry that I suddenly appeared with the others, but unlike them, I was just wearing trousers and a short-sleeved shirt by then soaked in sweat for it was approaching midday. I joined in a part of the Eucharistic prayer in English, and immediately Mass was over many of the crowd came up to us, warmly and unselfconsciously embracing us, the children hugging and kissing us. I could not but reflect what the reaction to this would be in England with its present concern regarding paedophilia.

The Sisters' bungalow comprised three very small bedrooms, together with an equally small but adequate kitchen, shower room, and all this giving on to a central sitting and eating area. When the Sisters moved in, the roof was of corrugated iron but they improved it by having it tiled. However, there was no ceiling, and when lying in bed I perceived daylight through the gaps in the tiles, and one night there was a storm, which even the local people considered to be one of the worst they had known. The thunder, God's ghetto-blaster, made the noise from Bunny's Bar seem a mere whisper, and the spray coming in through the roof made the morning shower almost superfluous.

The two Sisters living there, in a multitude of ways, helped and inspired the various Christian communities around them, as well as running an important healing centre. These flourish throughout Brazil and the Sisters see their role as instigating them and as in Rio, training local personnel to run them. I found it well equipped, with use being made of natural medicines – no drugs at all. There were natural remedies for every sort of ailment, made mostly from herbs, which grew in the wild undergrowth all around. Just a few were cultivated specially in the Sisters' tiny garden. One evening I was doing the washing up – one didn't need to know Portuguese to do that – and I threw some eggshells into the waste bin. This provoked an exclamation and a slight reprimand from Sister. Eggshells had to be washed, dried in the sun, carefully crushed to a fine powder before being used as the principal constituent in a multi-mixture medicine for pregnant mums. This was important as so many babies were born under-nourished. The seeds and pips from various fruits were also used. It seemed that the small black seeds of papaya, crushed up, are good for people with cancer.

At the centre, the Pastoral da Crianca as it was called, the elderly were also involved. I saw some lovely baskets made out of tightly rolled up pieces of newspaper varnished over, which surprisingly seemed quite strong. There were also classes in reading and writing. However, it was the young who shone most by their involvement in all aspects of life in this poor region. Erivelton, for example, was a lad of twenty-one who had been elected leader of his Christian community. After being out of work, he had recently got a job in a large store, but wanted to go on to university to read law in order to use his skill in the struggle for human rights in Brazil. In most towns human rights groups are active. Many are financed from voluntary organisations in Germany and young people, like Erivelton, are involved.

Just before I arrived, the president of the Tocacins, who had his palace in Palmas had proposed constructing a tarmacadam tree-lined avenue up to his palace. Within less than two kilometres from him there were people living in shacks by the side of muddy, potholed roads and with no electricity and no clean water. The human rights group staged a peaceful demonstration to protest about this. Often notice was taken by the authorities and change occurred.

The human rights group in Palmas, run by two young women with the voluntary help of a lawyer, dealt in a practical way with the problems occurring in the community. They organised educational programmes, as well as dealing with adolescent pregnant women who had been left high and dry by the man in the picture; they accompanied people who had been treated violently by the police; they ensured that a youngster of twelve was not put in with hardened criminals when put into prison; they tried to deal with the problem of street children and glue sniffing which was rampant in the centre of Palmas; and then there were small firms around Palmas and sometimes rogues came with false documents to claim the land back and so there would be a dispute as to who really had a right to the land.

However, problems with children were the most common. Some could be dangerous. Psychologists claimed, I think rightly, that the reason for so many of these problems was that many kids lacked love and a suitable occupation. It was important that moral values were passed on. Many children were high on drugs, had knives in their clothes and sometimes if teachers resisted them they would run the risk of being attacked and killed themselves. Terasina, who was a good friend of Sister Katy's and lived just round the corner from her, was a Notre Dame nun teaching in a local school, and she was trying on one occasion to negotiate between three different gangs, but had to be escorted back home at night because she was nearly killed herself.

Early one morning there was an accident just outside our bungalow. A motorcyclist had crashed over a hole in the road. He was not badly injured but had to be taken to hospital. Our concrete road had been built only a year or so previously, but the sewerage channel ran quite near the surface and at intervals there were round holes with concrete covers. However, some of these covers to the manholes had been broken, probably because they were not very well made in the first place. This was the case of the one outside and it had merely been marked in the road by a couple of pieces of wood placed over the hole. The cyclist had hit these and throughout the remainder of my stay there the sewerage welled up into the roadway: not a very healthy situation.

The last days of Holy Week and of Easter will always remain as the most memorable and meaningful of my life. The expressive and relevant liturgies, led by young people, brought the whole redemptive drama of our faith to life. This, coupled with the warmth of the welcome given to me on each occasion, although I was unable to communicate with the people in Portuguese, was unforgettable. The Way of the Cross on Good Friday, when hundreds of us walked in the heat through some of the Christian communities, stopping at crossroads and corners to witness the re-enaction of a scene from the Passion rendered by altogether some eighty young people, dressed for the part, from Father Pedro's youth group. Tears came to my eyes: I felt so much a part of it, and even more so when arms stretched out towards me whenever I paused to take a sip of cold water from the flask I had been advised to take with me. The Way of the Cross took nearly three hours and well before we reached the marketplace where the crucifixion took place with Padre Pedro on the cross, my water flask was empty through having shared it with so many, and we were all thirsty with the Lord. Pedro, as he hung on the cross, added to the words of Jesus, and cried out in a loud voice that as long as we have the unemployed, as long as we have bad health care, as long as we have children suffering and people who are poor and oppressed, then Jesus will not come down from the cross. He continues to suffer in and through us.

Padre John, another priest helping in the parish, celebrated the Easter Vigil, introducing me to the people packed into the church, which held about three hundred. One man, seated near the front, immediately stood up and reiterated what Padre John had said, agreeing that everyone there was so pleased that I was with them that evening. It was so spontaneous and genuine.

A great fire was blazing outside the church and although it did not happen on this particular occasion, often each person who came would bring a piece of wood to throw on to the fire. This symbolised their old life, their sins and failings and they were burnt to ashes by the fire. Four Easter candles were lit from the fire and they were held by members of the four different communities taking part. Lots of people brought bottles of water, which were placed on a table by the altar and were blessed during the vigil. People then took them home. As would be expected, it was a lively liturgy and several times the congregation, more or less spontaneously, sang out their joy at the Lord's resurrection. At the end, as seemed customary, crowds of people swarmed around both Padre John and me, hugging and kissing and shaking hands, and occasionally showing off one or two words of English.

We all adjourned afterwards to Terasina's house and had a bite to eat. The night was short and Bunny's Bar had its ghetto-blaster going at its loudest and there were people dancing outside. This was apparently very common, particularly on Holy Saturday evening. There was also a country custom whereby after midnight you could go and steal a chicken and cook it for lunch on Easter Sunday! We did in the event have chicken but I do not think it was stolen! In fact, for Easter Sunday lunch we were many kilometres distant from Palmas.

There were three rural communities, some sixty to seventy kilometres away, who had not seen a priest for about four months. Each group of Christians in these villages was held together and coordinated by a small community of nuns. However, in the first, at Aparecida, it would be truer to say that it was just one German Sister, Irene, who animated the Christians, and, indeed most of the thousand or so inhabitants of the village. Sister Irene possessed a strong and vibrant personality and not only held the Christian community together leading the Sunday liturgy, but she also ran a vast compound for training the local people in farming techniques, fish breeding and other agricultural skills, to say nothing of lessons for children in the three Rs, painting, carpentry, religious education and music. However, perhaps her greatest accomplishment had been to train a considerable number of leaders.

Some of the young people would come in from a distance of forty to sixty kilometres. In the fish reservoirs there were as many as three thousand fish and they were really the only things that made any sort of profit, although I was surprised to find that she reckoned that it was only a third self-supporting. I think this was partly because she seemed to give a lot of things away, including the meals, and the local people were unable to buy much of the produce especially the fish, which they liked, because they had no money. Furthermore, half of the proceeds of what was sold was divided amongst the children. I saw quite a lot of cocoa trees and I was given a stone to suck off the soft surround and the technique was then to put the stone out to dry and then roast it. The result would be cocoa! There were banana trees, sweetcorn and an enormous variety of other produce. There was great poverty in the village itself as those who did work were very poorly paid and sometimes the motivation in going to help Sister Irene, or going to learn something from her project, was simply in order to get a free meal. It turned out that often they had no food on Sunday when they didn't go to see her and so they were quite hungry when they turned up again on Monday.

I was with Father Matt Ryan, the Irish vice-provincial of the

Redemptorists, of whom quite a few work in this part of Brazil. We celebrated the Easter Mass with Sister Irene's community of villagers, had lunch with her, and then sped to another village, Novo Accordo, where three more religious Sisters looked after the Christian community there. Another Easter Sunday Mass was celebrated before visiting a third even more rural and remote community, Novo Horizon, where Sister Madeleine, a French nun, welcomed us. She and her companion Sister came from near Strasbourg, but the second nun was absent in France visiting her aged mother.

The cottage in which the two Sisters lived – Madeleine actually had a friend staying there just for a short time – was only built about two years previously, and it was a fairy-tale building. The floor was concrete, the thatch was enormously thick and apparently made out of thirty thousand pieces of straw. When it rained heavily, you could hardly hear the rain: it was just a soft distant murmur, so Madeleine enthusiastically informed us. I was pleased that she was French as she was one of the few people with whom I could really communicate directly, and in consequence I learned a lot from her. The concrete floor of the cottage, as also in Katy's bungalow, and in most other places we visited, was ordinary rough concrete which was burned with a machine and through which multicolours were impregnated so that the end result was quite smooth and looked quite attractive. Both the Sisters were quite artistic and had made all sorts of interesting carvings and plaques from local wood, coconut shells and various products of nature. Matt was also very much at home there and we had hardly set foot in the cottage when he led me down to the stream. This was in a hollow surrounded by a great deal of vegetation and here it was that Matt had his wash in the nude as also did the three ladies – after he had finished. I went down more modestly a little later. The only spectators to what must have been quite an amazing scene were a horse and a donkey which we passed on the way.

A further quite lively Easter Mass was celebrated there in a newly built Pastoral Centre which Madeleine was hoping to equip rather in the same way that Katy had done in her community, with alternative medicines, rooms for classes, lessons, and so on.

The main room was quite full for the Mass and the chairs were arranged in a semi-circle with an excellent music group, guitar, drums, and several of the youngsters dressed up in very dignified Middle-Eastern costumes to enact the Gospel of the Resurrection. Madeleine's touch was very evident in all this and the Mass was a most enjoyable event, although I felt the sweat literally running down my back and chest underneath my shirt and alb. Even the locals were commenting that it was very hot – over 40°C.

When we came out of Mass it was pitch dark and although it was only about one hundred and fifty yards to Madeleine's cottage I found it very difficult to see my way. There were, of course, no street lights. The inhabitants if they wanted to go to the bigger village, Novo Accordo, on the other side of the river, had to get a boat down or walk round the way that we had come in the car, but I gathered that was not usual.

I looked up at the stars for a long time. The quietness, the peace, and the darkness and the little cottage and the whole atmosphere of the place, together with Madeleine herself, charmed me beyond words. I was to sleep in a room, the third bedroom in the cottage, and Katy and Gina who had come with us were to sleep in hammocks in the Pastoral Centre. I was concerned about this because I knew that neither of them would sleep very well in a hammock as they'd already mentioned this to me. Also there would be no mosquito nets and that could be a problem. However, they insisted that this was how it should be and so I had a tiny room with a bed, a very hard mattress and a mosquito net. There were no inside doors in the cottage, just a curtain hanging over the entrance to each of the three bedrooms. There was a main room with a table and just inside the front door a gas cooker and fridge, and opposite that, a small area which was made into a prayer room with two prayer stools and matting and a couple of focal points in the way of pictures on the wall. As I was about to go into my own room I noticed on the floor by the curtain covering the doorway what I thought was a doorstop and I was about to question why there should be a doorstop rather like a toad when there was no door, when it started moving: it was a toad.

Matt opted to sleep in one of the poorest cottages in Novo

Accordo. It had a mud floor and was inhabited by an elderly lady with her daughter who was paralysed and in a wheelchair. When she was eighteen years old, she had been shot in the spine by another youngster. Matt knew the family well from previous visits, and a hammock had already been hung up for him across the corner of the living space. He explained to me later that his principle, when travelling from place to place, was always to stay not in a comfortable family dwelling, but with the poorer ones.

We made our way back the following day along the long dusty track to Palmas, and I was grateful for having experienced this excursion into the rural heart of Brazil, and of having seen the Church functioning in difficult situations and without, for most of the time, a resident priest. No sooner back in the Sisters' cottage in Palmas than the bush telegraph must have been active, and within half an hour there were several callers. Because of the heat, the door and windows were always open, and this was, at the same time, an invitation for anyone to walk in. It made no difference if one was busy with some work or engaged in conversation, the caller would invariably enter as if it was his or her home, and often go straight to the fridge and help himself to a cold drink. Privacy, and this was even more true amongst the poor, did not exist. If one was having a meal, it was not unusual for several to come in, sit down and share what we had.

Many people would come to Sister Katy with their problems. Some wanted money or food, as unemployment was rife. Most of the population of Palmas comprised people from the very poor north-east of Brazil who had come to Palmas hoping to find work, as it was a new city, expanding all the time. Ten years previously it had a population of two thousand people, and in that time this had increased a hundredfold. Then, because of the poor living conditions, disease was common and the Sisters were, with their natural remedies, like a magnet for the sick people. However, some had to be taken down to the hospital, and I saw this happening when Katy was awakened in the early hours of one morning.

The open door and consequent hospitality to everyone was taken for granted, and one felt that it was the Gospel being lived out at its best. Occasionally discretion would be exercised and the caller would poke his head through the open window to see, first of all, if anyone was inside. However, for those of us brought up in a different culture it could at times be quite draining and exhausting, even though, in my case, I was experiencing it for only a short while. Nevertheless, when the time came for my departure, I realised that my welcome by the people in Palmas had been so warm and genuine, that I felt a deep emptiness on leaving.

At the airport I found I was travelling once more on a small twelve-seater TAM aircraft, bound for Belem and thence on for a further visit to Jamaica. I checked in my luggage and the girl behind the desk said, 'You know the plane only has one engine.' I do not know whether she thought my case was particularly heavy and the plane might have difficulty taking off with just one engine, although I could hardly think this as I was as usual travelling fairly light, especially considering I was away for seven weeks. Or she may have been for some unknown reason trying to put me off embarking! Once on the plane I found that I was one of only seven passengers in this little twelve-seater and I occupied a single seat immediately behind the pilot.

Flying at an altitude of nine hundred feet, I could see very clearly what the countryside was like, although we did pass through a certain amount of cloud. After a while I saw that the pilot had handed over to the co-pilot and was reading a book which I noticed immediately was a book on how to speak English. I saw no notice, such as one sees on many buses, forbidding one to speak to the driver, so I tapped him on the shoulder, explained that I was English, and offered to help him. He seemed grateful and I then proceeded to give him a mini-English lesson in mid-air. He asked where I was going.

'Belem,' I said.

'So am I,' he replied.

'I hope so!' I added with relief.

He explained the various places we were flying over and told me that he was studying for an exam in English as he wanted to qualify to fly jets and English was necessary for this. I have often wondered whether he passed his exam.

A longer journey by jet took me on another occasion to Brisbane.

A great-uncle had emigrated to Australia and his daughter had sent regular food parcels to our family back in England during World War Two. Correspondence between the two branches of the family continued, and I eventually decided, in spite of current DVT (Deep Vein Thrombosis) scares, to go out to meet them all. I was welcomed in the warm and generous laid-back way typical of those 'down under', and enjoyed sharing family memories with Margaret and Doug and those who sported a trickle of the same blood. It was a most enjoyable and moving experience, and apart from some 30°C difference in the temperature, the attractive Queenslander houses, not to mention kangaroos and koala bears that peed when you cuddled them, it was difficult to realise that one was not in England, but over sixteen thousand kilometres away. Happily, modern technology through the telephone, fax and email can enable me to continue and deepen the bonds they generated by their hospitality and love, as well as softening the sadness of separation.

Now back to the northern hemisphere where I have experienced wonderful hospitality in several countries, notably Greece, Norway, Switzerland, Italy and France, to name but a few. In Greece the openness and unhesitating welcome of so many islanders is typical of a warmer clime. In both Switzerland and Norway, where doors so often have to be closed on account of the cold, this is compensated for by the innate warmth of their temperament. Many holidays have been spent in Greece, particularly on some of the smaller islands, and many books have already been written about them. My brief experience of Norway and the Arctic Circle had its beginning on a boat plying between two Greek islands and is worth recounting.

John and I were spending a week on the north coast of Samos when we decided one day to take a boat from Pythagoria on the south of the island to Patmos. It was a day trip and an early start, which meant that we had missed our Morning Prayer, so we decided to remedy this once we were ensconced in the bows of the boat where it was fairly quiet. Halfway through the prayer in our breviary, I noticed two ladies, one probably in her forties and the other in her twenties, seated facing us about fifteen feet away.

I was unable to hear what language they were speaking but shortly afterwards one of them produced what appeared to be a New Testament and started reading it and commenting on it to her companion. At this point I looked across and made a remark about the need to prepare for the visit to Patmos by reading the Apocalypse. Conversation began, and we found we were talking to two Norwegians who spoke English fluently, the older, Ruth, who was an ordained Lutheran pastor, and the younger, Kristin, who had studied theology and was awaiting ordination. We talked our way to Patmos, as well as on the return two-hour journey to Samos. They were both very well read, putting us somewhat to shame with their knowledge of Greek and Hebrew, though not quite convincing us of the rightness of women priests! A further meeting occurred later in the week, and this resulted the following year in an invitation to Kristin's ordination in a village near Tromso in the north of Norway. We decided to accept.

This involved flying to Oslo and staying for a few days in Elverum, accepting Ruth's hospitality. She introduced us not only to Oslo, freshly caught shrimps, the café which Ibsen regularly frequented (it is said that you could tell the exact time by the moment he entered the café), but also the Euro-Asian pine forest which stretches to Vladivostok, confirmation in a Lutheran church, traditional log cabins, and Third World involvement in Namibia, to mention only a few items of interest.

A further journey by air, in distance as far as London to Oslo, took us to Tromso, which is within the Arctic Circle. Here we were met by Kristin and, after having a meal with some of her relatives, were driven to Moen, the village where the ordination was to take place. The ceremony, a few days later, was colourful and impressive in a modern brightly and artistically decorated church with the sun streaming in. John and I sat on the front row whilst several Lutheran clergy 'concelebrated'. We were invited to join the family, together with the local mayor, for a meal afterwards, and hours later, after midnight, we were drinking coffee outside the house in full daylight, it being the end of May and the time of the 'midnight sun'. One felt strangely disorientated.

The Catholic cathedral in Tromso is probably one of the smallest in the world; it cannot hold more than about one hundred and fifty people at the very most. It is one hundred and twenty-six years old and Tromso was originally, in the last century, the centre for Catholicism for the whole of the north. Priests went from Tromso to Iceland, to Scotland and to other areas of the Arctic. This seems to have been the reason why the cathedral was actually built there. It is a wooden structure and is very near the centre of the town.

As I approached I caught sight of a figure leaning out of an upstairs window of the adjacent house talking to two young people with rucksacks, and I looked up and before he disappeared from the window I called up, asking him if he was the bishop, to which he replied, 'Yes, wait a minute and I'll come down.' I introduced myself and he greeted me warmly and we talked for some time – he was very ready to talk about the situation in Tromso. He himself had been bishop there for eight years, previously administrator I think, in the south. He had two Polish priests assisting him and six priests altogether in the diocese! In fact it is the cathedral the furthest north of any in the world and probably about the smallest diocese in the world. None of his clergy were Norwegian and most of them preferred to stay in the south. He could only get one or two up occasionally to preach a retreat or perform some special mission. Norway had three dioceses and about twenty-two thousand Catholics in all.

About fifty to sixty people go each Sunday to Mass in the winter, and about eighty or so in the summer. The organist who comes every Sunday of the year travels one hundred kilometres to get to the church and one hundred kilometres back. Sometimes he comes during the week as well for a choir practice. That is an example of fidelity! Much of the bishop's time, of course, is spent travelling, and he confessed that he had probably more to do with the Lutherans than with his own people, finding them very close in faith and in practice to ourselves.

Within the Arctic Circle most people have very little sleep in the summer, but catch up on it when winter comes and it is dark and the snow is piled high against the windows. That is also when, for many, depression sets in. The rhythm of life is annual rather than daily. The friendliness and welcome of everyone we met, the clarity of the unpolluted atmosphere, the texture of light reflecting off the snow on the hills and mountains, the frozen lakes, the cold calm fjords, the midnight sun, and the joy of being a part of the celebrations to which our Norwegian friends had invited us, all contributed to making our stay a wonderful experience. There may be disagreements on theological issues, but what really mattered was our respect for one another and the importance, in an age when Christians were a minority, of being united in our love of the Lord and of one another, united in prayer and work together.

Back in Oslo we saw the *Ra II* boat that Thor Heyerdahl and his friends had built for crossing the Atlantic, as well as the *Kon Tiki* raft. It was quite incredible how seven men had lived in a space of approximately twelve feet by six feet, men of different nationalities, for over one hundred and fifty days together. It was impressive also seeing the timber and papyrus that they had used for both the raft and the boat.

Later the same year Ruth and Kristin came to stay with me in Northampton, and one evening we invited Bishop Frank Thomas to have dinner with us and with several other friends. The conversation over the meal was both serious and profane, and at one point the bishop asked how Ruth and Kristin had known us. Ruth immediately jumped in with, 'Well, Bishop, you know some ladies would drop their handkerchief, but we decided to get out our New Testament!'

Another clean and also well-organised country is, of course, Switzerland, and many exchanges of hospitality have taken place from the time in the seminary when I came to know a Swiss student, Ernst, who was later ordained priest. A rather different sort of welcome occurred when I assisted at the wedding of Marcel, his younger brother, to Cécile. The ceremony itself seemed to lack a little of the warmth and informality that might have been experienced in England. However, that was remedied by the ensuing celebrations. There was sherry for everyone outside the church immediately after the wedding, and then the invited guests were taken in a bus, and some in cars, to the nearby lake. We walked from the car and I thought at first that we were going to a hotel on the edge of the lake. However, we soon realised that we were, in fact, boarding a boat which had been commandeered especially for the occasion. There was no one else on board apart from the wedding guests, and there on the boat were more drinks and a few nibbles. After some twenty minutes the boat set off on the lake. Sherif, my Egyptian friend, was there and a number of other people I knew who spoke English and we all thought that this was 'it', but such was not the case. For half an hour we chugged across the lake and then to my amazement ended up at another jetty near which was an enormous See-Hotel, Rigi-Royal. We were ushered into the reception hall and were each given a small round stick to which a piece of twine was attached. The twine led at its other end into a banqueting room, where the tables were all set for what turned out to be a very splendid meal of six courses. We were told to wind the twine on to the stick and, as it were, follow it to where it ended up at the seat allocated to us. However, the problem was to follow the twine whilst everybody else was doing the same thing at the same moment. I found myself at one point underneath the table banging my head against somebody else's head. It was a good thing it wasn't another part of their anatomy. The ice was broken, and conversation erupted amongst all. The various courses of the wedding dinner were punctuated with music and dancing and a slide show of Marcel and Cécile from the time of their birth down to the present moment, showing various interesting snippets from their lives, and with suitable amusing commentary. Marcel's youth group also performed; moreover, they had also 'performed' very efficiently and rather brutally back stage, for when we finally got back to Marcel and Cécile's flat at about 3.30 a.m. we found that it had been really wrecked. There was the inevitable toilet paper everywhere and the windows were painted with different colours with the names of Marcel and Cécile and various comments in German which I didn't understand. Every one of their books had been taken out of the bookshelves and laid flat on the floor so that the whole floor was paved with them. There were balloons in the toilet and, worst of all, three live fish (at least two seemed to be more or less alive, whilst I think one had died) floating in the bath three quarters full of water. Gerry immediately picked up the live fish – a second one died while we were looking at it – and took it off and threw it in the lake. The others, he said, we might possibly have for breakfast in the morning. I looked at Sherif and remarked that perhaps we might leave before breakfast to catch our plane back to England. The youth group's welcome to the newly-weds was barbaric and beyond the parameters of good humour.

Another ongoing and constant exchange of welcome also dates from seminary days and began, as already recounted, on the day of my ordination with the hospitality shown by Jeanne Lochet and her family. They, together with the Thorntons in Stone, one of the first Catholic families I ever knew, helped me to see that hospitality need be very simple and that sharing whatever you have in the way of food or shelter, no matter how little, invariably works out. It has rightly been said that 'Little is always much in the hands of Christ'.

A good example was shown me once by a priest in France. It was late afternoon one day towards the end of April when I, together with three other seminarians, drove up in a borrowed car and parked outside the church at Issoire. Our primary thought was food and shelter. Perhaps the parish priest could help and direct us, impecunious as we were, to somewhere quite cheap. He opened the door of the presbytery in answer to our knock.

'Ah,' he said, 'you'd like to see the church!'

'And to know where we could eat and sleep,' we added.

'Let me show you the church first,' he replied. 'Whilst the light is still good,' he added.

We agreed, little knowing that he would spend between two and three hours explaining the many fascinating details and taking us up to the tribune, where few visitors ever went. Finally, he shared what little food he had in his house and took us to the parish hall where we slept, not too uncomfortably, on the floor.

Thirty-five years later I revisited Issoire, spoke to a lady selling postcards in the church and who reminisced about their former curé, Père Ferrandou, the one whom we had met and who had since died.

'Ah,' she lamented, 'he has not been replaced by clergy of the same calibre and with the same enthusiasm for the Church and for his people.'

Mention of France would not be complete without paying tribute to the great work of Taizé, dedicated as it is to the whole area of reconciliation between peoples. People of all ages, although predominantly young, from the world over, come to Taizé travelling by bus, air, train, car, coach, bicycle or on foot. Latterly, my visits have meant taking the TGV from Paris to Macon, and shortly before arriving at Macon you can see in the distance on the left near the horizon a small cluster of stone buildings and a matting of tents comprising different coloured rectangles, squares and other shapes, with several other concrete structures merging into the whole. This is Taizé and the view is very soon replaced a few kilometres further on by the prominent Romanesque tower of the ruins of the great medieval monastic centre of Cluny.

On descending from the train at Macon, taking a bus, which winds back near the much straighter line taken by the TGV, you arrive at the top of the hill in the middle of the tiny village of Taizé. As you descend from the bus your first sight is that of a board proclaiming 'Welcome' in many different languages. This could well be accompanied by a young person smilingly presenting you with a small bunch of wild flowers as a sign that you really are welcomed with love and concern. As Gerard Hughes has written: 'Taizé communicates Christ's welcome to all men. Visitors are not proselytised, coerced or threatened, but given a glimpse of what they can become in Christ and an opportunity to meet, reflect and pray together on the meaning of their lives.'

The story of how it all began is well known, and is best summed up in the words of the Brothers:

> In August of 1940 Brother Roger, 25 years old, settled alone in Taizé. It was wartime and he wanted first of all to help people going through difficulties. He began to offer hospitality to refugees, Jews in particular. He intended to create a community that would be a "parable of communion". After two years, his first brothers joined him.
>
> Today the community numbers more than 100 brothers, Catholics and of different Protestant backgrounds, from twenty-five different countries. Small groups of brothers live among the

poor in Asia, Africa and Latin America.

Since the end of the 1950s, tens of thousands of young adults from every continent have come to Taizé. The intercontinental meetings held each week enable them to pray, to reflect on the sources of the faith, to look for meaning for their life, to prepare themselves to be creators of trust and reconciliation in the places where they live. The European or intercontinental meetings held in large cities are stopping-points on this "pilgrimage of trust on earth" undertaken by Taizé.

The style of prayer at Taizé is important and combines a certain structure with freedom and particularly freedom for the sort of contemplation that we Catholics so often miss in our present liturgy. When it was in Latin, with the priest rather remote, the Mass was a sort of background to contemplative prayer, and each person had great freedom to pray as the spirit moved them. This is now to a large extent missing in the vernacular liturgy where there are all too few moments of silence. The Common Prayer of Taizé involves great spaces of silence, a joyful unison of prayer in singing, combined with the mantra which enables one to attain, without any particular training or intellectual thought or preparation, a depth of contemplation which is so vital for the growth of the spirit in our lives. I find Taizé one of the few places where prayer somehow becomes easy.

Because of the ever-increasing number of people going to Taizé, especially those aged between eighteen and thirty, not only the various facilities, but also the church itself, have had to be enlarged. It is probably the only church in the world that, since it was built in 1962, has been extended at least four times. Its bare concrete and wooden structure is not aesthetically pleasing, but the subdued lighting, the candles, the simple prayer stools, the ikons and, most of all, the Blessed Sacrament, make it a place where people are drawn to prayer both by day and night.

In Brother Roger's letter for the Millennium he writes:

Wherever you may be across the continents, you want to become aware of the mystery that lies at the heart of your heart: can you sense the profound beauty of the human soul? What is this hidden beauty? It lies in the audacity of a longing. Even if we are unaware of it, one of the most intimate desires of our being is to love. Without love, could our life find meaning? God loves me – and this reality sometimes seems almost beyond our reach. But the day of a discovery can dawn: when I let myself be touched by God's love, my life opens up to others.

And this is surely what hospitality is all about.

One is also reminded vividly of the truth of this when visiting the extensive ruins of the great Greco-Roman city of Ephesus in western Turkey. It was here that St Paul verbally combated the pagan worship of the goddess Artemis. But here, also, are the considerable remains of two great basilicas dating back to the early years of Christianity. One is dedicated to St John, the Apostle, and covers his tomb, whilst the other is dedicated to Our Lady. At that time it was the custom to dedicate a church to a saint only when that person had lived in the flesh there. Hence these are strong indications that the dying Christ's request to his mother and to his Apostle, John, was fulfilled at Ephesus: 'Jesus said to his mother, "Woman, this is your son." Then to the disciple he said, "This is your mother." And from that hour the disciple took her into his home.' (John 19:27)

For centuries Christians venerated a site on the hill outside Ephesus as the place where Mary lived in the care of John, and from where she was assumed into heaven. Through the vision of a German nun, who had never visited the place, excavations revealed the foundations of an ancient house, over which there is now built a chapel, commemorating Mary having lived in that place. It is known as 'Meryem Ana', and is holy to both Christians and Muslims. Father Tarcy Mathias, one of the Capuchin priests who live adjacent to the shrine, writes in a leaflet about the place:

> Whatever the religious attitudes of those who visit, all feel an intimate and warm welcome inside this poor house. They feel free and relaxed. Young lovers experience a deeper and richer meaning in their mutual love, and they symbolise it by their tears of joy, and by lighting and joining two candles together. Who could be a better guide to a life of love than Mary, whose life was filled with the Holy Spirit of Love?

Curious people – people who want to discuss and argue the

historicity of the place – become quiet and reflective. Who could be a better answer to their many questions than Mary Herself?

People who do not believe seem to experience a quiet peace and a conversion. For their inner life of being 'reborn' in the Spirit, who could be a better mother than Mary Herself?

Others experience Mary in a very concrete and visible way. Mary is excited and happy to see her people. She moves in the midst of them, welcoming everyone. Her happiness and joy are contagious. Like children in a family in the presence of the mother, all are happy and talking around Mother Mary. Perhaps some religious persons are scandalised by all the talking and noise and complain to Our Lady, saying that this is a sacred place – a place of silence and prayer. Mary replies to them, 'Silence and prayer are a result of inner peace when one is welcomed and made to feel like a member of a family. You must do with your hands what I do without mine. Welcome them with love and patience. Do not judge their way of life. Lead them by your example of love to silence and prayer.'

Chapter XI

THE WELCOME OF DEATH: THE CLIMAX OF OUR LIVES

In my Father's house there are many places to live in... I am going now to prepare a place for you.

John 14:2

Death, like birth, is one of the greatest moments of our lives. It is the climax of our lives here on earth, and the great moment of welcome by God into the fullness of life in eternity. This is our belief as followers of Christ. However, we are experiencing an age and culture which, whilst displaying death second-hand through the media, is reluctant to face up to it in reality. For the most part, people are left to die without the help and support of a hand held by a loved one; because, though it is a great and significant moment of our journey, it can be tinged with fear, and I return to the quotation about dying by Gwen Ffrangcon-Davis, mentioned in an earlier chapter, when she said, 'I suppose you're always a little nervous of doing something for the first time.'

For Christians and for many others the final farewell is the final welcome. Apart from the possible suffering involved prior to death, the main cross of death is surely, for many, the parting from those we love and the abandonment of unfinished business – all this assuming that our mind is still functioning effectively. President Mitterrand of France, who died towards the end of the last century, and who for many years lapsed from his Catholic faith, nevertheless found faith in his later years and some while before he died was interviewed on television. In the course of the interview he was asked, 'If God exists what would you like to hear from him after your death?'

Mr Mitterrand replied, 'Welcome home.'

'And what would your reaction be?' continued the interviewer.

'At last I know,' replied Mitterrand.

The pattern or rhythm of death and resurrection is built into the whole of creation. Bede Griffiths makes this point very succinctly:

> It is the law of growth for all matter, for all life and for all human existence.
>
> When two atoms of hydrogen combine with an atom of oxygen to form water, they have to die to their existence as gases and be reborn to a new existence as water. Again, when water is absorbed by a plant, its molecules have to die to their separate existence as water and rise again to a new existence as the components of a living cell. Again when the plant is eaten by an animal, it has to die to its existence as a plant and rise again to a new life in the tissue and organs of the animal. Finally, when the animal becomes food for man, it dies as an animal and comes to birth in the bloodstream of a human being, eventually feeding the brain, which gives rise to thought and human consciousness. Thus the whole process from inorganic existence to life and consciousness takes place through a series of deaths and resurrections. The death and resurrection of Jesus was the final act in this drama, when a human body, fashioned from atoms and molecules and living cells passed from a human state of existence and consciousness to a divine state, that is, to a state no longer conditioned by time and space and the ordinary laws of causality.

He goes on to say that this pattern is found in our own daily lives. Each night we die to our state of consciousness and then rise to a new state in the morning. In our human growth, we die to our childish ways to become adolescent, adult, and so on through each stage of our lives.

Let us now look briefly at the events that may be connected with that final farewell and welcome into the fullness of life. Suffering and pain, old age and the messiness of illness are often the first circumstances that come to mind in association with death. This, combined with the aforementioned fear, can be quite traumatic for all concerned. I can recall the sleepless night I had once, when, only half-recovered from pneumonia, a friend, one of the best doctors in Dublin, gave me a further examination and concluded that there seemed to be some sort of occlusion in my right lung. I asked him if it was possibly cancer, to which he replied, 'Well, you can't rule that out. Never mind,' he added, 'trust in the mercy of God.'

Several good happenings resulted from what later transpired to be a false alarm. The following day at the De Mello spirituality conference I was attending at the time, I was asked at the last minute to be the principal celebrant and to preach at the Mass. It was the feast of the Assumption, and I homed in on the words of the angel, 'Mary, do not be afraid', at the Annunciation, relating something of my own thoughts and fears of the previous night. I discovered afterwards that it was a great help to quite a few who were there. For me, it became a most fantastic personal spiritual exercise, even more effective than De Mello's meditation on 'The Deliverance' in his book *Wellsprings*, in which the author helps one to think about the reality of one's death, as this is the best way of seeing life as it really is. On returning to England it also resulted in my changing doctors and finding one who could not have been more helpful and caring when my father, who some years later became ill, died just four months short of being a hundred.

Prayer, throughout our lives, is essential and helps us to be fully human. For the elderly it can become a special vocation, and my father in his latter years spent hours daily communing with God. He had a remarkable memory for people and even their names. One evening towards the end of our monthly shared meal which concluded the 'Prayer of Reconciliation' in the style of Taizé, Roger Sawtell, the coordinator of the group, banged on the table to get silence and then announced that fifteen months ago one of his nephews, Peter Brown, a young child, had been very ill with heart complications. Roger had asked my father to pray for him. Over a year later Roger had seen my father again, who had asked him how Peter Brown was. He had remembered the name and had, it appears, been praying for him each day. Roger commented, 'We often pray for people, and then after a while stop. I was like that, but then, after my visit to Ken's father, I contacted Peter Brown's family and found that the boy was not completely well, but had made, nevertheless, an extraordinary recovery.'

Sometimes prayer for the sick is answered in unexpected and wonderful ways, and suffering, as Rene Danford remarked when we were viewing Monet's garden near Paris one wet afternoon, is like rain on the flowers: it shows up the colours better. This was certainly true in the extraordinary account of David and Nuala's death. I had not been living in Aylesbury very long when Anne Holt phoned me to ask if I would visit a friend of hers, Nuala, who had just been told that she had terminal cancer, and wanted to find a sympathetic priest with whom she could talk. I was unsure whether I would fit the bill, but nevertheless drove out to the country cottage where Nuala lived with her husband, David, who was a leading gynaecologist.

I found Nuala somewhat bewildered and saddened by her illness. She had been a lively, vivacious lady in her forties, who had been known for her parties and her hospitality to all. She came from Dublin and ten years previously had married David who accepted Nuala's Catholicism, although he himself would have described himself as a non-believer. I got on well with both of them, giving, of course, considerable help to Nuala through the sacraments. Soon after I began to visit, David was diagnosed also as having bone cancer. It was in the early spring and Nuala's prognosis was that she would probably last until the summer whilst David would live until the end of the year.

They had no children, and both family and friends were in constant attendance. Nuala had parents, a sister and two brothers who came frequently and regularly from Dublin to see her, Maeve, her sister staying most of the time to look after her. I came to know the family well. By August both David and Nuala were at home confined to bed. Nuala prayed that, in spite of the prognosis, David would die before her, as she felt that she could cope with the bereavement better than he could. And this is exactly what happened. David died with Nuala lying in the bed beside him, praying and holding his hand. She herself died just over two days later. Their joint funeral Mass, which I celebrated, was a moving experience and was the first since the Reformation in the little village Anglican church. The vicar assisted, and most of the villagers and a vast number of friends as well as relatives filled the building.

Throughout those months I had come to know Nuala's family well, and in later years was able to taste something of the typical Irish hospitality and humour when I visited them in Dublin. On one occasion my father accompanied me and Maeve and her brother Harry took him to the Dublin zoo. As the three of them had got their tickets and passed through the entrance lobby the ticket collector said to Harry, 'Is that gentleman a senior citizen?' – to which Harry replied 'Well, yes, yes, I suppose he is really; in fact, indeed he is because he's got a son who is nearly a senior citizen.' My father was given a half-price child's ticket!

Maeve herself had had her share of suffering, having lost her husband in an air crash at Heathrow, leaving her to bring up three young sons. When in later years she had a hysterectomy she phoned me from the hospital shortly afterwards, already bubbling over in spite of being sedated. She recounted that the cleaning woman had come into the room that morning following her operation and said in a typically Irish way, 'Well, how are ye now that you've had all your furniture removed?' So Maeve chuckled and replied, 'Yes, I'm an unfurnished woman.'

Some deaths are sudden and the Church's Advent readings with their insistence on 'staying awake' and 'being prepared' are good reminders of this. Calls often used to come in the night, summoning me to CCU or ITU at the hospital. Once awake and having driven the two miles to the hospital I invariably found a relieved welcome on arrival – by relatives of the sick person and by the nursing staff. Even in situations of crisis I usually experienced an atmosphere of calm and stillness and intimacy, accentuated by the dimmed lighting of the ward and the attempt not to disturb other patients. Nurses must always be patient-centred, rather than caught up overmuch in administration or regarded as consultants' handmaids, and I think this concern for the patient is seen most clearly as paramount in the night emergencies.

Whilst the welcome into eternity comes abruptly and suddenly for some, for others it is at the end of a very long and slowly debilitating illness. This was the case with Betty Sheffield. I had known Betty for many years and she suffered from a weakening heart disease as well as other minor maladies. Doctors had forecast her death years before it eventually occurred. Her faith and love and acceptance of her situation were exceptional and unforgettable. She said to me once when I called on her at home, apologising for having been away and not having visited, 'Father Ken, if you come, it's wonderful; if you don't come, it's wonderful: I accept whatever happens.' Then she added that she was really beginning to put the de Mello spirituality exercises into practice. Betty was the sort of person from whom, after visiting her, you came away feeling almost 'on a high'. I remember on one occasion I was particularly depressed, annoyed and in a pretty bad frame of mind when I called on her. I didn't let her know, of course, how I felt myself; and the conversation went on to death and her funeral and various other matters. I left pretty well on cloud nine: all my own little problems had vanished.

She had had a difficult life, her husband having left her many years previously and she had brought up four daughters and a son on her own As they grew to be adult, she had turned to counselling and helping in many and varied ways all sorts of people. She had also been involved in the Charismatic Renewal when it had first started in England, and she found it a great help when I prayed over her. However, on one occasion there had been a healing service in the cathedral led by an American priest, a Father Peter Rookey, who had gone over to her where she was sitting in her wheelchair and hadn't listened to what she was trying to tell him – that she was not paralysed – and in fact one of Father Rookey's assistants came and started rubbing her legs and then tried to haul her out of the chair. This made Betty really angry. I countered this by saying that I too was angry at quite a few aspects of the service, which put a certain question mark against some of the practices of the Renewal movement, although, in common with many others, I had gained a lot through it.

Betty was a gentle person, and before she finally died, any inner resentment against her husband had vanished, and both he and all her family gathered around during the final hours of her journey to the next life, and expressed their prayer and thanksgiving for her at her funeral.

It was a little like that with Molly Ravensden who was elderly and very traditional, frequently harkening back to the days before Vatican II, and extremely critical of many more recent customs in the Church. I discovered from her doctor and others that she was similarly disposed to disapproval of various modern medical practices and other current observances. Her most common expression was, 'Why don't we do so and so?' or 'Why don't we do it like that?' The annoyance and irritation she felt showed in her facial expression and the lines of anxiety.

Molly fell ill with cancer whilst on holiday abroad. She returned to hospital in England, where she died just a week later. On the day I anointed her and gave her communion she lay back in the bed, and somehow all her lines, all her worries and all her criticisms had completely vanished.

She lay there looking just like a young girl and I said to her, 'Molly, you look beautiful, and you are beautiful,' and she gave me such a lovely smile. It was a great grace that those little niggles and aggravations which had probably caused many of her wrinkles and lines seemed to have completely disappeared.

Perhaps Molly experienced something of the sentiments so well expressed by Teilhard de Chardin:

> When the signs of age begin to mark my body (and still more, when they touch my mind); when the ill that is to diminish me or carry me off strikes from without or is born within me; when the painful moment comes in which I suddenly awaken to the fact that I am ill or growing old; and above all, at that last moment when I feel I am losing hold of myself and am absolutely passive within the hands of the greatest unknown forces that formed me; in all those dark moments, O God, grant that I may understand that it is You (provided my faith is strong enough) who are painfully parting the fibres of my being in order to penetrate to the very marrow of my substance and bear me away within Yourself...

That moment of death is in God's hands. However, the temptation today is to act as God and for man to control both the beginning and end of human life. We must remember that 'God is in charge', so relax! And that moment at the conclusion of our earthly pilgrimage becomes rather like the moment of birth. Just as a baby emerges from the darkness and security of the womb into a totally different environment, so at death we are reborn into a completely new and different form of life in a purely spiritual realm. The medievals usefully likened it to the emergence of the butterfly from the caterpillar–larva state. This theme is excellently set out in Trina Paulus's little book, *Hope for the Flowers*. It is the story of a caterpillar who had trouble becoming what he really was, but finally felt he had to let go of everything. That is what, here and now, we have to prepare for at the moment of our death. To help someone to this is invariably a great privilege, and there have been occasions when in the middle of giving a dying person the Sacrament of the Sick, and praying aloud for a seemingly unconscious person, the eyelids have flickered or the hand I have been holding has tightened, and I know they have been aware and have heard and within minutes or even seconds, have passed on to the welcome awaiting them in the next life. I suspect that, like birth, the transition to this next life is sometimes on our time scale, a slow and gradual change, and for others, it is much more rapid.

To our way of thinking it may often come at just the wrong time – on Christmas Day, or just after retirement, or whilst on holiday. This is because we are like people looking at the wrong side of a hand-woven Turkish carpet. The ends droop and dangle, there is no pattern and the colours seem to clash. It is only when finally we are viewing our lives, as it were, from the right side of the carpet in the next life, that we will appreciate the beautiful pattern. For those looking on and who are hit hard by the loss of a loved one, many have to pass through the various stages of bereavement during which it is difficult to appreciate any sort of pattern.

Then there are occasions when tragedy and sorrow are mixed with humour. One such time was when there had been a lot of rain and the funeral director warned me that the village church-yard, which sloped down towards a river, was muddy and wet. The cortege wended its way through the not particularly short grass to the grave, which I immediately, to my horror, found was half full of water. Fortunately, the family stood fairly well back and it is possible that they could hardly see the water in the grave.

As soon as was appropriate I indicated that I wanted the coffin lowered so that at least it would cover up the water but I then found that it was gently bobbing to and fro near the surface of the water. The family were neither Irish nor Italian and so did not wish to come and peer into the grave and sprinkle holy water on the coffin. I, for my part, had been so anxious to cling on to my umbrella that I had anyway forgotten to take with me the holy water. Perhaps the rain, which was by then pouring down, made up for my forgetfulness.

Other experiences of a somewhat macabre nature included finding the grave too small for the coffin at the moment when the undertakers attempted to lower it; and another occasion when an undertaker bent over to look into the grave to make sure the coffin was resting neatly and his spectacles fell in!

Some years ago I noted the following in my journal:

> Our lives are very uneven and ragged in many ways – moments when we feel close to God, and others when we feel that God is far away when we are immersed in the practicalities of living. Probably most of the time we feel the latter, but we have to draw on the high moments in the past. More and more I think this is important in ministering to people: to draw especially on the moments of grace, the sacraments, and other occasions when the Lord has seemed to be real, in order that we grow in an awareness of His reality all the time. In some ways I suppose it's like water pouring through a garden sprinkler. At any particular moment a piece of ground may be quite wet or quite dry, but the overall picture is of gentle watering, and the growth occurs. I do sometimes ask myself what is the purpose of it all, and have to remind myself of the basic reality that I exist, that others exist, that we have been created, that God has shown His love in Christ, and the whole purpose of living is precisely to live through death and resurrection, darkness and light, aridity and fruitfulness, and eventually to the fullness of reality after death. I think this is what young people need to be guided towards, and it is through prayer and through silence that we find meaning…

Returning to the experience of Taizé, it is something more than a small miracle that the young people, and indeed the not so young, are literally thrown into the silence of Taizé, those deep wells of silence after the readings and the silence in the church between the various public prayers. It is rather like someone who has no idea whatsoever of how to swim being caught up and thrown into the deep end of the swimming pool. There is a temporary drowning, and then you find that something is happening, you are beginning to come up, perhaps you are beginning to float, perhaps you start flapping your arms and legs and you are moving. The Taizé experience is rather like that and it is precisely that experience that so many want to take back with them, combined with that of simplicity and of community. Our search for God, which seems to be so well typified in all its dimensions at Taizé, consists in knowing ourselves, in finding ourselves, in finding the presence of God within us, in finding that presence, perhaps recognising that presence in the most unlikely people around us, and in allowing ourselves to be lifted up by the divine, the Spirit, in those solid pregnant moments of silence.

It is perhaps most of all in the experience of silence and a life lived simply that we learn to die and gain a glimmering, a foretaste of the loving welcome of God's presence. I like the story of the American who called on a certain Polish rabbi. The rabbi's room was very bare, with just a table, a chair and a few books. The American asked the rabbi: 'Where are all your belongings?'

And the rabbi turned to the American and replied, 'Where're yours?'

To which the American responded, 'Oh, I'm just travelling around; just a visitor; I'm just passing through.'

'So am I,' said the rabbi.

I conclude this chapter with a poem written by Joan Murphy, a friend who used to come to me with her questions and difficulties. It seems to sum up much of what I have been attempting to write.

On the Day of My Death

It will be an authentic time then,
When bone and flesh contrive together towards silence;
The moving of organic life
Towards quiet.
Birds
May shrill on chimneys
In England's quaintly mysterious suburbs.
Gardens may riot with peony and wallflower –
Wealth of the simple, the easily pleased.
Laburnum
May droop its yellow tassels
Over endless trimmed lawns,
Yet for me on that day there will be hardly any blood
Moving through its complex network;
Not much heart activity either, no, hardly any;
While kidneys and liver will
So slowly, yet with a grand finality, shiver to rest.
Hardly any movement in those eyeballs,
Those skin cells that worked ceaselessly
Among the rockeries and dusty mantelpieces
Of houses I called home.
That will be a strange day
When my being goes away
Without fingernails or ankles.
Moving out of my bit of flesh,
My only possession.
Every piece of me has a certain singularity,
Even uniqueness, but then
There will be hardly any activity left,
No, hardly any, even in bone marrow.
The work of my intricate mechanism
Will be almost over, that was so delicate,
So highly tuned.
Too good
A thing really for one person
To have to itself; without at least a perfect work

To show for it.
That day
When silence and rest take over my body,
It will start to change.
Hardly any time left in its present form,
But every cell has always longed for change.
Every component part
Will soon draw away separately,
Ready to start again.
Hardly any flesh can work as it did,
No, hardly any; now it begins
Its inevitable journey outwards to make pigs
And nasturtiums, earth-worms and ash-trees
And I am glad for it, glad and joyful as I slide from my home.
How strange! My face no longer moves,
Not even the tongue.
Voiceless, I move into my future,
Stripped of all baggage,
Doing what my fathers did
I am achieving, at last, my purpose.
It always seemed obscure, unlikely.
Yet today,
In hardly any warmth
I am completed.

Conclusion

And so we come to the end of this attempt to explore in a somewhat pragmatic manner the giving and the receiving of hospitality. It has involved an account of experiences gained through travel in other climes, experiences unique to a priest engaged in pastoral work, and, hopefully an account of just a little growth in love and trust. My hope is that it may be in some small way an inspiration and encouragement to others.

I have learned much from others, but perhaps most of all from the brief visits to the Third World. You do not need a lot in order to be hospitable. A little is enough. Jesus showed this in a dramatic way when he invited thousands of people to share a meal with him. Simple shared meals where everyone brings just a little prove this. I can still enjoy a good meal in good company, but somehow, lurking in my mind, there is always the memory of the simple basic fare of the Brothers in Jamaica.

It has I think rightly been said that the greatest suffering experienced by many today is that of loneliness. It is at the root of many of today's evils – alcoholism, drug-taking, the obsession with sex, and so on. It is encountered by most people in some form or other at some time during their lives, but most acutely felt by the bereaved, the separated and divorced, the unmarried mother, the single and even the celibate clergy. Marriage is not necessarily the answer: over half of the world's population, anyway, are not married. Nor may living in community be the answer either. However, an important step as an antidote to the malaise of loneliness is, I would suggest, to live more in communion with others, to open the door of one's home and one's heart to others, especially those in need, and at times to invite the perhaps socially undesirable to sit down at one's table. It requires courage and means taking risks, but it could so easily begin for some by continuing the sign of peace with one's neighbour at

Mass and an invitation to share the Sunday meal, or taking someone from a nearby old people's home or nursing home to share one's food. There are many opportunities of welcoming others just as Christ has welcomed us, for the glory of God; and loneliness will vanish.

I conclude with three quotations: the first is from Gerard Hughes's book:

> I enjoy both being alone and being with people. When alone you want to be with people, and when you are with people, you want to be alone. Solitude helps me to appreciate company and company helps me to appreciate solitude, but there is a time for speaking and a time for being silent.

The second is from Brother Roger of Taizé:

> An inner freedom can blossom within us when the Church keeps open the gates of joy and a great simplicity and when, even with almost nothing, it becomes welcoming, close to human suffering, present in history, attentive to the neediest.

And the third is from an unknown source:

> So much of our lives are spent
> In keeping other people out.
> We have private rooms, private houses,
> Private clubs and so on.
> Of course there are times
> When everybody needs to be alone.
> Yet there is a sense in which our size
> As human beings can be measured by the
> Circles we draw to take other people in.
> The smaller the circle, the smaller the person.
> A strong person isn't afraid of people who are different.
> A wise person welcomes them.
> By shutting them out we deny ourselves
> The riches of other people's experience.
> We starve our minds and harden our hearts.

When we name our brothers and sisters
We draw no circle smaller
Than the first one ever drawn on the earth.
In the beginning God gave the earth its shape
And made it round.
God included everybody.
So should we.

Showing hospitality and being a 'welcoming' person is, then, all a question of loving and the different and varied ways that we can show this, depending on our culture, our way of life and the means at our disposal. It involves both giving and receiving, and I have intentionally left it to the reader to fathom out and identify the multiple steps and varying shades of welcoming and sharing and loving.

Bibliography

Arrupe, Pedro, *Hunger for Bread and Civilisation*, Rome, Sedos, 1976

Barclay, William, *The Daily Study Bible*, St Andrews Press

Ciferni, Andrew, *First Things First*

Gibran, Kahil, *The Prophet*, Heinemann Ltd, 1926

Graham, Kenneth, *The Wind in the Willows*, London, Methuen, 1908

Hoban, Mary, *Fifty-One Pieces of Wedding Cake*

Horwood, William, *The Willows in Winter*, London, HarperCollins Publishers Ltd

Hughes, Gerard, *Walking to Jerusalem*, Darton, Longman and Todd

——, *In Search of a Way*, Darton, Longman and Todd

Johnson, Vernon, *One Lord, One Faith*, Sheed and Ward, 1929

Morton, H V, *In the Steps of St Paul*, London, Methuen

Nouwen, Henry, *Reaching Out*, London, HarperCollins Publishers Ltd

Payne, John Henry, *Chronicles of a Century*, London, Minerva Press

Teilhard de Chardin, *The Divine Milieu*, Paris, Editions du Seuil

Thurston, Hazel, *The Traveller's Guide to Cyprus*, published by Jonathan Cape. Reprinted by permission of The Random House Group Ltd

Walker, Kenneth, *Diagnosis of Man*, London, Random House

All Biblical quotations, with permission of Darton, Longman and Todd, from the New Jerusalem Bible. Similarly, the quotations from Brother Roger of Taizé and from the Taizé Calendar 2002 are all quoted with permission.

Father Tarcy Mathias, an unpublished leaflet, by permission of the writer

Bede Griffiths and Teilhard de Chardin quotations, by permission
of *The Tablet*, April 1981

Joan Murphy, unpublished poems, by permission of her husband,
James Murphy